Revised Third Edition, 1995

FLAGSTAFF HIKES

by
Richard & Sherry Mangum

HEXAGON PRESS
FLAGSTAFF, ARIZONA

NON LIABILITY STATEMENT

While we have worked hard to guarantee accuracy and have personally taken every one of these hikes, errors in field notes, transcription and typesetting can occur. Changes also occur on the land and some descriptions that were accurate when written may be inaccurate at press time. One storm, for example, can change a trail or road. In addition to the problem of accuracy, there is the problem of injury. It is always possible that hikers may sustain harm while on a hike. The authors, publishers and all those associated with this book, directly or indirectly, disclaim any liability for accidents, injuries, damages or losses that may occur to anyone using this book. The responsibility for good health and safety while hiking is that of the user.

Look for Our Companion Book

Cover photo by Sherry G. Mangum
Cover design by Joan Carstensen, Northland Graphics
Produced by Northland Graphics, Flagstaff

© Richard K. Mangum and Sherry G. Mangum
Berne Convention and all other rights reserved
Revised Third Edition, 1995
First Edition, April 1992
Revised Second Edition, June 1992
ISBN 0-9632265-7-6

Printed on recycled paper

TABLE OF CONTENTS

FOREWORD

In April, 1992 we came out with the first edition of *Flagstaff Hikes*, followed that June by the revised second edition. Since then we have had the pleasure of talking to many people who have used and enjoyed our book.

The main thing that we have learned in talking to people is that they are using the book in ways that we did not foresee. Many newcomers to Flagstaff come here to enjoy the natural features of the area—the forests, mountains, canyons, deserts. They use the book not only for hiking information but as a guide to the area.

With this in mind, we have decided to expand the scope of the book. We now see *Flagstaff Hikes* as an outdoor guide to the natural features of the Colorado Plateau, using Flagstaff as a base. This means reaching out, but never going farther than a comfortable day's drive. Our hikes are still day hikes—no overnighters or excessively long trails.

Flagstaff is the Gateway to the Grand Canyon, and some of the finest hikes in the world. We have experimented with day hiking on Grand Canyon trails and have included four fine Grand Canyon hikes in the book, because we think every reasonably fit hiker should at least sample these Grand Canyon trails. They require some effort because they are so steep, but they are all superb.

We have also included several hikes in The Rim country. Although Flagstaff is a short distance from the Mogollon Rim, when area residents talk about The Rim Country, they mean the area southeast of Flagstaff, going towards Payson. We think you will enjoy the beautiful green country there.

We have dropped our coverage of mountain bike trails, because we found that the needs of bikers and hikers are so different. A good hike may be way too short for a satisfying bike ride.

The book is bigger and better. We have re-written some hikes, cast out some, added others, and have generally upgraded the book to make it better and more useful. There are **48 brand-new hikes** in the book. All of the maps have been re drawn to make them clearer. We have also included some aids, such as the Access Map on pages 10 and 11 and a Hike Locator. You will find some handy charts with useful information on page 6.

We are constantly on the trail or poring over maps, talking to people and scouting to find good hikes. Let us know if you know about a good trail that we have missed.

ABOUT THE AUTHORS

RICHARD K. (DICK) MANGUM

Dick was born in Flagstaff. From childhood he has enjoyed getting out into the woods, canyons, hills and mountains surrounding his birthplace.

After graduating from Flagstaff High School, he attended the University of Arizona, where he obtained his BS and law degrees. He returned to Flagstaff and engaged in the general practice of law for fifteen years, then became a Superior Court Judge in Flagstaff in 1976.

He retired in November, 1993, in order to devote full time to his two favorite hobbies, hiking and writing. He wrote the articles, drew the maps and typeset the book.

SHERRY G. MANGUM

Although Sherry was not born in Flagstaff, she has lived there since she was seven years old. Like Dick, she enjoyed getting into the outdoors from the time she was a toddler.

Inheriting her love for photography from her parents, both professionals, she has refined her skills to produce the photographs used in this book.

Adept at all aspects of photography, she prefers landscapes. Her work has been published in books and periodicals since 1978. Sherry's camera of choice is a Nikon F4.

TIPS ON FLAGSTAFF HIKING

WATER

Don't count on finding water anywhere. Take your water with you.

HIGH ALTITUDE

Hikes in Flagstaff start at 7000 feet and go all the way up to 12, 643 feet, the highest point in Arizona. High altitudes mean:

1. You won't have the energy you are used to.
2. Hiking will be a lot harder on your heart.
3. You will be drier than usual.
4. You will sunburn more easily.
5. It will be much colder than normal, especially at night.
6. Alcohol is much more intoxicating.

THE TERRAIN

Flagstaff country is generally benign. You can get lost in the woods, but you won't if you stay on the hikes described in this book.

ROCK CLIMBING

We do not provide any rock climbing information. If you want to go rock climbing, you are on your own.

VARMINTS

Because Flagstaff is cool and has long winters, you won't find many mosquitoes. Pests like chiggers are absent. Ticks are rare in the high country. There are a few black widow spiders around, but no scorpions. Rattlesnakes are not entirely out of their range, but they are not plentiful. Even so, don't do anything stupid like reaching blindly under a rock or brush pile.

WEATHER

Flagstaff's regular snow season is anytime between Halloween and Easter. Don't count on hiking in the high country then. Summers are perfection, though rain is common between the Fourth of July and Labor Day.

ACCESS

Some of these hikes are totally unavailable in winter. Hikes in the high mountains are impossible then because of snow. The average snowfall in Flagstaff is 110 inches, and the mountains get even more. In addition to the obvious road problems caused by snow, some of the back roads are barred by locked gates during the winter. Call the Forest Service for road data.

HANDY CHARTS AND DATA

Hours of Daylight

	JAN	FEB	MAR	APR	MAY	JUNE	JULY	AUG	SEPT	OCT	NOV	DEC
SUNRISE	7:35	7:26	6:57	6:14	5:36	5:14	5:16	5:35	5:59	6:21	6:48	7:16
SUNSET	5:26	5:55	6:22	6:48	7:12	7:35	7:45	7:30	6:54	6:11	5:33	5:15

Normal Precipitation—inches

JAN	FEB	MAR	APR	MAY	JUN	JUL	AUG	SEP	OCT	NOV	DEC
2.04	2.09	2.55	1.48	0.72	0.40	2.78	2.75	2.03	1.61	1.95	2.40

Normal Temperatures—High and Low

JAN	FEB	MAR	APR	MAY	JUN	JUL	AUG	SEP	OCT	NOV	DEC
42.2	45.3	49.2	57.8	67.4	78.2	81.9	79.3	73.2	63.4	51.1	61.0
15.2	17.7	21.3	26.7	33.3	41.4	50.5	48.9	41.2	31.0	22.4	15.8

Converting Feet to Meters

Meters	910	1212	1515	1818	2121	2424	2727	3030	3333	3636
Feet	3000	4000	5000	6000	7000	8000	9000	10000	11000	12000

Average Walking Rates

Time	1 Hour	30 Min.	15 Min.	7.5 Min.
Miles	2.0	1.0	0.5	0.25
K M	3.2	1.6	0.8	0.4

CLIMATE

Flagstaff, elevation 7,000 feet, is situated on a volcanic plateau at the base of the highest mountains in Arizona. The climate may be classified as vigorous with cold winters, mild, pleasantly cool summers, moderate humidity, and considerable diurnal temperature change. The stormy months are January, February, March, July, and August.

Based on the 1951-1980 period, the average first occurrence of 32 degrees Fahrenheit in the fall is September 21 and the average last occurrence in the spring is June 13.

Temperatures in Flagstaff are characteristic of high altitude climates. The average daily range of temperature is relatively high, especially in the winter months, October to March, as a result of extensive snow cover and clear skies. Winter minimum temperatures frequently reach zero or below and temperatures of -25 degrees or less have occurred. Summer maximum temperatures are often above 80 degrees and occasionally, temperatures have exceeded 95 degrees.

The Flagstaff area is semi-arid. Several months have recorded little or no precipitation. Over 90 consecutive days without measurable precipitation have occurred. Annual precipitation ranges from less than 10 inches to more than 35 inches. Winter snowfalls can be heavy, exceeding 100 inches during one month and over 200 inches during the winter season. However, accumulations are quite variable from year to year. Some winter months may experience little or no snow and the winter season has produced total snow accumulations of less than 12 inches.

—National Climatic Data Center, U. S. A.

HOW TO USE THIS BOOK

Alphabetical arrangement. The 134 hikes in this book are arranged from A-Z.

Index. The index starts at page 262. It groups the hikes by geographical area and by special features.

Layout. The text describing a hike and the map of the hike are on facing pages so that you can take in everything at once.

Maps. The maps are not to scale but their proportions are generally correct. The main purpose of the maps is to get you to the trailhead. The **maps** show mileage point-to-point. The **text** gives cumulative mileage.

Larger scale maps. For the big picture, we recommend using a Forest Service recreation map.

Bold type. When you see a trail name in **bold** type it means that the hike is described in this book.

Ratings. We show hikes rated as *easy, moderate* and *hard.* We are middle-aged hikers in normal condition, not highly conditioned athletes who never tire. Hikers should adjust our ratings for their own fitness level. The hike-in-a-box on each map may best show how hard a hike is.

Mileage. Driving distance was measured from Flagstaff City Hall located at the junction of Route 66

and Humphreys Street. All hikes start from this point. Milepost locations are also shown on the maps (as MP) on highways that have them. Hike mileage was measured by a pedometer.

Access roads. To reach many of these hikes, you will have to travel unpaved roads, some of them rough. Our Toyota Tercel has 4-wheel drive but not much clearance. Our access ratings were based on how well the Tercel handled the roads. Some drives require a high clearance vehicle.

Safety. We avoid taking risks on hikes. None of these hikes requires technical climbing.

Wilderness Areas. The Flagstaff area is blessed by having many of its hiking places included within federally designated Wilderness Areas. This is great for the hiker. Please read the Rules of the Trail on page 9.

Cairns. These are stacks of rocks used as trail markers. Some are officially placed, while others are made by hikers.

Mileposts. Major Arizona highways are marked every mile by a sign about three feet high on the right side of the road.

RULES OF THE TRAIL

Artifacts: Leave potsherds, arrowheads, and other artifacts where you find them.

Bikes: Stay on roads and trails. You cannot ride a bike inside a Wilderness Area. Some people will go into an open area on a road and then sneak from it onto a wilderness trail. These scofflaws cause road and trail closures. Abuse it and lose it.

Cabins: Northern Arizona's climate is hard on cabins and they are scarce. Treat the few remaining ones gently. Don't climb on them, pry boards off, or go digging for buried treasure.

Dogs: If you take your dog along on a hike, it should be on a leash.

Garbage: Pack it in, pack it out.

Rock Art: Do not touch it. Skin oils cause deterioration. Professionals don't even apply chalk in order to photograph rock art today, because it causes damage.

Ruins: Just look, don't touch. Preserve them. Don't pot hunt, climb walls or do anything else that harm a ruin. Help them survive.

Trails: Stay on trails. They have been designed not only to provide access but also to bypass areas that can be harmed by people walking on them. Don't cut across switchbacks. It is disheartening to see how fast a trail can be destroyed by careless use.

Wilderness Areas: These are special places. The goal is to leave them unimpaired for future use and enjoyment. In the wilderness, the hiker is king. No mechanized travel is permitted in Wilderness Areas, not even bicycles. Horses are not allowed. Although Wilderness Areas may appear to be very rugged, they are quite fragile. Use them lightly. Leave no trace. They are a gift that we must all act to protect and preserve.

NAPHS

Hiking Grand Canyon—1900

Access Map

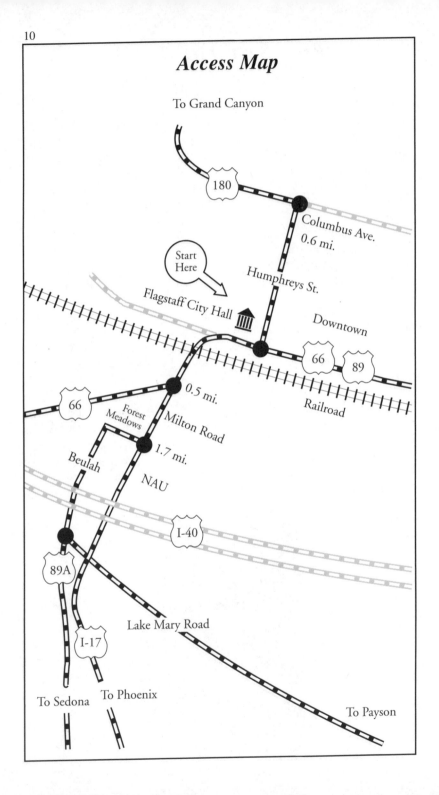

To Grand Canyon

180

Columbus Ave.
0.6 mi.

Start Here

Humphreys St.

Flagstaff City Hall

Downtown

66 89

0.5 mi.

66

Forest Meadows

Milton Road

Railroad

1.7 mi.

Beulah

NAU

I-40

89A

I-17

Lake Mary Road

To Sedona   To Phoenix

To Payson

Access Map

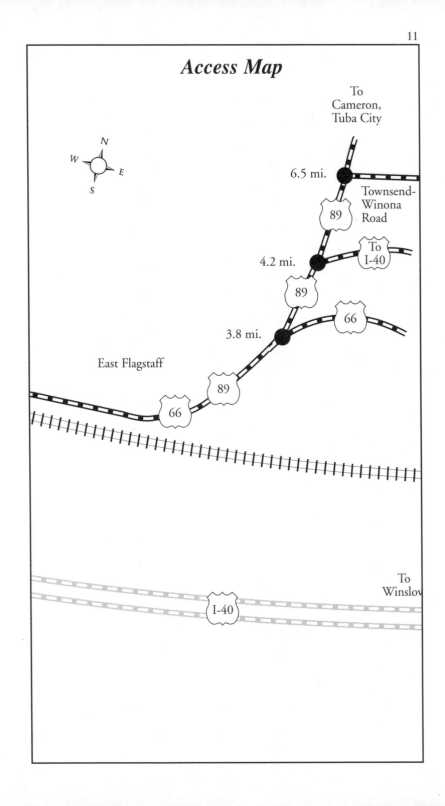

HIKE LOCATOR

LOCATION MAP

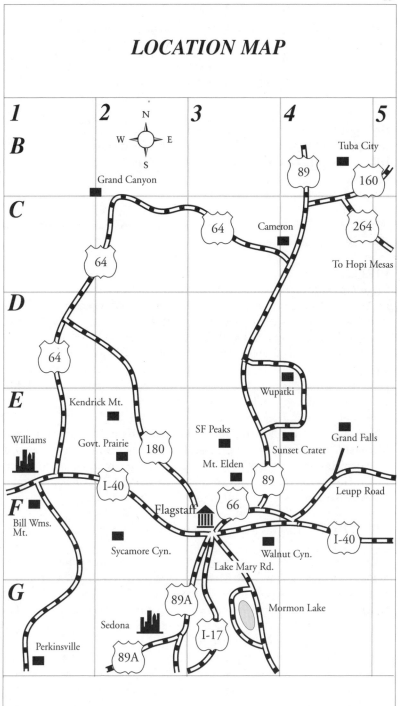

A-1 MOUNTAIN

General Information
Location Map E2
Bellemont and Flagstaff West USGS Maps
Coconino Forest Service Map

Driving Distance One Way: 9.9 miles 15.84 *km* (Time 30 minutes)
Access Road: All cars, Last 4.4 miles *7.04 km* good gravel road
Hiking Distance One Way: 1.0 miles *1.6 km* (Time 40 minutes)
How Strenuous: Hard
Features: Landmark hill north of Flagstaff

NUTSHELL: This hike takes you to the top of a prominent landmark on the Flagstaff horizon.

DIRECTIONS:
From Flagstaff City Hall Go:
    West a block on Route 66 (Santa Fe), then south, beneath the railroad overpass, see Access Map, page 10. At 0.50 miles *0.8 km* you will reach a Y intersection. The right fork is Route 66. Take it. You will soon leave town, driving on a stretch of fabled Highway 66. At the 5.0 mile *8.0 km* point you will merge onto Interstate-40 West. Look for Exit 190 at the 5.3 mile *8.5 km* point, and take it. Turn right at the stop sign and take gravel road FR 506. Follow it to the 7.5 mile *12 km* point, where you will be on top of Observatory Mesa. Here you will meet FR 515 forking to the right. Go left here, staying on FR 506, the main road. It will curl around toward A-1 Mountain. At 8.2 miles *13.12 km* there is a fork. Go left, again on the main road, which is now FR 518B. At 9.7 miles *15.5 km* you will come to a radio tower. Go beyond it on a rocky road to the 9.9 mile *15.84 km* point, turning left where it forks, and park just before a fenced stock tank.

TRAILHEAD: There is a road going uphill to your left. Walk the road.

DESCRIPTION: Before you walk up the mountain, take a minute to look at the stock tank. You will see what looks like a large corrugated metal shed roof resting on the ground. It slopes downward. A gutter catches all the rain water that runs off the roofing and channels it into a pipe that flows into a large round metal tank from where it feeds out into a trough. This is an upscale version of the old rain barrel.
    The hike: as you walk this road uphill, you will wonder who made it and why. It goes as straight up a mountain as a road can, with impossibly steep grades for driving. Was it a fire break? The area around A-1 Mountain was the subject of one of the largest forest fires in Flagstaff's history in 1951.

A-1 Mountain is one of those mountains that does not have a single top. You will reach the first knob at 0.20 miles *0.32 km*. You can see a higher knob ahead of you. Here the road really gets steep. You climb it to the half mile point, where you are in the basin of a volcano. In spring, this may be a small lake. There is a right fork in the road at 0.6 miles *0.96 km*. Take it. The road straight ahead dwindles down to nothing. The right fork takes you to a higher knob and ends on the north face of the mountain at about one mile. One of the main reasons for climbing a mountain is to have views. Unfortunately, the forest on this top is so heavy that you only get glimpses of the countryside—too bad, as this mountain is well located.

This mountain was named after the huge Arizona Cattle Company, which had its headquarters in Ft. Valley, from 1885-1899. Its brand was the A-1.

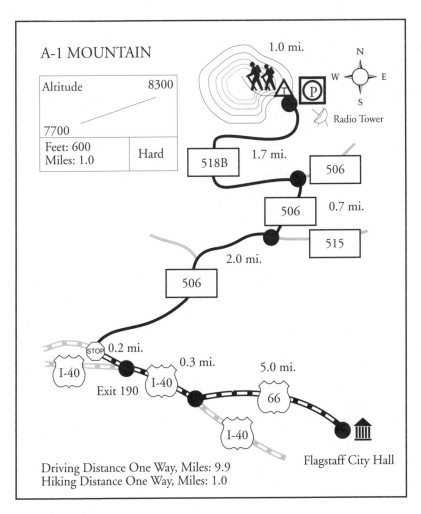

ANTELOPE HILLS

General Information
Location Map E2
Wing Mountain USGS Map
Coconino Forest Service Map

Driving Distance One Way: 18.5 miles *29.6 km* (Time 40 minutes)
Access Road: All cars, Last 4.0 miles *6.4 km* good gravel road
Hiking Distance One Way: 0.8 miles *1.3 km* (Time 45 minutes)
How Strenuous: Moderate
Features: Views

NUTSHELL: This mountain 18.5 miles *29.6 km* north of Flagstaff is located at the northeast end of Government Prairie and gives tremendous views of the prairie to the south.

DIRECTIONS:
From Flagstaff City Hall Go:
   North on Humphreys Street for 0.60 miles *0.96 km*. See Access Map, page 10. Turn left at the stoplight onto Columbus Avenue and follow it around a big curve to the north. You will see the street signs call this road Columbus at first, then Ft. Valley Road and then Highway 180. Stay on Highway 180 to the 14.5 mile *23.2 km* point (MP 230), where an unpaved road takes off to the left. Turn left onto this road, FR 245, and follow it to the 17.6 mile *28.16 km* point where it intersects FR 171. Turn left onto FR 171 and follow it to the 18.25 mile *29.2 km* point, where FR 812 goes off to the right. Turn right on FR 812 and take it to the 18.5 mile *29.6 km* point. Park there.

TRAILHEAD: You will see the Antelope Hills to your right (north). You will also see a primitive road going to it and then going straight up the side of the mountain. Hike near this road.

DESCRIPTION: There are several hills surrounding Government Prairie. While they all have features in common, each has its own distinct characteristics and personality. The Antelope Hills are the farthest north of the group, situated at the north end of the prairie, close to Kendrick Peak.
   The trail was not made for hiking. Kamikaze four-wheelers created it by charging straight up the mountain in a *falter-and-die* test of their machines. Government Prairie is now closed to off-road travel, so the scar is healing. Help it heal by hiking alongside it, but not on it.
   The Antelope Hills have two knobs. The southern knob that you climb first is bare. As a result it provides some great views. You can see particu-

larly well to the south, where the whole sweep of the Government Prairie is in view, although your ability to see beyond the midpoint is restricted to the opening between Klostermeyer Hill and Rain Tank Hill. The views east are also fine, as you look onto the western side of the San Francisco Peaks. We were here in October and saw a great display of yellow and red aspen leaves on the slopes of the peaks.

Once you reach the top you will find that there is only a small drop in elevation to the saddle between the knobs and that it is easy to walk down to the saddle and then up to the top of the north knob. Sad to say, the views to the north are not good because of heavy timber on the north knob.

On your way up or down, check out the ruins of an old cabin and out-buildings at the foot of the hill to the east of the trail about thirty yards. You will also see a couple of platforms about eight feet high. These are part of an NAU research project into the life of the prairie dog. There is a large prairie dog colony surrounding the platforms.

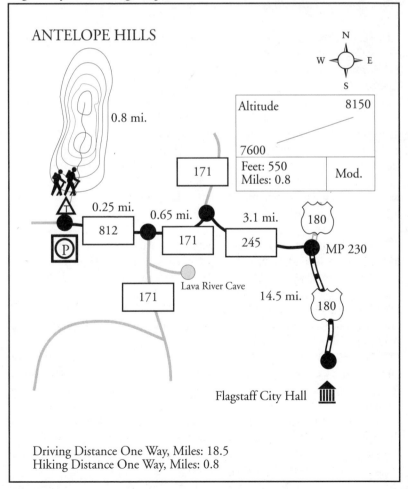

ANTELOPE HILLS

N
W ← ⊕ → E
S

Altitude   8150

7600

Feet: 550
Miles: 0.8   Mod.

0.8 mi.

171

0.25 mi.

812   171   245   MP 230
0.65 mi.   3.1 mi.   180

P

Lava River Cave

171   14.5 mi.   180

Flagstaff City Hall 🏛

Driving Distance One Way, Miles: 18.5
Hiking Distance One Way, Miles: 0.8

A(U)BINEAU CANYON #127

General Information
Location Map E3
Humphreys Peak and White Horse Hills USGS Maps
Coconino Forest Service Map

Driving Distance One Way: 24.9 miles *40 km* (Time 50 minutes)
Access Road: All cars, Last 5.3 miles *8.5 km* gravel, in medium condition
Hiking Distance One Way: 2.4 miles *3.9 km* (Time 2 hours)
How Strenuous: Hard, Steep trail, High altitudes
Features: Alpine scenery, Vast views

NUTSHELL: This is a killer hike up the north face of the San Francisco
Peaks about 25 *miles 40 km* north of Flagstaff.

DIRECTIONS:
From Flagstaff City Hall Go:
North on Humphreys Street, 0.60 *miles 1.0 km* to the stoplight. See
Access Map, page 10. Turn left on Columbus Avenue and follow it north
around a curve, where the road changes its name to Ft. Valley Road, and
later is posted as Highway 180. At 19.6 *miles 31.4 km* (MP 235.2) turn right
on the upper Hart Prairie Road, FR 151. At 21.2 *miles 34 km*, turn left on FR
418 and continue on it to the 24.3 *miles 39 km* point, where you will see a
sign for the Bear Jaw and Abineau Trails. The access road to the trailhead is
marked FR 9123J. Turn right onto it and follow it to the 24.7 miles point,
where you fork left, then to the 24.9 miles *40 km* point, where you will reach
the parking area. Park at the parking lot

TRAILHEAD: The cinder road on which you drove in is blocked by a row
of boulders at the parking lot. Walk past the boulders and go on down to the
end of the road. The trail takes off to your right, uphill, and is marked

DESCRIPTION: You actually start this hike on a connecting trail that
climbs about 0.4 *miles 0.64 km* from the parking lot and then meets the
Abineau Trail. Here you turn right and go uphill.
The Abineau Trail was used by sheepherders years ago as a means of
taking their sheep to high summer pastures. The first mile of the trail was a
road from Reese Tank. The Reese Tank part of the trail is now bypassed by
the new routing.
The present trail starts rather mildly, moving through a nice forest, then
the pitch changes to a steeper grade. Soon it will become obvious to you that
you are in a canyon. Just above the 9000 foot level, the forest is entirely
spruce and the trail is very rocky and steep.

Near the top, you break out into a small park, treeless in spots. The view is quite breathtaking. Ahead of you (south), is the towering top of Mt. Humphreys, highest point in Arizona at 12,643 feet. Behind you (north), you can see forever. From this spot it's a hard haul up to FR 146, the end of the trail, at 2.4 *miles 3.9 km* from the parking area.

If you want to do a loop, walk along east on FR 146 for a distance of 2.0 *miles 3.2 km* to the Bear Jaw Trail (signed) and go down it. This will add 2.0 *miles 3.2 km* to this hike, for a loop total of 7.05 *miles 11.3 km*, compared to a total of 4.8 *miles 7.7 km* going up and down the Abineau Trail only.

You will find two spellings for this trail. Most of the old sources show it as "Aubineau." Recently the name began to appear as "Abineau." We show both spellings so people will know it is the same trail. It is named after Julius Aubineau, Flagstaff mayor in 1898, who is regarded as the father of the Flagstaff municipal water system.

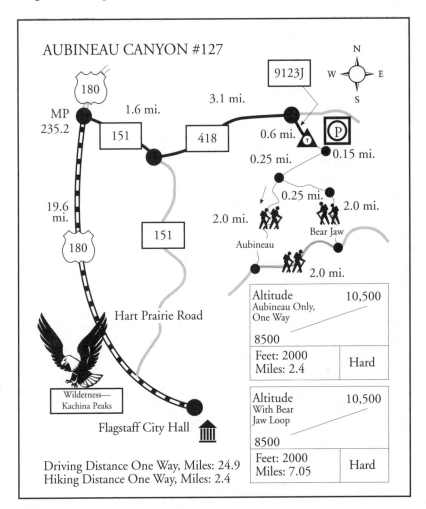

A(U)BINEAU PIPELINE TRAIL

General Information
Location Map E3
Humphreys Peak and White Horse Hills USGS Maps
Coconino Forest Service Map

Driving Distance One Way: 21.6 miles *34.6 km* (Time 45 minutes)
Access Road: All cars, Last 4.5 miles *7.2 km* medium dirt road
Hiking Distance One Way: 6.7 miles *10.7 km* (Time 4 hours)
How Strenuous: Moderate, except for high altitudes
Features: Beautiful forests, marvelous views

NUTSHELL: You start this hike on Locket Meadow, high on the east side
of the San Francisco Peaks 22.0 *35.2 km* north of town. From the meadow
you follow the Inner Basin Trail (an old service road) to Jack Smith Spring.
Then you branch off onto another closed road that takes you around the
north side of the peaks through a beautiful forest to a bare spot from which
you have vast views. A great trail in October when aspen leaves are turning.

DIRECTIONS:
From Flagstaff City Hall Go:
   East on Route 66. This will take you through the city, heading first easterly and then north out of town. See Access Map, pages 10-11. Route 66
veers off to the right in about 3.8 miles *6.08 km*. Go straight here, on
Highway 89. At 17.1 miles *27.4 km* (MP 431.2)—just past the entrance to
Sunset Crater—turn left onto FR 552 and take it to the 18.3 mile *29.3 km*
point, where you will see a sign for Lockett Meadow. Go right. From here
the road is a winding narrow gravel route which zigzags up the face of the
mountain, giving great views of the Painted Desert as you go. At 21.3 miles
34 km you reach Lockett Meadow. Go to your right into the campground.
Park anywhere around the 21.6 mile *34.6 km* point.

TRAILHEAD: Use the Inner Basin trailhead, which you will find by driving all the way back into the trees among the campsites. The trailhead is
posted with a big sign to the left of a toilet.

DESCRIPTION: The first part of this hike follows the **Inner Basin Trail**
for 1.5 miles *2.4 km* to Jack Smith Spring. This is a beautiful part of the trail,
a lush alpine habitat with plenty of aspens, firs, ferns and other vegetation.
You are walking along a maintenance road used by the City of Flagstaff. Its
purpose is to allow city vehicles to get to the springs in the Inner Basin,
which are part of Flagstaff's water supply. The road is closed to all other
vehicular traffic, so it makes an excellent hiking trail.

At Jack Smith Spring you will find a couple of old green cabins and a supply dump with water pipe and other materials lying about. A road comes in from the left here. It is FR 146, which goes down to the Schultz Pass Road. FR 146 road is used as a hiking trail, see **Tunnel Road.** What you want to do at this point is take a road to the right, which goes uphill. You will soon see that it is not maintained.

This old road goes around to the north side of the Peaks. It is not used by vehicles and is not maintained, but makes a fine hiking trail. It takes you on a gradual climb, curving around to the north.

The **Bear Jaw** and **Aubineau Canyon** hiking trails terminate on this road near its end.

You will pass through heavy aspen forests, so it is a great place to come in the fall to see the changing leaves. Mid-October is the right time for this. The road/trail ends in a bare spot on the side of the mountain, where there are sweeping views to the north.

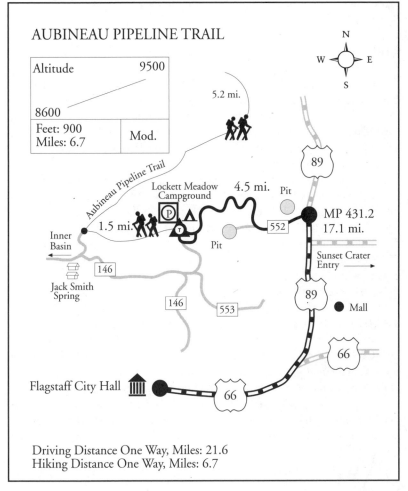

Mangum

BABE'S HOLE

General Information
Location Map F2
Sycamore Point USGS Map
Coconino Forest Service Map

Driving Distance One Way: 24.1 miles *38.6 km* (Time 1 hour)
Access Road: High clearance needed for last 1.8 miles *2.9 km*
Hiking Distance One Way: 1.2 miles *1.9 km* (Time 1 hour)
How Strenuous: Moderate
Features: Remote hidden spring, Virgin forests in a Wilderness

NUTSHELL: Located 24.1 miles *38.6 km* southwest of Flagstaff, this trail takes you to a remote and beautiful spring hidden away on the east side of Sycamore Canyon.

DIRECTIONS:
From Flagstaff City Hall Go:
    West one block on Route 66 (Santa Fe), then left (south) beneath the railroad overpass. See Access Map, page 10. At 0.50 miles *0.8 km* you will reach a Y intersection. The right fork is named Route 66. Take it. You will soon leave town. At 2.6 miles *4.2 km* you will reach a road going to the left. This is the Woody Mountain Road, FR 231. Take it. It is paved about a mile and then turns into a cinder road. At 16.6 miles *26.6 km* you will intersect FR 538. Turn right onto FR 538 and follow it to the 22.3 mile *35.7 km* point, where it intersects FR 538E. Turn right on 538E. At 22.7 miles *36.4 km* you hit another intersection, where FR 538E forks to the left, going to Dorsey Spring Road. The road is rough beyond here. Keep straight, now on FR 538G, and follow it to its end at 23.7 miles *37.9 km*, where it meets FR 527A. Turn left onto the Kelsey Trail road, going to the 24.1 mile *38.6 km* point, the parking area. This last 0.4 mile *0.64 km* stretch is terrible, a real tire-eater. You might want to walk this bit.

TRAILHEAD: You will see a big sign at the parking area.

DESCRIPTION: This trail shares the same right of way with the **Kelsey Spring Trail**, and you have to pass through Kelsey Spring to reach Babe's Hole. The comments about the Kelsey Spring hike apply here.
    The parking lot is located right on the edge of the rim, so the trail immediately plunges down into the canyon. It is steep but not slippery. It passes through a beautiful forest, which gets more beautiful and interesting as you go.
    Kelsey Spring is easily reached in 0.5 miles *0.8 km*, on a shelf of level

land. Enjoy it and then continue down the canyon. As you leave Kelsey Spring, you enter an unusual life zone where the prevailing pines disappear, to be replaced with oaks and other deciduous trees. The area seems to get a lot of moisture, so the vegetation is heavy.

At Babe's Hole several hill folds come together to make a small protected pocket of land. You can see why it got the name "hole" as it really is a small and enclosed area. Babe's Hole is a beautiful place. It looks otherwordly, with many bent trees overarching and protecting the spring, which is lined with a small circle of rocks and roofed over with poles. It is very quiet. A fantastic place.

From Babe's Hole you can continue downhill another 0.15 miles *0.24 km*, where there is a trail junction. The **Kelsey-Winter Trail** takes off to the left, to **Dorsey Spring** and then **Winter Cabin Spring**, while the trail to **Geronimo Spring** goes down to the bottom of the canyon.

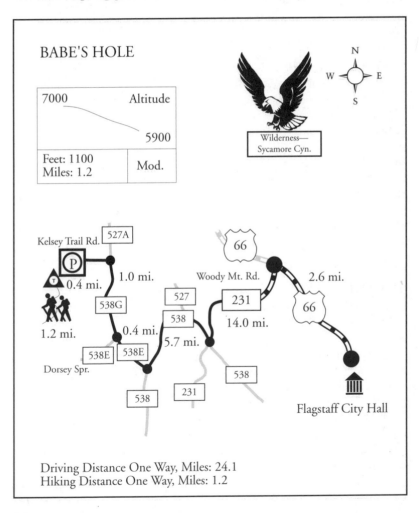

BABE'S HOLE

7000	Altitude
	5900
Feet: 1100 Miles: 1.2	Mod.

Wilderness— Sycamore Cyn.

Kelsey Trail Rd. 527A
0.4 mi. 1.0 mi.
66
Woody Mt. Rd. 2.6 mi.
538G
1.2 mi. 527
538 231 66
0.4 mi. 14.0 mi.
5.7 mi.
538E 538E
Dorsey Spr.
538
538 231
Flagstaff City Hall

Driving Distance One Way, Miles: 24.1
Hiking Distance One Way, Miles: 1.2

Mangum

BALD HILL

General Information
Location Map E2
Kendrick Peak and Wing Mt. USGS Maps
Coconino Forest Service Map

Driving Distance One Way: 22.4 miles *35.8 km* (Time 45 minutes)
Access Road: All cars, Last 8.3 miles *13.3 km* good gravel road
Hiking Distance One Way: 1.1 miles *1.76 km* (Time 1.0 hours)
How Strenuous: Moderate
Features: Views

NUTSHELL: Bald Hill is a foothill located to the south of Kendrick Peak. Because the top is bald, it provides great views.

DIRECTIONS:
From Flagstaff City Hall Go:
   North on Humphreys Street for 0.60 miles *1.0 km*. See Access Map, page 10. Turn left at the stoplight onto Columbus Avenue and follow it around a big curve to the north. You will see the street signs call this road Columbus at first, then Ft. Valley Road and then Highway 180. Stay on Highway 180 to the 14.5 miles *23.2 km* point (MP 230), where an unpaved road takes off to the left. Turn left onto this road, FR 245, and follow it to the 17.6 mile *28.2 km* point where it intersects FR 171. Turn right on FR 171 and follow it to the 20.7 mile *33.2 km* point, where you will see a sign for the **Kendrick Mountain Trail**. Turn right on the drive to the Kendrick Mountain trailhead, which you will reach at 21.1 miles 33.8 *km*. Here you will see a sign for FR 190 going uphill to your left. Follow it to the 22.8 mile *36.5 km* point, where there is a logging road to the left. Park near the intersection.

TRAILHEAD: On the north side of FR 190 you will see a blocked road going uphill. The beginning of the road has been scarified. It has a sign, "Closed to motor vehicles, foot travel welcome."

DESCRIPTION: FR 190 takes you through a saddle between Newman Hill on your left and Bald Hill on your right. You will find some pretty landscape in this little-traveled place, particularly on the north side of Newman Hill, where there is a stand of aspen near Newman Tank.
   Beyond Newman Tank you will go downhill. Where the road flattens out, you will find a road to your right that is not on any official map. This goes to the top of a small knoll on the side of Newman Hill. We think it must be a recent logging road.
   Park near this place and then look across FR 190. You will see a road

going up the side of the mountain. It looks red. Where the mouth of the road meets FR 190, the Forest Service has closed the road to motor vehicle travel. The closed road makes a fine hiking trail.

You will make a fairly gradual climb as you walk along the road, which goes generally eastward. The road ends at 0.8 miles 1.3 *km* at a ravine. From this point you can see the crest of Bald Hill before you. We generally like to keep hikers on roads or trails, but sometimes a bit of bushwhacking is worthwhile. We think that this is such a case, because you will not get lost and the footing is okay. Just hike up to the top.

When you top out on the crest, you will be rewarded, with fine views all around. The views of Kendrick, which is very close, are splendid. You can also see the San Francisco Peaks, Government Prairie, and many other worthwhile sights.

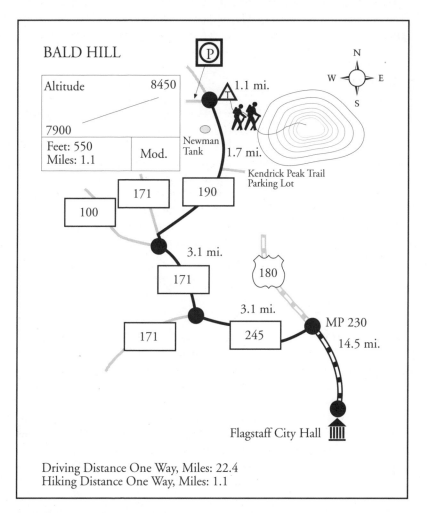

BEALE ROAD ON GOVT. PRAIRIE

General Information
Location Map E2
Parks and Wing Mt. USGS Maps
Kaibab (Williams) Forest Service Map

Driving Distance One Way: 24.3 miles *38.9 km* (Time 40 minutes)
Access Road: All cars, Last 11.0 miles *17.6 km* good gravel road
Hiking Distance One Way: 2.3 miles *3.7 km* (Time 1.5 hours))
How Strenuous: Easy
Features: Historic road, Views

NUTSHELL: This stretch of the Beale Road crosses Government Prairie. The old wagon tracks are visible and have been marked. A hike across the prairie would be worthwhile in its own right, but with the added bonus of the wagon road, it becomes a fascinating experience.

DIRECTIONS:
From Flagstaff City Hall Go:
    West a block on Route 66 (Santa Fe), then south, beneath the railroad overpass. See Access Map, page 10. At 0.50 miles *0.8 km* you will reach a Y intersection. The right fork is Route 66. Take it. You will soon leave town. At the 4.8 mile *7.7 km* point you will merge onto Interstate-40 West. Look for Exit 185, "Transwestern Rd., Bellemont" and take it. It is at the 10.8 mile *17.3 km* point. From the exit turn right and go to the frontage road, where you turn left onto FR 146. You are now following another stretch of U.S. 66. Stay on this to the 18 mile *28.9 km* point, where you will see FR 107 fork right. Take FR 107 and follow it to the 24.3 mile *38.9 km* point, where FR 107 and FR 100 join. Park off FR 107 on the right (east) just below the intersection.

TRAILHEAD: At the gate.

DESCRIPTION: The Beale Road was scouted in 1857 by a government party led by Lt. Edward Beale. It was this *government* sponsorship leading to the establishment of a *government* road that gave the name Government Prairie. Beale returned with work crews in 1858 and 1859 to develop the road and it was used as a major east-west road until the coming of the railroad in 1882. On the first expedition Beale used twenty camels, an experiment to see how well they could handle American deserts. This explains why a camel is used as a symbol for the road. You will see the camel burned onto the posts that mark the trail. Beale loved the camels but the cowboys (camelboys?) hated them and they never caught on.

At the junction of FR 107 and FR 100 you will see a fence to your right with a gate. Go through the gate to begin walking the Beale Road. You will pick up markers there. The right of way is marked with posts, rock cairns, blazes and brass caps. In 0.15 miles *0.24 km* you will come upon an old homestead to your left. There isn't much left, but you can make out the outlines of stones that were used as footings.

At 0.3 miles *0.48 km* you will leave the road you are walking and go across country. This takes you from open land, through woods. At 1.3 miles *2.1 km*, you break out onto the main part of the prairie where you will see the wagon tracks clearly and follow them. You cross FR 793 at the 1.4 mile *2.3 km* point. When you reach the 2.3 mile point, the road leaves the prairie and enters a wooded area in front of **Wild Bill Hill**. We end the hike here (the road continues) as crossing the prairie makes a good day hike.

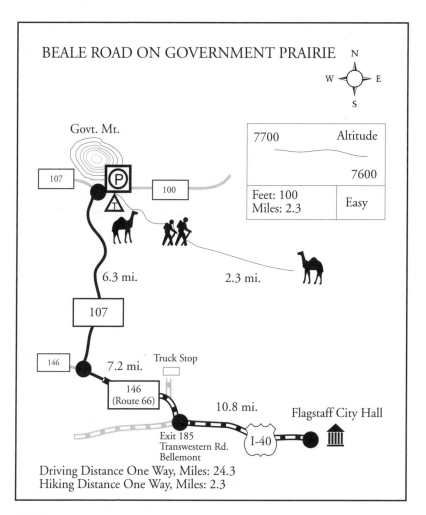

BEALE ROAD—LAWS SPRING

General Information
Location Map E2
Squaw Mountain and Williams, USGS Maps
Kaibab (Williams) Forest Service Map

Driving Distance One Way: 37.6 miles *60 km* (Time 1 hour)
Access Road: All cars, Last 10.1 miles *16.2 km* good gravel roads
Hiking Distance One Way: 0.25 miles *0.4 km* (Time 30 minutes)
How Strenuous: Easy
Features: Spring with petroglyphs, Historical 1850s wagon route

NUTSHELL: This hike takes you to Laws Spring, an attractive historical site with an interpretive sign, rock art (both ancient and modern), and then onto the Beale Road.

DIRECTIONS:
From Flagstaff City Hall Go:
    West a block on Route 66 (Santa Fe), then south, beneath the railroad overpass. See Access Map, page 10. At 0.50 miles *0.8 km* you will reach a Y intersection. The right fork is Route 66. Take it. You will soon leave town. At the 4.8 mile *7.7 km* point you will merge onto Interstate-40 West. Drive I-40 West to the 24.5 mile *39.2 km* point (MP 172), where you will take Exit 171 for Pittman Valley. Turn left at the stop sign and take paved road FR 74, toward the Compressor Station. The paving will end at 27.3 miles *43.7 km.* At 32.2 miles *51.5 km* you will intersect FR 141 and go right on it. At 32.7 miles *52.3 km* you will see a sign for Boulin Tank and intersect FR 730. Turn left on FR 730 and follow it to the 34.95 mile *55.9 km* point where you join FR 115. Turn left onto FR 115 and follow it to the 36.85 mile *58.9 km* point. There you will see a road to your left, with a Laws Spring sign. Take this road to the parking lot, where you park at 37.6 miles *60 km.*

TRAILHEAD: Posted at the parking lot.

DESCRIPTION: The Beale Road was a heroic undertaking. The United States acquired Arizona north of the Gila River in 1848 after the Mexican War, and Congress sent Beale to explore it and find a travel route across northern Arizona to California in 1857. Beale's party included camels to deal with deserts. Beale located a good route roughly following the thirty-fifth parallel. In 1858 and 1859 he returned under a Congressional grant and developed the road for travel. About seventy-five percent of the old road has been located, thanks largely to the efforts of Flagstaff's Jack Beale Smith. The Forest Service joined with Smith in the project of marking the road, and their efforts made this hike possible.

The trail takes you gently down the bank of a small stream, where you will find a rock basin at the bottom. Look for Indian rock art along the way, and you will see a few symbols. Laws Spring fills the rock basin, and seems to be perennial. It was an important water source for travelers on the Beale Road. The words, "Laws Spring" were chiseled into a rock in 1859 by a member of Beale's crew. Look carefully and you will see other rock art, both ancient Indian and modern. The Forest Service has placed a nice explanatory plaque on the face of a boulder at the spring.

After you have enjoyed the spring, take the rest of the trail, up the other bank, again a gentle climb. At the 0.25 mile *0.4 km* point, you will find the Beale Road marker in a field. This is officially the end of the hike, but you might want to walk part of the old road. Turn right at the marker and follow the cairns and posts as far as you wish.

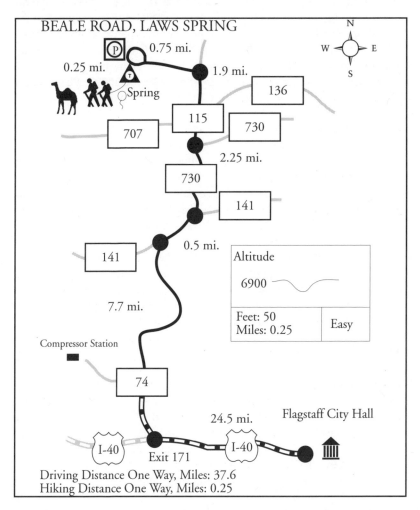

BEAR CANYON, OVERLAND ROAD

General Information
Location Map F1
Williams South, May Tank Pocket USGS Maps
Kaibab Forest Service Map

Driving Distance One Way: 46.55 miles *74.5 km* (Time 1.25 hours)
Access Road: High clearance needed for last 0.9 miles *1.44 km*
Hiking Distance One Way: 2.25 miles *3.6 km* (Time 1.5 hours)
How Strenuous: Moderate
Features: Historic Overland Road (1860s), Beautiful wild canyons

NUTSHELL: The Overland Road was built in 1863 to give access from the Beale Road (at a point where Flagstaff was founded 17 years later) to the gold fields near Prescott. It was used until rail transportation made it obsolete in 1882. In 1988 the portion of the old road through the Kaibab Forest was located and marked. On this hike you will enjoy hiking part of the Overland Road, as it crosses the head of Bear Canyon and then goes across country to join the paved Perkinsville Road south of Williams.

DIRECTIONS:
From Flagstaff City Hall Go:
    South on Route 66 under the railroad overpass. Be sure to follow Route 66 when it turns right at the second stoplight. See Access Map, page 10. In about five miles *8.0 km* you will merge onto I-40 West and stay on it to the 30.3 miles *48.5 km* point, the Williams Exit, #165. Take that exit and at the stop sign go left to Williams. Go into town on Railroad Avenue to the 32.9 mile point *52.6 km* where you will find Fourth Street. Turn left on Fourth Street. As it leaves town its name changes to the Perkinsville Road (FR 173). Stay on this road to the 45.65 mile *73.0 km* point, where you will turn left on FR 57. At the 45.85 mile *73.4 km* point, you reach the junction with FR 57A. Turn right (south) on 57A and follow it to the 46.55 mile *74.5 km* point, where you will find a cattle guard. Park off the road there.

TRAILHEAD: Start at the cattle guard.

DESCRIPTION: The Overland Road is marked with 4x4 posts, large cairns (rock piles), brass pins and blazes. You will see some of these along FR 57A, which was part of the Overland Road. Walk down FR 57A to a point 0.5 miles *0.8 km* from the cattle guard, where you will see a burro marker on a 4x4 post. Walk 25 paces beyond it and you will see markers where you leave the roadway and take off cross country to your right (west). Follow these markers from now on. You can seldom see the path, so be sure to follow the markers. They are well located. Never guess where the hike is going. Keep a marker in sight at all times.

The Overland Road's builders had many challenges. One of the major ones was the problem of avoiding the canyons that seem to cut this area everywhere. You will see how they met this challenge, as you go across Bear Canyon at its head, where it is a tiny ravine. You will skirt three other canyons as you go.

Once the road builders had dodged the canyons, they got onto a finger ridge that took them down from the Mogollon Rim to the Verde Valley, the route still used by the present Perkinsville Road, which you will meet at the end of this hike. The place where you come out onto the Perkinsville Road is at MP 170.4.

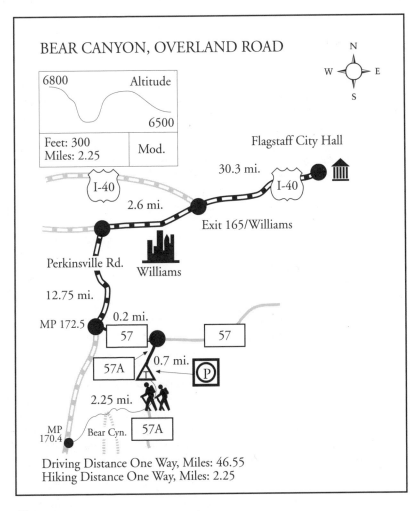

BEAR CANYON, OVERLAND ROAD

Altitude
6800
6500
Feet: 300
Miles: 2.25
Mod.

Flagstaff City Hall
30.3 mi.
I-40
2.6 mi.
Exit 165/Williams
Perkinsville Rd.
Williams
12.75 mi.
0.2 mi.
MP 172.5
57
57
57A
0.7 mi.
2.25 mi.
MP 170.4
Bear Cyn.
57A

Driving Distance One Way, Miles: 46.55
Hiking Distance One Way, Miles: 2.25

Mangum

BEAR JAW CANYON #26

General Information
Location Map E3
Humphreys Peak and White Horse Hills USGS Maps
Coconino Forest Service Map

Driving Distance One Way: 24.9 miles *40 km* (Time 50 minutes)
Access Road: All cars, Last 5.3 miles *8.5 km* gravel, in medium condition
Hiking Distance One Way: 2.65 miles *4.2 km* (Time 2 hours)
How Strenuous: Hard, Steep trail, High altitudes
Features: Alpine scenery, Vast views

NUTSHELL: This is a killer hike up the north face of the San Francisco Peaks about 25 miles *40 km* north of Flagstaff.

DIRECTIONS:
From Flagstaff City Hall Go:
   North on Humphreys Street, 0.60 miles *1.0 km* to the stoplight. See Access Map, page 10. Turn left on Columbus Avenue and follow it north around a curve, where it changes name to Ft. Valley Road, and then to Highway 180. At 19.6 miles *31.4 km* (MP 235.2) turn right on upper Hart Prairie Road, FR 151. At 21.2 miles *34 km*, turn left on FR 418 and continue on it to the 24.3 mile *38.9 km* point, where you will see a sign for the Bear Jaw Trail. The road to the trailhead is marked FR 9123J. Turn right on it and follow it to 24.7 miles *39.5 km* and take the left fork, to the parking area, at 24.9 miles *40 km*. You will see a parking area to your left.

TRAILHEAD: The cinder road on which you drove in is blocked by a row of boulders at the parking place. Walk past the boulders and continue 0.15 miles *0.24 km* to the end of the road. The trailhead takes off to the right (south) uphill there.

DESCRIPTION: The Forest Service recently changed the trailhead from its old location at Reese Tanks to this new location. The information in the first printing of this book was for the former trail layout. The new alignment shortens the hike and makes it less demanding.
   From the end of the road, you will hike up a trail segment, newly built, which meets the Aubineau Trail in about 0.25 miles *0.4 km*. From here you walk a 0.25 mile *0.4 km* leg of the old Aubineau Trail to the left.
   At the end, 0.65 miles *1.0 km* from the parking area, you reach the old Bear Jaw-Aubineau trailhead. Go right, uphill. From here the trail moves through beautiful woods, featuring heavy stands of aspens. You will pass through some old sheepherder camps, complete with herders' names carved

on the aspens. The trail is steep and goes up and up without respite.

You will climb through these woods for about 2.0 miles *3.2 km*, to the end of the trail at the 10,500 foot point, where it terminates at Forest Road FR 146, and you will see a sign there showing the Aubineau Trail 2.0 miles *3.2 km* to your right (west). You can return the way you came for a 5.3 mile *8.5 km* total hike or you can make the hike a 7.05 mile *11.3 km* loop using FR 146 as a connector to the Aubineau Trail.

To use the Aubineau loop, walk west (your right) on FR 146 a distance of 2.0 miles *3.2 km*, a beautiful and fairly level walk through a magnificent forest. The Aubineau Trail intersects FR 146 in a treeless park, a great view platform. FR 146 continues beyond the Aubineau connection and ends against the side of Mt. Humphreys where some digging has taken place, where the City of Flagstaff tapped a spring.

The Aubineau Trail is 2.4 miles *3.8 km* long, the upper portion being very steep and rocky.

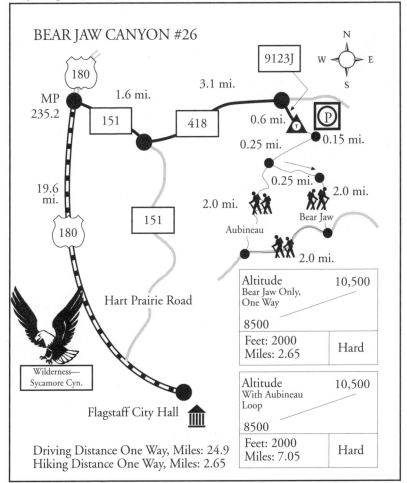

Mangum

BENHAM TRAIL #38

General Information
Location Map F1
Bill Williams Mountain USGS Map
Kaibab (Williams District) Forest Service Map

Driving Distance One Way: 36.85 miles 59.*0 km* (Time 60 minutes)
Access Road: All cars, All paved except last 0.25 miles *0.40 km*
Hiking Distance One Way: 4.5 miles *7.2 km* (Time 2.75 hours)
How Strenuous: Hard
Features: Beautiful forest, High mountain, Views

NUTSHELL: This hike takes you to the top of Bill Williams Mountain outside the Town of Williams, about 30 miles *48 km* west of Flagstaff.

DIRECTIONS:
From Flagstaff City Hall Go:
    South on Route 66 under the railroad overpass. Be sure to follow Route 66 when it turns right at the second stoplight. See Access Map, page 10. In 5.0 miles *8.0 km* you will merge onto I-40 West and stay on it to the 30.3 miles *48.5 km* point, the Williams Exit, #165. Take that exit and at the stop sign go left to Williams. Go into town on Railroad Avenue to the 32.9 mile point *52.6 km* where you will find Fourth Street. Turn left on Fourth Street. As it leaves town its name changes to the Perkinsville Road (FR 173). Stay on this road to the 36.6 miles *58.6 km* point, where you turn right onto the signed trail access road. Take this road to the 36.85 miles *59.0 km* point, the trail parking area, which is equipped with a restroom and also has horse facilities: corrals and trailer parking.

TRAILHEAD: You will see a sign marking the trailhead at the parking area.

DESCRIPTION: The sign at the trailhead indicates that this trail was built in 1920. It was abandoned in 1951 when the nearby FR 111 (the present road to the top) was built. It was reopened as a recreational trail in 1976. The trail was named after H. L. Benham, who was the Ranger for the Williams District from 1910 to 1911.
    It is hard to tell whether this trail was built as a road or as a pack trail. There are places where it is wide enough for a road, but the upper half looks only wide enough to have been a pack or foot trail. In any event, the trail was well engineered so that it climbs 2000 feet gradually. This means a lot of zigging and zagging.
    The trail goes up the east and south faces of the mountain. It does not get

as much moisture as the **Bill Williams Mountain Trail** on the north side. Consequently, the forest is mostly pine with a lot of oak, until you reach aspen groves in the last mile *1.6 km*. There are some open areas for views, but generally the forest is heavy.

At about the 1.5 mile *2.4 km* point you will enter into a gorgeous grove of oaks, really special. Mile posts have been inserted along the trail to mark your way. According to Dick's pedometer, they are accurate. You will cross the road, FR 111, five times as you go up the mountain. The fifth time is at the 4.0 mile *6.4 km* point, where the trail ends. You then walk the road the final half mile *0.8 km* to get to the lookout tower. Until you reach the 3.5 mile *5.6 km* point, views are scarce because the forest is so heavy. At the top, however, the views are open and glorious.

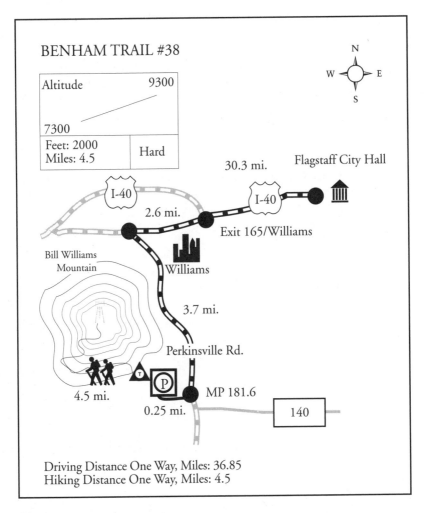

BENHAM TRAIL #38

Altitude	9300

7300

Feet: 2000 Miles: 4.5	Hard

N
W ←○→ E
S

30.3 mi.   Flagstaff City Hall

I-40   I-40

2.6 mi.   Exit 165/Williams

Bill Williams
Mountain

Williams

3.7 mi.

Perkinsville Rd.

4.5 mi.

0.25 mi.   MP 181.6   140

Driving Distance One Way, Miles: 36.85
Hiking Distance One Way, Miles: 4.5

Mangum

BILL WILLIAMS MTN. TRAIL #21

General Information
Location Map F1
Bill Williams Mountain USGS Map
Kaibab (Williams District) Forest Service Map

Driving Distance One Way: 35.3 miles *56.5 km* (Time 50 minutes)
Access Road: All cars, All paved except last 0.20 miles *0.32 km*
Hiking Distance One Way: 4.4 miles *7.04 km* (Time 3 hours)
How Strenuous: Hard
Features: Beautiful forest, High mountain, Views

NUTSHELL: This hike takes you to the top of Bill Williams Mountain outside the Town of Williams, about 30 miles *48.0 km* west of Flagstaff.

DIRECTIONS:
From Flagstaff City Hall Go:
    South on Route 66 under the railroad overpass. Be sure to follow Route 66 when it turns right at the second stoplight. See Access Map, page 10. In 5.0 miles *8.0 km* you will merge onto I-40 West and stay on it to the 30.3 miles *48.5 km* point, the Williams Exit, #165. Take that exit and at the stop sign go left to Williams. Go into downtown Williams. The main street through town is divided. You will be on Railroad Avenue headed west. Stay on this through town. At the 34.4 miles *55.0 km* point you will be on a frontage road. There you will see a paved road turning left and going uphill toward Days Inn motel. Take this lefthand road. At 35.0 miles *56.0 km* you will reach the turn for the Forest Service's Williams District Ranger Office (also called Camp Clover). Go left at this turn and head toward the camp. At 35.3 miles *56.5 km*, just before the fence going into the compound, you will see a road going left. It is signed. Turn left on this road and follow it a short distance until you see a trailhead sign to your right. Pull in there and park.

TRAILHEAD: You will see a sign marking the trailhead at the parking area.

DESCRIPTION: This trail was built in 1902 as a toll trail for horse riders, and is 3.8 miles *6.08 km* long. It is also known as the Camp Clover Trail.
    The 3.8 miles *6.08 km* indicated by the sign takes you to the point where the trail intersects FR 111, the road to the lookout tower, yet the mileposts along the trail treat this segment as being 3.0 miles *4.8 km* long. From FR 111 it is another 0.6 miles *1.0 km* to the tower. We think the sign understates the distance.
    Whatever the mileage, this is a steep and strenuous trail. The first mile

is fairly gradual, going through a nice pine forest, where we were lucky enough to see a bobcat strolling along in front of us. From that point, the trail climbs sharply and the forest changes character, becoming almost a rainforest, with lots of fir and spruce and incredible stands of tall aspens.

Because of this heavy forest you won't have any views until you reach FR 111, but from that point upward, the views are marvelous. Try to make it to the tower, for the views from there are as good as any in the region, since the mountain is situated so that you see interesting country all around.

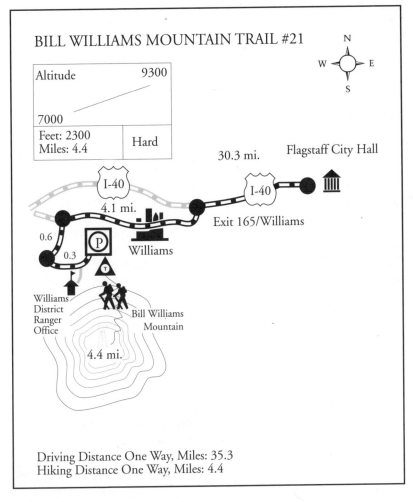

BILL WILLIAMS MOUNTAIN TRAIL #21

Altitude   9300

7000

Feet: 2300
Miles: 4.4   Hard

30.3 mi.   Flagstaff City Hall

I-40

4.1 mi.   I-40

0.6   Exit 165/Williams

0.3   Williams

Williams
District
Ranger
Office   Bill Williams
                   Mountain

4.4 mi.

Driving Distance One Way, Miles: 35.3
Hiking Distance One Way, Miles: 4.4

Mangum

BISMARCK LAKE ELK PRESERVE

General Information
Location Map E3
Humphreys Peak and Wing Mountain USGS Maps
Coconino Forest Service Map

Driving Distance One Way: 17.2 mile *27.5 km* (Time 35 minutes)
Access Road: All cars, Last 7.0 miles *11.2 km* gravel, in good condition
Hiking Distance One Way: 1.0 mile *1.6 km* (Time 30 minutes)
How Strenuous: Moderate
Features: Aspen groves, Meadow views

NUTSHELL: Located on the San Francisco Peaks, about 15 mile *24 km*s north of Flagstaff, this short, easy walk displays the alpine beauty of the area.

DIRECTIONS:
From Flagstaff City Hall Go:
North on Humphreys Street for 0.60 miles, *1.0 km* to the stoplight. See Access Map, page 10. Then take a left onto a street marked Columbus Avenue, which changes to Ft. Valley Road as it makes a curve to the north. Outside the city limits, the road becomes Highway 180, a major route to the Grand Canyon. At 10.2 miles *16.3 km* (MP 225.1), turn right onto FR 151, the lower Hart Prairie Road, and follow it to the 16.6 mile *26.5 km* point, where it intersects FR 627. Take FR 627 to the right and drive to the 17.2 mile *27.5 km* point, where you will find a fenced parking place. Park there.

TRAILHEAD: You will see a sign at a gate in the parking area fence.

DESCRIPTION: The Hart Prairie Road is a loop road that intersects Highway 180 at two points. One point is 10.2 miles *16.3 km* north of Flagstaff and the other is 19.6 miles *31.3 km* north. If you hear someone talking about taking the Hart Prairie Road, be sure to find out whether they are talking about the upper or lower end of the loop.

To make this hike, you walk through the fence and follow a road which has been closed, as no vehicle traffic is allowed inside the Bismarck Lake Elk Preserve. At 0.3 miles *0.5 km* you will come to Ki Tank. Don't take the fork to the right that appears there. At 0.7 miles, *1.1 km* the trail forks again. Take the left fork, which goes uphill to a grassy ledge.

When you top out on the ledge you find yourself on a sizable meadow ringed with aspen, pine and fir. The lake is hardly deserving of the name most of the time, usually appearing as a cattle tank about 20 feet in diameter except during the spring thaw, when it is at its fullest. In dry Arizona any body of water more than ten feet across is likely to be called a lake.

The forest is beautiful here. The area gets a lot of moisture, so in addition to the trees, there are many ferns, mosses, mushrooms and flowers.

The hike is an easy one for the Peaks area, as the climb is gentle, the trail is short, and the altitude is not terribly high.

This is a perfect place for elk, as they have everything they need here: grass, water and shelter. Best time to see them is just at dusk. We have been here five times and have heard but not seen elk each time. If you are in elk country in the autumn, you may hear the bull elks bugling. We have heard this twice at Bismarck Lake Elk Preserve, both times in mid-October. Once it erupted from a thick grove of trees nearby and made us jump. The elk bugle is a weird sound and if you are unprepared for it, you would have no idea what you are hearing. It sounds like the hokey trumpeting of elephants that you hear in a Tarzan movie. The bulls, normally passive, are quite aggressive when they are bugling, so don't bugle back.

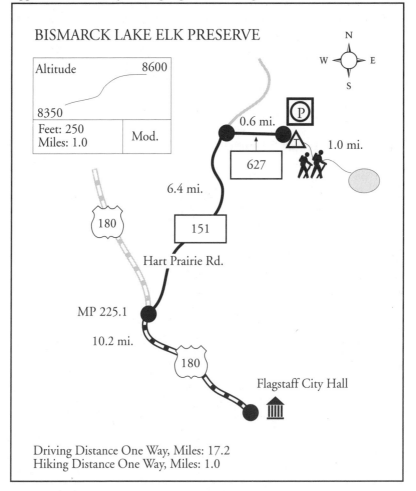

BISMARCK LAKE ELK PRESERVE

Altitude   8600

8350

| Feet: 250 Miles: 1.0 | Mod. |

0.6 mi.

627

1.0 mi.

6.4 mi.

180

151

Hart Prairie Rd.

MP 225.1

10.2 mi.

180

Flagstaff City Hall

Driving Distance One Way, Miles: 17.2
Hiking Distance One Way, Miles: 1.0

Mangum

BIXLER SADDLE TRAIL #72

General Information
Location Map F1
McLellan Reservoir, Williams South USGS Maps
Kaibab (Chalender) Forest Service Map

Driving Distance One Way: 43.65 miles *69.8 km* (Time 1 hour)
Access Road: High clearance for last 2.0 miles *3.2 km*
Hiking Distance One Way: 2.0 miles *3.2 km* (Time 1 hour)
How Strenuous: Hard
Features: Beautiful forest, Views

NUTSHELL: Bill Williams Mountain dominates the skyline of the Town of Williams, located about 30 miles *48 km,* west of Flagstaff, in the same way that the San Francisco Peaks dominate Flagstaff. The **Benham Trail** takes you up the east and south faces of Bill Williams Mountain, and the **Bill Williams Mountain Trail** takes you up the north face. This little known but excellent new trail takes you around the west face of the mountain.

DIRECTIONS:
From Flagstaff City Hall Go:
South on Route 66 under the railroad. See Access Map, page 10. Turn right at the stoplight at 0.5 miles *0.8 km.* You will merge onto I-40 headed west in about 5.0 miles *8.0 km.* Go past Williams, to the 39.1 mile *62.6 km* point, the Devil Dog Exit 157, and turn off onto a loop which will bring you to a stop sign. Take the fork to the right here and go south under I-40. You will come to another intersection at 39.6 miles *63.3 km.* Take the left fork (west). The paving ends in a few feet at a cattle guard. You will now be driving FR 108. At 40.0 miles *64.0 km* you will come to a junction where FR 744 goes to your right. Stay on FR 108 and turn left (east). At 40.4 miles *64.6 km* you will reach a corner where the road ahead is blocked with a barrier. Turn right here, still on FR 108. At 40.55 miles *65.0 km* you will meet FR 45 to your left (east). There is a sign reading, "Primitive Use Road" but don't be deterred by this. If you have high clearance you will have no trouble if the road is dry. At 41.65 miles *66.6 km* FR 45 makes a 90° turn to the right. Straight ahead you will see another blocked road. Turn right on FR 45, which will now begin to climb to the 43.65 mile *69.8 km* point, its end. There are spots where the road is quite narrow and there are exposed rocks in many places, but considering other roads we have driven, it is not bad. You will top out at Bixler Saddle, a bare shelf surrounded by forest.

TRAILHEAD: At the saddle.

DESCRIPTION: As you climb toward Bill Williams Mountain you will soon catch sight of the lookout tower, but the trail then turns away from it, toward the north. You hike through a nice pine forest that has healthy stands of oak. The trail was added to the system in 1993 and is in good condition.

As you near the mountain you will see some interesting volcanic columns, giant sheer crags rearing up hundreds of feet. Their walls are covered with beautiful multi-colored lichens. The trail winds north, then curves to the west in about 0.5 miles *0.8 km,* where it begins to climb. At the 0.75 mile *1.2 km* point it ascends sharply by switchbacks and then moves to the northeast.

At the 2.0 mile 3.2 km point, you will intersect the **Bill Williams Mountain Trail** as it comes down from the summit..

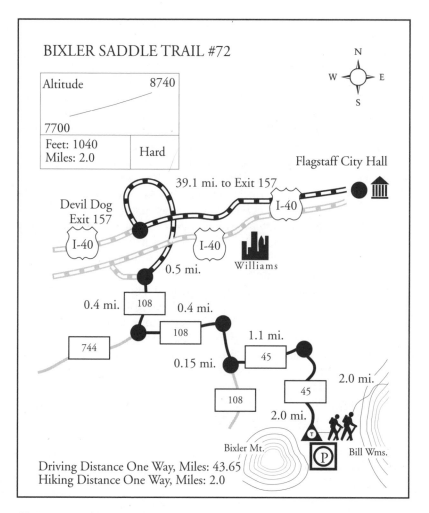

BLUE CANYON

General Information
Location Map C5
Begashibito Cyn., Pillars of Hercules
and Rocky Ridge NW USGS Maps

Driving Distance One Way: 126 miles *201.6 km* (Time 2.5 hours)
Access Road: All cars if road is dry
Hiking Distance One Way: 2.0 miles *3.2 km* (Time 1 hour)
How Strenuous: Easy
Features: Superb scenic canyon, Painted Desert, Indian reservation

NUTSHELL: In a region full of colorful canyons, this one stands out for its vivid beauty and unique sculptures.

DIRECTIONS:
From Flagstaff City Hall Go:
    East and then north on Route 89. See Access Map on pages 10-11. Stay on Highway 89 for 67.8 miles *108.5 km* (MP 480.8), where Highway 160 intersects it on the right. Turn onto Highway 160 and head east for 10.4 miles *16.64 km*. At the stoplight in Tuba City, which is at the junction of Highways 160 and 264, turn right on 264 and follow it for 33.5 miles *53.6 km* to MP 355.6. Here you will see an unpaved road to your left. It is the only one in the vicinity, so you can't miss it. You will pass over a cattle guard at the fence. There is a major road to the left here. Do not take it. Go straight ahead. Once you correctly get established on the right road at this point, you can't go wrong, as your way is obvious to the end. The road has no number posted, but it is the main road and is in good condition. We were able to drive it at speeds of 40 to 50 mph. Once you get to the rim of the canyon about 13.5 miles *21.6 km* from the beginning of the road, you come to one of the two tricky parts. You will see that the road now takes a sharp dip into the canyon. The road on the steepest part on this dip is full of soft sand and potholes. Slow down and take it carefully. Also think about how tough this will be going up on your way back home. The other tricky part is at the bottom where you cross the wash. Here you also find deep soft sand, but it is at a level place. Drive across the canyon toward the dark red and highly sculpted formations on the north side. The road comes near them and then begins to turn away. Just here, at 14.1 miles *22.6 km*, you will see a primitive road turning sharply to your right. Take this and drive as close to the "fantasy rocks" as you can.

TRAILHEAD: There is no trail.

DESCRIPTION: The name Blue Canyon seems a misnomer. There are some subtle blue hues, but the canyon is ablaze with astonishing whites and reds.

The area is composed of sandstones deposited one on top of the other like a layer cake, then tilted through faulting. You will see white bands on the bottom and red bands on the top. The stone is very soft, almost a mud. The red formations look like fantastic blobs of Play Doh stuck together imaginatively so as to form an eye-catching field of strange rounded and tapered sculptures. The white layer has weathered into pinnacles and spires. There are countless miles of sedimentary formations on the Colorado Plateau but nothing else looks quite like this.

There is no hiking trail on the north side of canyon, but the floor is wide and flat. When it is dry you can drive almost anywhere. Pick out a place that looks interesting and then drive or walk over to it and explore. This part of Blue Canyon is a photographer's dream. Enjoy it.

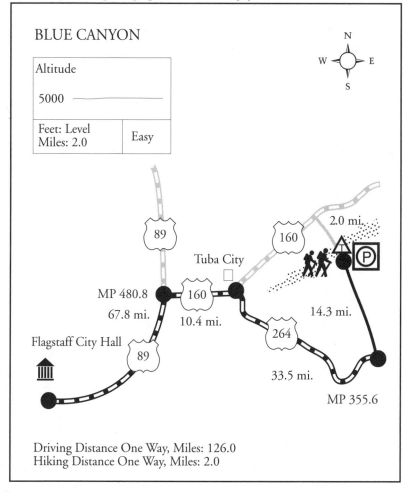

BLUE CANYON

Altitude

5000 ———

Feet: Level
Miles: 2.0   Easy

N
W —O— E
S

89

160

2.0 mi.

Tuba City

MP 480.8

160

67.8 mi.

10.4 mi.

14.3 mi.

Flagstaff City Hall

89

264

33.5 mi.

MP 355.6

Driving Distance One Way, Miles: 126.0
Hiking Distance One Way, Miles: 2.0

Mangum

BRIGHT ANGEL TRAIL

General Information
Location Map B2
Bright Angel USGS Map
Kaibab (Tusayan) Forest Service Map

Driving Distance One Way: 82.8 miles *132.5 km* (Time 2 hours)
Access Road*:* All cars, All paved
Hiking Distance One Way*:* 1.5 miles *2.4 km* (Time 1.5 hours)
How Strenuous*:* Hard
Features*:* The main Grand Canyon trail

NUTSHELL: You will sample the most famous hiking trail in the world, by taking a day hike down the first 1.5 miles *2.4 km*. You will enjoy the color, history and romance of the Grand Canyon.

DIRECTIONS:
From Flagstaff City Hall Go:
     North on Humphreys Street 0.60 miles *1.0 km* to a stoplight. See Access Map, page 10. Go left on Columbus Avenue and follow the curve north. Street signs will show the street first as Ft. Valley Road, then Highway 180. This is a major road to the Grand Canyon. At 50.4 miles *80.7 km* (MP 265.8), you will intersect Highway 64, coming out of Williams, at Valle. Go right at this junction and follow the highway to the south entrance to the Grand Canyon National Park, where you will have to pay an entrance fee. Once inside the park, go to the 79.8 mile *128 km* point, where you intersect the East Rim Drive. Turn left, toward Grand Canyon Village. You will reach the village area, then stay on the main road just past the Bright Angel Lodge, which is uphill, to your right, at 82.8 miles *132.5 km*. Look for a trail sign at the end of the Bright Angel parking lot and turn right, going past the cottages to the trail parking lot at the rim. Parking is scarce in high season and you may have to hunt for a place in the area.

TRAILHEAD: Follow the signs at the parking area.

DESCRIPTION: The Bright Angel Trail began as an ancient Indian path. In 1890 it was developed as a privately-owned mining trail, later converted into a tourist toll-trail. The Hermit Trail, built by the Santa Fe Railroad; and the South Kaibab Trail, built by the Park Service, were created to avoid these tolls. The Park Service acquired Bright Angel in 1928.
     This is the trail used by the famous mule rides to go down to Phantom Ranch. It is not a wilderness experience. In fact, one of the attractions of the trail is people-watching. You will hear many languages spoken.

Serious hikers backpack on this trail, using it as access for a multi-day experience. Overnight hikes require permits (which are scarce) and a great deal of preparation and training. For a day hike, you do not need a permit, but please be prepared. Take water (one quart per person), wear suitable shoes, and allow enough time for a comfortable experience.

As you descend, the temperature increases. Take this into account in deciding how much water to carry and how to dress.

You will pass through two tunnels, and end your hike at the First Rest House. This is a hike of 1.5 miles *2.4 km*, which seems mild, but it requires a steep climb of 1131 feet on the way back up. You will enjoy gorgeous views of the canyon all the way.

We recommend that every able-bodied visitor go down into the Grand Canyon, even if it is for a very short distance, for it is the only way to get a feel for the canyon's immensity. A good shorter hike is to go to the Second Tunnel, a hike of 0.87 miles *1.4 km*, a drop of 597 feet.

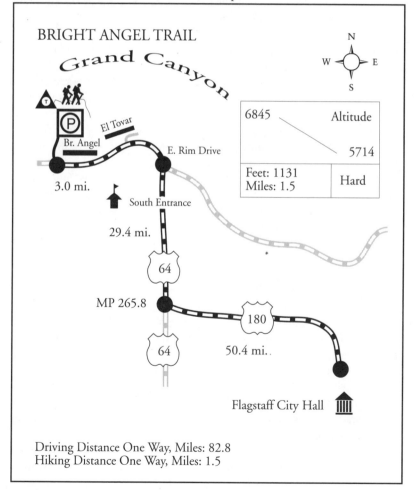

BRIGHT ANGEL TRAIL

Grand Canyon

6845	Altitude
	5714
Feet: 1131 Miles: 1.5	Hard

Br. Angel

El Tovar

E. Rim Drive

3.0 mi.

South Entrance

29.4 mi.

64

MP 265.8

180

64

50.4 mi.

Flagstaff City Hall

Driving Distance One Way, Miles: 82.8
Hiking Distance One Way, Miles: 1.5

Mangum

BROOKBANK TRAIL #2

General Information
Location Map E3
Humphreys Peak & Sunset Crater West USGS Maps
Coconino Forest Service Map

Driving Distance One Way: 6.5 miles *10.4 km* (Time 30 minutes)
Access Road: All cars, Last 2.9 miles *4.64 km* medium gravel road
Hiking Distance One Way: 5.0 miles *8.0 km* (Time 3 hours)
How Strenuous: Hard
Features: Views, Forests

NUTSHELL: This is a marked and maintained trail that starts at a point on the Elden Lookout Road and climbs to Sunset Park near the top of Mt. Elden north of Flagstaff.

DIRECTIONS:
From Flagstaff City Hall Go:
    North on Humphreys Street for 0.60 miles *1.0 km*. See Access Map, page 10. Turn left at the stoplight onto Columbus Avenue and follow it around a big curve to the north. You will see the street signs call this road Columbus Avenue at first, then Ft. Valley Road and then Highway 180. Stay on Highway 180 to the 3.1 miles *5.0 km* point (MP 218.6), where the Schultz Pass Road, FR 420, goes to the right. Follow FR 420. At the 3.6 mile *5.8 km* point it curves left where you will see the unpaved Elden Lookout Road (FR 557) going straight. Take the right fork and follow FR 557 to the 6.5 mile *10.4 km* point, where you will park.

TRAILHEAD: There is a closed road to your left. The sign is located about twenty yards up this road.

DESCRIPTION: This trail is part of the Dry Lake Hills-Mt. Elden trail system, so it is marked and maintained. The trail goes up a closed ranch road for about a mile *1.6 km*, beyond which it turns into a footpath. At the 1.1 mile *1.8 km* point you will reach a trail junction. The unmarked trail to your left goes uphill to the **Dry Lake Hills** trail, which is not part of the trail system, but is written up in this book.
    Take the right fork here. It goes around a long loop that hugs the shoulder of one of the hills. At the toe of the loop you will have good views of the San Francisco Peaks. Then you curve south, toward Mt. Elden, walking through high north-facing forests of spruce and fir.
    At the 3.4 mile *5.5 km* point you will reach a trail junction. Here you want to turn right onto the Sunset Trail. The signs here are confusing, so

please follow our directions.

The trail will take you down a fold between the Dry Lake Hills and Mt. Elden and will then climb up a slope of Mt. Elden through a very nice alpine forest. You will reach a ridge crest on Elden in about a mile *1.6 km*. From here the trail goes over the crest a short distance and then follows along on the shoulder of the crest to Sunset Park.

This last half mile *0.8 km* burned in a huge forest fire caused by human carelessness in 1978. Only now is the forest starting to heal. The fire made the mountain bare here so you have clear views to the east. They are spectacular.

We end the hike at Sunset Park, where there is a trail junction, just above the Elden Lookout Road. You can go on a mile *1.6 km* to the lookout tower. We like this as a two-car hike, parking one car at the 6.5 mile *10.4 km* point and the other at the 9.4 mile *15.0 km* point on the Elden Lookout Road, then hiking downhill.

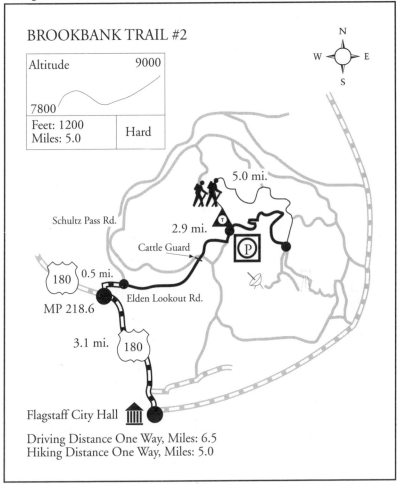

BROOKBANK TRAIL #2

Altitude 9000

7800

Feet: 1200
Miles: 5.0

Hard

5.0 mi.

Schultz Pass Rd.

2.9 mi.

Cattle Guard

180 0.5 mi.

Elden Lookout Rd.

MP 218.6

3.1 mi. 180

Flagstaff City Hall

Driving Distance One Way, Miles: 6.5
Hiking Distance One Way, Miles: 5.0

Mangum

BUFFALO PARK

General Information
Location Map E3
Flagstaff West USGS Map
Coconino Forest Service Map

Driving Distance One Way: 2.3 miles *3.7 km* (Time 10 minutes)
Access Road: All cars, All paved
Hiking Distance: THREE TRAILS. **Trail #1** is 0.5 mi. *0.8 km*,
    Trail #2 is a 2.0 mi. *3.2 km* loop, **Trail #3** runs 0.5 miles *0.8 km*
    downhill.
How Strenuous: Easy/Easy/Moderate
Features: Urban Trails. Easy to reach, Easy to walk

NUTSHELL: Buffalo Park is owned by the City of Flagstaff. Located on top of a flat mesa, it features three well maintained trails. *One* is a straight half-mile road. *Two* loops around a Vita Course. *Three* follows the old road alignment downhill.

DIRECTIONS:
From Flagstaff City Hall Go:

North on Humphreys Street to the stoplight at 0.60 miles *1.0 km*. See Access Map, page 10. Turn right here onto Columbus Avenue and go one block east to the next stop sign, which is at Beaver Street. Turn left onto Beaver Street and go up the hill. At the 1.0 mile *1.6 km* point you will reach Forest Avenue. Turn right on Forest and follow it to its end at a hilltop. Here, at 1.9 miles *3.04 km*, you will find Gemini Drive. Turn left onto it and at 2.3 miles *3.68 km,* you will come to Buffalo Park. Park in the parking lot.

TRAILHEADS: At the entrance arch.

DESCRIPTION: Buffalo Park is an open plain extending back about a half mile from the archway at its entrance. In the 1960s it was run as a zoo but failed due to lack of funds. You can see some vestiges of this operation near the entrance, where a welcoming arch and buffalo statue survive.

Trail No. 1: As you stand under the arch and look ahead, you will see the main trail running in a straight line due north. This trail runs almost exactly 0.5 miles *0.8 km* to the fence marking the rear boundary of the park. There is nothing fancy about this trail. It runs across the open park like an arrow. You will find a couple of metal buildings behind a chain link fence near the trail's end, where it veers to the northeast and you come to a gate where the **Oldham Trail No. 1** begins. If you are doing a timed or measured mile, you simply turn around and go back the way you came.

Trail No. 2: This trail is a Vita Course. You will encounter 20 stations with placards describing some kind of exercise to be done on each spot. In some places there are devices such as chinning bars. There are mileage markers every quarter mile. The course runs in a loop. If you do the entire loop you will do two miles *3.2 km*. Walk north from the archway about 100 yards, where you will see a cindered path forking to your right (NE). Turn right onto the path. From here it is easy to follow your way because you can see the exercise stations ahead. The first leg of the trail loops around to the east of Trail No. 1, then turns west and crosses it. The second leg loops around west of Trail No. 1 and is more scenic. Near the end of this trail take the right fork that goes down into dense woods.

Trail No. 3: This trail does not go into the park. Follow the old alignment of Cedar Road from outside the gate. You will go downhill to the corner of McPherson Park, then curve south to join the new road at its intersection with Turquoise Drive, a distance of 0.5 miles *0.8 km*.

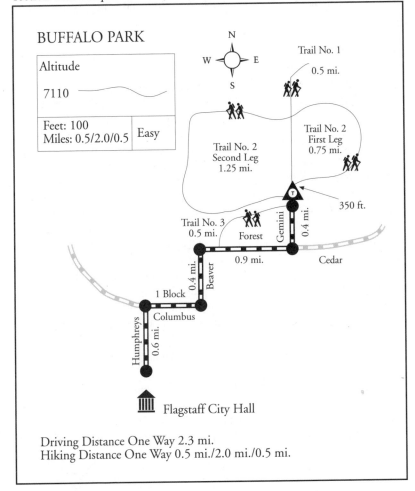

Mangum

BULL BASIN TRAIL #40

General Information
Location Map E2
Kendrick Peak, Moritz Ridge and Wing Mt. USGS Maps
Coconino Forest Service Map

Driving Distance One Way: 34.55 miles *55.3 km* (Time 1.25 hours)
Access Road: All cars, Last 20 miles *32 km* good gravel road
Hiking Distance One Way: 4.5 miles *7.2 km* (Time 3.0 hours)
How Strenuous: Hard
Features: Fine forests, Ten thousand foot peak, Views

NUTSHELL: This trail, located 34.55 miles *55.3 km* north of Flagstaff, takes you up the north side of Kendrick Peak, the second highest mountain in the region.

DIRECTIONS:
From Flagstaff City Hall Go:
   North on Humphreys Street for 0.60 miles *1.0 km*. See Access Map, page 10. Turn left at the stoplight onto Columbus Avenue and follow it around a big curve to the north. You will see the street signs call this road Columbus at first, then Ft. Valley Road and then Highway 180. Stay on Highway 180 to the 14.5 miles *23.2 km* point (MP 230), where an unpaved road takes off to the left. Turn left onto this road, FR 245, and follow it to the 17.6 mile *28.2 km* point where it intersects FR 171. Turn right on FR 171 and follow it to the 24.8 mile *39.7 km* point, where you will see a sign for the Pumpkin Trail. Go just beyond this, to the 24.9 mile *39.8 km* point and turn left on FR 171. Follow it to the 27.7 mile *44.3 km* point, where it meets FR 144 and turn right on FR 144, taking it to the 29.2 miles *46.7 km* point, where it intersects FR 90. Turn right on FR 90 and drive it to the 33.9 mile *54.3 km* point, where you will see FR 90A to the right. Take FR 90A to the 34.45 mile *55.1 km* point, where you will see a sign marking a road to the right to the Bull Basin trailhead. You can see the parking lot from this point. Turn right, downhill, and you will reach the parking area at 34.55 miles *55.3 km*.

TRAILHEAD: Well marked with a sign at the parking area.

DESCRIPTION: There are three trails that take you to the top of Kendrick Peak: The Bull Basin Trail, The **Kendrick Mt. Trail** and The **Pumpkin Trail**. We think Bull Basin is the best, with Pumpkin running a poor third.
   From the parking area you will walk a closed road along the west side of Bull Basin, a large grassy meadow. At 0.9 miles *1.4 km* you will come to a trail junction where you will see the **Connector Trail** to the right.

Up to this point the land has been flat. Beyond it you begin to climb the mountain, with the trail following some old logging roads up to the 1.5 mile *2.4 km* point. The forest on this north side of the mountain has many spruces and firs, and seems to have recovered from logging better than pure pine forests do.

Beyond the 1.5 mile *2.4 km* point the trail becomes a footpath and begins to climb steeply. The trail is well designed so that the grades are not too steep. The pines thin out and soon you are in a forest of spruce, fir and aspen.

At 3.0 miles *4.8 km* you will emerge onto a small saddle and follow a ridge line to the top. From here the forest is all spruce and there are many huge boulders. You will emerge from this dark forest at 4.0 miles *6.4 km* at the Old Ranger Cabin, built in 1911-1912 and in remarkably good shape. From the cabin it is another half mile *0.8 km* to the lookout tower.

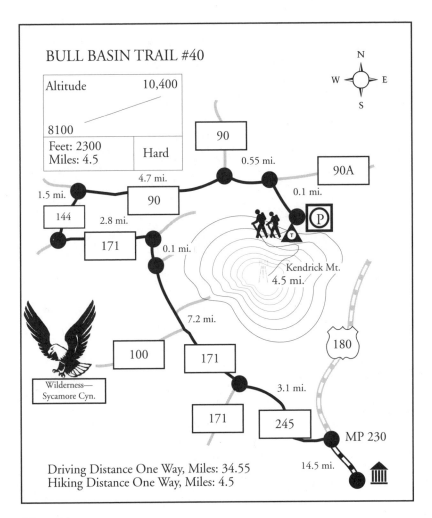

CASNER MOUNTAIN TRAIL NORTH

General Information
Location Map F2
Loy Butte, Sycamore Point USGS Maps
Coconino Forest Service Map

Driving Distance One Way: 29.0 miles *46.4 km* (Time 60 minutes)
Access Road: High clearance only, Last 25.0 miles *40 km* unpaved, rough
      spots
Hiking Distance One Way: 4.0 miles *6.4 km* (Time 2.5 hours)
How Strenuous: Moderate
Features: Views

NUTSHELL: Located 29.0 miles *46.4 km* southwest of Flagstaff, this hike
follows the top of a ridge that connects Casner Mountain to the Mogollon
Rim.

DIRECTIONS:
From Flagstaff City Hall Go:
    West a block on Route 66 (Santa Fe), then south, beneath the railroad
overpass. See Access Map, page 10. At 0.50 miles *0.8 km* you will reach a
Y intersection. The right fork is Route 66. Take it. You will soon leave town.
At 2.6 miles *4.2 km* you will reach a road going to the left. This is the Woody
Mountain Road, FR 231. Take it. It is paved about a mile *1.6 km* and then
turns into a cinder road. At 16.6 miles *26.6 km* you will intersect FR 538.
Turn right onto FR 538 and follow it to the 26.1 mile *41.8 km* point, where
FR 538B branches off to the right. Take FR 538B. It follows the path of the
huge power line you can see overhead. The road is pretty good down to the
28.25 mile *45.2 km* point but from there it becomes very rough with lots of
exposed tire-eating rock. It ends at 29.0 miles *46.4 km* at a bare spot on the
ridge, where you park, near the power line.

TRAILHEAD: You walk the power line service road.

DESCRIPTION: This trail began its life as a sheep driveway. Years later
engineers followed this same route to bring a major power line down to the
Verde Valley and the sheep trail was converted into a service road for the
line.
    A major attraction of this trail is that the ridge you walk is so narrow that
you can see off into the Sycamore side or the Sedona side in many places.
Both are spectacular. There are very few trees growing along the side of this
trail, so it is mostly unshaded and can be hot. Take lots of water.
    At the 0.25 mile *0.4 km* point on the hike you will come to a three-point

wilderness trail intersection where the Casner Mountain, Mooney and **Taylor Cabin** trails meet. You can see the Mooney Trail going down diagonally to your left into the Sedona back country. The Taylor Cabin Trail drops down steeply into Sycamore Canyon on your right.

The Casner Mountain Trail is not level. As it follows the contours of the ridge it dips and rises. At 2.0 miles *3.2 km* it makes a major dip into a saddle where you reach bottom at 2.5 miles *4.0 km*. From there you begin the mile *1.6 km*-long ascent that will take you onto Casner Mountain.

You reach a false top on Casner at 3.5 miles *5.6 km* and then make the final push to hike's end, the real top, at 4.0 miles *6.4 km*.

The trail continues, going down the mountain on its south face. It is about 3.0 miles *4.8 km* to the bottom on the south. Instead of trying to make this a killer day hike, we think it is better described as two hikes. The **Casner Mountain Trail South** and **Mooney Trail** are described in our other book, *Sedona Hikes*.

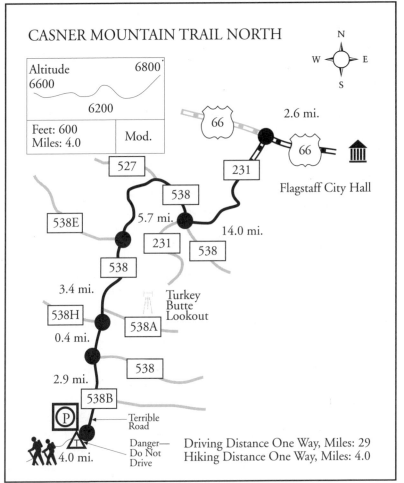

CASNER MOUNTAIN TRAIL NORTH

Altitude 6800
6600
6200

Feet: 600
Miles: 4.0   Mod.

527

231

2.6 mi.

66

66

Flagstaff City Hall

538

538E

5.7 mi.

14.0 mi.

231

538

538

3.4 mi.

Turkey Butte Lookout

538H

538A

0.4 mi.

538

2.9 mi.

538B

P

Terrible Road

Danger—
Do Not
Drive

4.0 mi.

Driving Distance One Way, Miles: 29
Hiking Distance One Way, Miles: 4.0

Mangum

CLOVER SPRING

General Information
Location Map F1
Bill Williams Mountain USGS Map
Kaibab (Williams District) Forest Service Map

Driving Distance One Way: 35.3 miles *56.5 km* (Time 50 minutes)
Access Road: All cars, All paved except last 0.20 miles *0.32 km*
Hiking Distance One Way: 1.25 miles *2.0 km* (Time 40 minutes)
How Strenuous: Moderate
Features: Beautiful forest, Views, Spring

NUTSHELL: This hike takes you to a spring on the flank of Bill Williams Mountain outside the Town of Williams, about 30 miles *48 km* west of Flagstaff.

DIRECTIONS:
From Flagstaff City Hall Go:
    South on Route 66 under the railroad overpass. Be sure to follow Route 66 when it turns right at the second stoplight. See Access Map, page 10. In 5.0 miles *8.0 km* you will merge onto I-40 West and stay on it to the 30.3 miles *48.5 km* point, the Williams Exit, #165. Take that exit and at the stop sign go left to Williams. Go into downtown Williams. The main street through town is divided. You will be on Railroad Avenue headed west. Stay on this through town. At the 34.4 miles *55.0 km* point you will be on a frontage road. There you will see a paved road turning left and going uphill toward Days Inn motel. Take this lefthand road. At 35.0 miles *56.0 km* you will reach the turn for the Forest Service's Williams District Ranger Office (also called Camp Clover). Go left at this turn and head toward the camp. At 35.3 miles *56.5 km*, just before the fence going into the compound, you will see a road going left. It is signed. Turn left on this road and follow it a short distance until you see a trailhead sign to your right. Pull in there and park.

TRAILHEAD: You will see a sign marking the Bill Williams Mountain Trail (also known as Camp Clover Trail) trailhead at the parking area.

DESCRIPTION: You will hike along the **Bill Williams Mountain Trail** for a distance of 0.67 miles *1.1 km*; then the Clover Spring Trail branches off to the left. It is marked by a sign. This first segment of the trail is moderately steep and passes through a typical ponderosa pine forest with lots of oak mixed in. There are a couple of places around the half mile *0.8 km* spot where you can look out over the Williams area.
    Once you leave the Bill Williams Trail, the Clover Springs trail goes

downhill a bit and around the side of the mountain. You will come upon a sign reading, "Clover Spring 1/2 Mile" that is inaccurate, as the spring is only 0.2 miles *0.32 km* from that point.

The spring appears on the hillside with no change in the appearance of the terrain, except for a row of green grass to mark where it flows. You are suddenly there, with a small sign to tell you that the place is Clover Spring.

There is a square concrete box at the head of the spring. When full, it overflows and runs downhill, cutting a channel. A piece of metal has been placed over the channel. About twenty feet down from the box, a small pool is formed and from there a trickle runs free down the mountainside, tracing a thin green line. The Forest Service tapped Clover Spring in the past and used the water at Camp Clover.

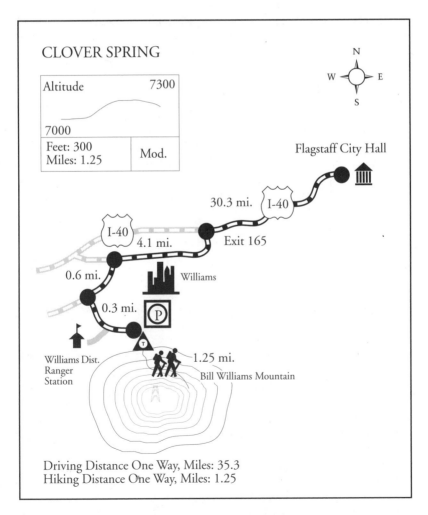

CLOVER SPRING

Altitude   7300

7000
Feet: 300
Miles: 1.25   Mod.

Flagstaff City Hall

30.3 mi.   I-40

I-40
4.1 mi.   Exit 165

0.6 mi.

Williams

0.3 mi.

Williams Dist. Ranger Station

1.25 mi.
Bill Williams Mountain

Driving Distance One Way, Miles: 35.3
Hiking Distance One Way, Miles: 1.25

Mangum

COAL MINE CANYON

General Information
Location Map C4
Coal Mine, Tuba City SE USGS Maps
Coconino Forest Service Map

Driving Distance One Way: 93.85 miles *150 km* (Time 2 hours)
Access Road: All cars, Last 0.9 miles *1.6 km* good dirt road
Hiking Distance One Way: 1.0 miles *1.6 km* (Time 1 hour)
How Strenuous: Moderate
Features: Gorgeous canyon

NUTSHELL: This requires a long drive but it is easy to reach on good roads. Though Coal Mine Canyon has incredible beauty, it is allowed to bask quietly in its splendor, host to the small number of people who know that it exists. It is home to the legendary Ghost of Coal Mine Canyon.

DIRECTIONS:
From Flagstaff City Hall Go:
    North on Highway 89 for 67.8 miles *108.5 km* (See Access Map, pages 10-11) to MP 480.8, where Highway 160 intersects 89 on the right. Turn onto Highway 160 and head east for 10.4 miles *16.64 km* to the stoplight at Tuba City (MP 321.4). Turn right there onto Highway 264. Drive past the Hopi village of Moenkopi, and enjoy looking down into Moenkopi Wash at the farms that line it. Soon you will climb a mesa. At a point 14.9 miles *24 km* from the stoplight (MP 336.8) take an unmarked unpaved road to your left. On this road, you will reach a junction in 0.3 miles *0.5 km*, where you go straight. At the next junction, 0.4 miles *0.64 km*, go right (NE). At the third junction, 0.55 miles *0.9 km*, take the middle road to the canyon: you will see that the right road goes to a windmill and the left road goes to a green house. You will reach the canyon rim at 0.75 miles *1.2 km*. Enjoy the view; then turn right and drive over and park at the picnic tables.

TRAILHEAD: WARNING: DO NOT TRY THIS HIKE IF THE GROUND IS MUDDY. Walk through the gate into the picnic area and turn toward the canyon, where you will find a low ridge with a footpath on its top. Turn right on this and walk along it about 125 paces, to a point where you will see a faint path going downhill to your left. This is the trailhead.

DESCRIPTION: The trail is not marked, but it is distinct. The first portion is the most difficult, a very steep drop of about 100 feet, over which the trail goes straight down. This stretch may be too much for some hikers. After that, the trail is more level and is decent walking.

You will be enthralled by the sights on this hike, as the canyon is a carnival of brilliant color, with lots of soft stone that has eroded into fascinating towers and sculptures. The color of the soil on the path changes continually. This place is heaven for photographers and geologists.

Keep watching the cliffs on your left (west). Where they end, you have reached the 0.66 mile *1.1 km* point. From here the trail dips down onto the canyon floor, where the canyon is much wider. Hikers can walk along the streambed for miles, but the best part is the first mile *1.6 km*.

THE COAL MINE. Near the top of the canyon you can see a black layer. This is a low grade bituminous coal seam that was mined from about 1908-1915 and again from about 1947-1955.

THE GHOST. We lack space for the legend here, but it is a wonderful story. Old accounts about how to see it are outdated, as it now impossible to drive to the east rim viewpoint that was used for ghost watching. There is no longer a campground. View it from the picnic area.

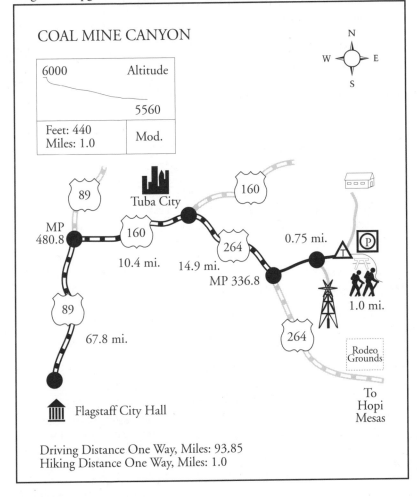

COCONINO RIM TRAIL

General Information
Location Map C2
Grandview Point USGS Map
Kaibab (Tusayan) Forest Service Map

Driving Distance One Way: 87.8 miles *140.5 km* (Time 2 hours)
Access Road: All cars, Last 15.3 miles *24.5 km* good unpaved road
Hiking Distance One Way: 3.0 miles *4.8 km* (Time 1.5 hours)
How Strenuous: Easy
Features: Grand Canyon views, Arizona Trail link

NUTSHELL: This trail goes along the crest of the Coconino Rim, a long ridge running southeasterly from Grandview Point at the Grand Canyon, 87.8 miles *140.5 km* from Flagstaff.

DIRECTIONS:
From Flagstaff City Hall Go:
   North on Humphreys Street 0.60 miles *1.0 km* to a stoplight. See Access Map, page 10. Go left on Columbus Avenue and follow the curve north. Street signs will show the street first as Ft. Valley Road, then Highway 180. This is a major road to the Grand Canyon. At 50.4 miles *80.7 km* (MP 265.9), you will intersect Highway 64, coming out of Williams, at Valle. Go right at this junction and follow the highway to the 72.5 mile *116 km* point (MP 235.5), which you will find just as you come into Tusayan. Go right on FR 302 and follow it to the 87.7 mile *140 km* point, where there is a junction. Turn left on FR 310 there, where the sign says, "G.C.N.P. 1" and in 0.1 mile *0.16 km* you will see a sign for the Grandview Lookout to your right. Turn right and park at the base of the fire lookout tower.

TRAILHEAD: At the parking area. There is a sign. The trail is marked by posts placed every half mile *0.8 km*.

DESCRIPTION: The Arizona Trail is an ambitious project to create a linked series of trails that go across Arizona from Utah to Mexico. A few segments have been completed and tied together, starting in the north. This trail is part of the system and for that reason it is difficult to give true mileage for this hike as theoretically it will go to Mexico.
   The Coconino Rim is the uplifted portion of a large fault that created a crescent shaped ridge about 500 feet high running southeasterly from the Grand Canyon, which goes east to west in the area. The hiking trail takes advantage of the rim to bring the hiker into the Grand Canyon off of the main roads and above the desert.

We recommend that you climb the fire tower before you hike. It provides great views, whereas the trail has few. Then, get underway. For the first mile *1.6 km* of the trail the Forest Service has provided a series of signs telling about the Dwarf Mistletoe, with examples pointed out in the forest. We were especially taken with the information that the mistletoe propagates by explosively shooting its sticky seeds as far as sixty feet.

You will pass through areas where the mistletoe was not attacked and another where infected trees were removed. In the thinned area you are able to see into the Grand Canyon but it is only a glimpse.

The trail runs through an attractive pine forest, typical of the area, with nothing special to recommend it. The forest is so heavy that you cannot see into the distance. This is the irony of this trail: although it passes through one of the great scenic areas of the world, you can't see more than a few feet through the trees. There are no bare vista points. We stopped at the 3.0 mile *4.8 km* post, a distance that makes a nice day hike.

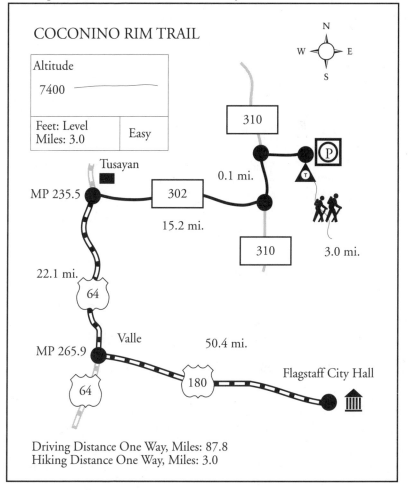

CONNECTOR TRAIL #80

General Information
Location Map E2
Kendrick Peak, Moritz Ridge and Wing Mt. USGS Maps
Coconino Forest Service Map

Driving Distance One Way: 34.55 miles *55.3 km* (Time 1.25 hours)
Access Road: All cars, Last 20 miles *32 km* good gravel road
Hiking Distance One Way: 2.0 miles *3.2 km* (Time 1.0 hour)
How Strenuous: Moderate
Features: Nice forest, Views

NUTSHELL: This sidehill trail is located on Kendrick Mountain, 34.55 miles *55.3 km* north of Flagstaff. After a brief climb it takes you from the **Bull Basin Trail** on the north side of the mountain to the **Pumpkin Trail** on the west side.

DIRECTIONS:
From Flagstaff City Hall Go:
    North on Humphreys Street for 0.60 miles *1 km*. See Access Map, page 10. Turn left at the stoplight onto Columbus Avenue and follow it around a big curve to the north. You will see the street signs call this road Columbus at first, then Ft. Valley Road and then Highway 180. Stay on Highway 180 to the 14.5 miles *23.2 km* point (MP 230), where an unpaved road takes off to the left. Turn left onto this road, FR 245, and follow it to the 17.6 mile *28.2 km* point where it intersects FR 171. Turn right on FR 171 and follow it to the 24.8 mile 39.7 *km* point, where you will see a sign for the Pumpkin Trail. Go just beyond this, to the 24.9 mile 39.9 *km* point and turn left on FR 171. Follow it to the 27.7 mile *44.3 km* point, where it meets FR 144 and turn right on FR 144, taking it to the 29.2 mile *46.7 km* point, where it intersects FR 90. Turn right on FR 90 and drive it to the 33.9 mile *54.3 km* point, where you will see FR 90A to the right. Take FR 90A to the 34.45 mile *55.1 km* point, where you will see a sign marking the access road to the Bull Basin trailhead. You can see the parking lot from this point. Turn right, downhill, and you will reach the parking area at 34.55 miles *55.3 km*.

TRAILHEAD: Use the Bull Basin Trailhead.

DESCRIPTION: From the parking area you walk a closed road along the west side of Bull Basin, a large grassy meadow. At 0.9 miles *1.4 km* you come to a trail junction where you see a trail to the right. A line of stones and poles indicate a trail junction mark the ground at this point. The **Bull Basin Trail** goes to the left, while the Connector Trail goes to the right.

The trail moves west along the base of Kendrick Mountain and then makes a gentle climb. After the climb, you will stay pretty much on the same level for the rest of the hike.

Because the trail is located on the north and west side of the mountain, the forest is more of a spruce and fir forest than a pine forest. It is quite attractive and is a pleasant walk. There are some aspens mixed in.

Along the trail there are some places where there are openings in the trees through which you can get views to the north. The landscape is one of wooded ridges below which a pastel desert begins abruptly and stretches to the Grand Canyon. About 0.1 mile *0.16 km* before the trail ends, you will enter a zone where the spruces stop and the pines begin.

The trail ends where it meets the Pumpkin Trail at a point 1.4 miles *2.25 km* from the Pumpkin Trailhead. There are signs at this junction. You could hike to the top of Kendrick on the Pumpkin Trail from here.

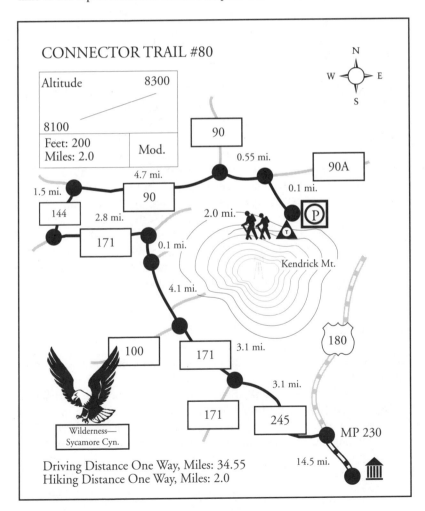

CONNECTOR TRAIL #80

Altitude   8300

8100
Feet: 200
Miles: 2.0   Mod.

4.7 mi.

90   0.55 mi.

90A

1.5 mi.   0.1 mi.

144   90

2.8 mi.   2.0 mi.

171   0.1 mi.

Kendrick Mt.

4.1 mi.

180

100   171   3.1 mi.

3.1 mi.

171   245

Wilderness—
Sycamore Cyn.   MP 230

Driving Distance One Way, Miles: 34.55   14.5 mi.
Hiking Distance One Way, Miles: 2.0

CRATER LAKE

General Information
Location Map E2
Kendrick Peak USGS Map
Coconino Forest Service Map

Driving Distance One Way: 21.7 miles *34.7 km* (Time 30 minutes)
Access Road: All cars, Last 1.0 miles *1.6 km* high clearance vehicle only
Hiking Distance One Way: 0.5 miles *0.8 km* (Time 15 minutes to the top)
How Strenuous: Moderate
Features: Charming hidden lake in a volcanic crater, Views

NUTSHELL: You can't see this little crater from the highway, but it is easy to reach and quite beautiful.

DIRECTIONS:
From Flagstaff City Hall Go:
    North on Humphreys Street for 0.60 miles *1.0 km*. See Access Map, page 10. Turn left at the stoplight onto Columbus Avenue and follow it around a big curve to the north. You will see the street signs call this road Columbus at first, then Ft. Valley Road and then Highway 180. Stay on Highway 180 to the 18.5 mile *29.6 km* point (MP 234.1), where a gravel road takes off to the left. Turn left onto this road, FR 760, and follow it to the 20.7 mile *33.1 km* point where a primitive unsurfaced road, FR 9009D appears to your left. Turn left on FR 9009D. This is a very rough road, with many large, exposed rocks. You may want to park at the junction and walk to the trailhead, which is 1.0 mile *1.6 km* from the fork. As you come near the trailhead, you will first see a sign announcing a travel restricted area. When you reach the trailhead, there is another sign saying "Official Notice." This is at a point where FR 9009D goes to the left, downhill. The hiking trail goes to your right, uphill.

TRAILHEAD: Not signed as a trail. Follow the old road, now closed.

DESCRIPTION: There are other hikes in the book that take the hiker up the north, west and south faces of Kendrick Peak, which is the tallest mountain in the region, save for the San Francisco Peaks. See the **Bull Basin**, **Pumpkin** and **Kendrick Mountain** trails. This is the only hike in the area of the east face of Kendrick, and it is on an adjacent volcanic crater.
    The hiking trail is an old road, so it makes for an easy walk. You start on the south face of the crater and move around, counterclockwise, to the east side, climbing about two hundred feet. As you climb, you have a few views into the surrounding area, but trees block your line of sight most of the time.

When you reach the bowl of the crater, you will find a fence with a maze-type gate. The road splits here. Take the right-hand road. It winds down to the floor of the crater, where you will find a charming lake with a horseshoe collar of aspens. This is a beautiful picturesque spot, perfect for a picnic. C. Hart Merriam saw this crater full to overflowing with rainwater in the summer of 1889.

After enjoying the lake, you might want to climb up to the rim of the crater and walk around it. There are some interesting red lava formations on the north end.

There are two Crater Lakes north of Flagstaff. The bigger and better known one is near the bottom of Hart Prairie, and is on private land that is posted with No Trespassing signs.

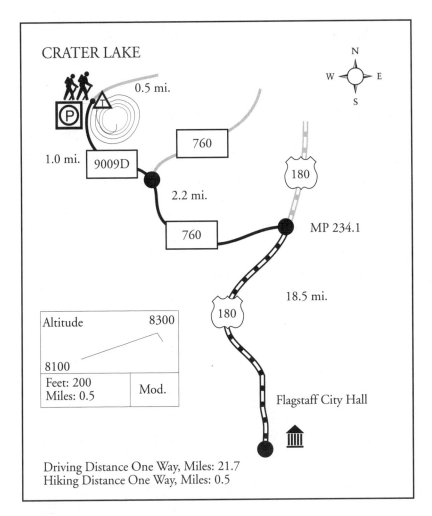

CRATER LAKE

0.5 mi.

760

1.0 mi. 9009D

180

2.2 mi.

760

MP 234.1

18.5 mi.

180

Altitude	8300	
8100		
Feet: 200 Miles: 0.5		Mod.

Flagstaff City Hall

Driving Distance One Way, Miles: 21.7
Hiking Distance One Way, Miles: 0.5

Mangum

DAVENPORT HILL TRAIL #63

General Information
Location Map F1
Bill Williams Mountain USGS Map
Kaibab (Williams District) Forest Service Map

Driving Distance One Way: 40.7 miles *65.1 km* (Time 60 minutes)
Access Road: All cars, Last 4.0 miles *6.4 km* good gravel road
Hiking Distances: One way 2.5 mi. *4 km* (Time 1.25 hours) / Loop—1.0 mi.
1.6 km (Time 30 min.) / Loop—1.8 mi. *2.9 km* (Time 1 hour)
How Strenuous: Moderate/Easy/Easy
Features: Beautiful forest, Nature trail, Lake

NUTSHELL: There are three hikes here: (1) Davenport Hill Trail, a 2.5 mile *4.0 km* trek to the top of a hill from which there are good views; (2) Ponderosa Nature Trail, an easy 1.0 mile *1.6 km* loop, (3) Dogtown Lake Trail, a 1.8 mile *2.9 km* loop around the lake.

DIRECTIONS:
From Flagstaff City Hall Go:
    South on Route 66 under the railroad overpass. Be sure to follow Route 66 when it turns right at the second stoplight. See Access Map, page 10. In about five miles *8.0 km* you will merge onto I-40 West and stay on it to the 30.3 miles *48.5 km* point, the Williams Exit, #165. Take that exit and at the stop sign go left to Williams. Go into town on Railroad Avenue to the 32.9 mile point *52.6 km* where you will find Fourth Street. Turn left on Fourth Street. As it leaves town its name changes to the Perkinsville Road (FR 173). Stay on this road to the 36.7 miles *58.7 km* point, where you turn left onto FR 140. You will see a sign for "Dogtown Lake" here. Take FR 140 to the 39.5 mile *63.2 km* point, where you turn left on FR 132 into the campground, which you will reach at 40.7 miles *65.1 km*. Follow signs to the boat ramp for hikes 1 and 2. You park at the parking area by the boat ramp for hikes 1 and 2. For hike 3, go to the picnic area.

TRAILHEAD: At the Boat Ramp for hikes 1 and 2; at the Picnic Area for hike 3.

DESCRIPTION: Hike 1: At about a quarter of a mile *0.4 km*, just after you have passed over a bridge and the nature trail begins to loop back to camp, you will find the Davenport Hill Trail branching to the left. There is a sign. You will walk along a level bench to the 1.0 mile *1.6 km* point, where you cross a road. You are now at the foot of the hill and begin to climb. This involves winding around the hill, which gives you different viewpoints, though the forest is so thick that you only get glimpses toward Bill Williams Mountain and toward Davenport Lake. You reach an intermediate top at 1.5 miles *2.4 km*, a good resting point, then begin the final ascent. Toward the top you hike through a dense forest of oak, pine, fir and spruce. It is really lovely. The trail takes you north to the farthest point on the hill where it stops at a large cairn. There is a sign here reading, "Davenport Hill, Elevation 7805."

Hike 2: Dogtown Lake (named after a Prairie Dog colony) is a pretty lake in a scenic basin. You start on the nature trail, which takes you along the valley where a stream would flow if it hadn't been dammed to form the lake. The valley is marshy and lush. A brochure is keyed to numbered points along the trail, which loops back to the start.

Hike 3: From the picnic area, you make a loop around the lake. This hike is easy and quite level.

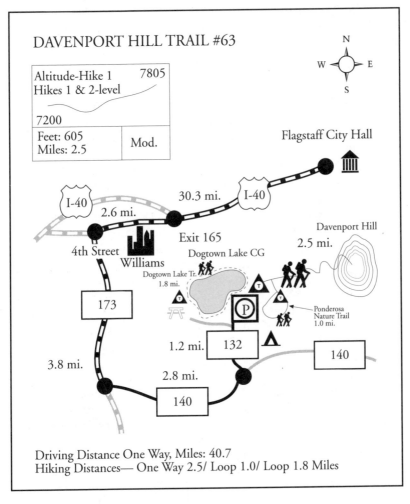

DONEY TRAIL #39

General Information
Location Map D4
Wupatki SW USGS Map
Coconino Forest Service Map

Driving Distance One Way: 42 miles *67.2 km* (Time 60 minutes)
Access Road: All cars, All paved
Hiking Distance One Way: 0.50 miles *0.8 km* (Time 30 minutes)
How Strenuous: Moderate
Features: Views, Indian ruins

NUTSHELL: This is a short easy trail located in the Wupatki National Monument northeast of Flagstaff. It takes you to the top of two cinder cones that give great unobstructed views of a fascinating volcanic field. You will also see some vestigial Indian ruins on this hike.

DIRECTIONS:
From Flagstaff City Hall Go:
East, curving to north on Santa Fe (Route 66). See Access Map, pages 10-11. Follow Highway 89 north out into the country. At 16.4 miles *26.24 km* (MP 430.3) you will reach the entrance to Sunset Crater National Monument. Turn right on the road into Sunset Crater. This road is also known as FR 545. At 18.4 miles *29.4 km* you will reach a ticket booth where you will have to pay admission. Just beyond that is the Visitor Center, which is worth a look.

At 26.0 miles *41.6 km* you reach the Painted Desert Vista. This is a look-out point where we recommend stopping to enjoy the view. Under the right lighting conditions it is superb. At 37.8 miles *60.5 km* you enter the Wupatki National Monument, which adjoins Sunset Crater, and you will see the road to the Wupatki Visitor Center to your left. This center is also worth a look.

Keep following FR 545 to the 41.9 mile *67.0 km* point, where you will see a road to your left going to the Doney Picnic Ground. Take it. At 42.0 miles *67.2 km* you will reach the parking area, where you park.

TRAILHEAD: You will see a sign at the parking area.

DESCRIPTION: The trail is obvious when you start the hike. It climbs twin cinder cones, one higher than the other. The trail leads to a saddle between the two cones at 0.13 miles *0.2 km*. Here you can decide whether to go left to the lower cone or right to the higher one. We recommend that you go left first. It's less than 0.10 miles *0.16 km* to the left top and is a climb of only 100 feet. You will see some informative signs along the path. Just below the top you will see the smallest, crudest Indian ruin imaginable. There are good views from the top and a bench to sit on.

Then it's on to the higher cone. It is 200 feet higher than the parking lot, so you get better views than you can from the lower cone. However, each summit offers a different angle, so both are worthwhile. On the trail you will see a small partially excavated pit house. At the top you will find a bench where you can sit and enjoy the views. There is a nice sign there with a sketch identifying the mountains you see to the west.

Because these tops are bare cinder cones your view is unobstructed. To the north you can see the Vermilion Cliffs and when the light is right you get a sense of the great cleft that is the Grand Canyon. To the east, you look at the Painted Desert. To the west you see the San Francisco Peaks and a long line of volcanic mountains, hills and cones. To the south is Sunset Crater.

Having a picnic at the picnic tables and then taking this hike makes for a nice family outing.

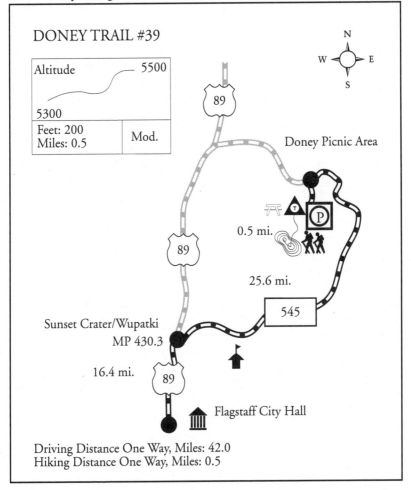

DONEY TRAIL #39

Altitude — 5500

5300

Feet: 200 Miles: 0.5 — Mod.

Doney Picnic Area

0.5 mi.

25.6 mi.

545

Sunset Crater/Wupatki MP 430.3

16.4 mi.

Flagstaff City Hall

Driving Distance One Way, Miles: 42.0
Hiking Distance One Way, Miles: 0.5

DORSEY SPRING TRAIL

General Information
Location Map F2
Sycamore Point USGS Map
Coconino Forest Service Map

Driving Distance One Way: 22.95 miles *36.7 km* (Time 60 minutes)
Access Road: High clearance for last 0.65 miles *1.04 km*
Hiking Distance One Way: 2.3 miles *3.7 km* (Time 1.50 hours)
How Strenuous: Hard
Features: Hidden spring, Virgin forests

NUTSHELL: Located about 25 miles *40 km* southwest of Flagstaff, this trail takes you part of the way into Sycamore Canyon to a beautiful spring.

DIRECTIONS:
From Flagstaff City Hall Go:
West a block on Santa Fe (Route 66), then south, beneath the railroad overpass. See Access Map, page 10. At 0.50 miles *0.8 km* you will reach a Y intersection. The right fork is named Route 66. Take it. You will soon leave town. At 2.6 miles *4.2 km* you will reach a road going to the left. This is the Woody Mountain Road, FR 231. Take it. It is paved about a mile *1.6 km* and then turns into a cinder road. At 16.6 miles *26.6 km* you will intersect FR 538. Turn right onto FR 538 and follow it to the 22.3 mile *35.7 km* point, where it intersects the Kelsey Spring Road, FR 538E. Turn right on 538E. The roads to this point are good, but beyond it they are rough. At 22.7 miles *36.3 km* you hit another intersection where FR 538E forks to the left. This is the Dorsey Spring Road. Turn left onto it and follow it to its end at 22.95 miles *36.7 km*, where you will find a parking lot.

TRAILHEAD: You will see a big sign at the parking area.

DESCRIPTION: The Dorsey Spring Trail does not take you into the inner gorge of Sycamore Canyon like its nearby neighbors the **Kelsey Spring Trail** and the **Winter Cabin Trail** do. It stops at Dorsey Spring. Also unlike those trails, the parking lot is not located at the canyon's rim.
From the parking area you will walk a closed jeep road. At 0.25 miles *0.4 km* you will see a closed road to the **Hog Hill** trailhead forking to the left. At 1.8 miles *2.9 km* you will reach the rim. From the rim area you will get a few views into the depths of the canyon, the only place on this trail where that is possible.
You will hike down into Sycamore along a side canyon. It is fairly steep but the footing is decent and you only have to go half a mile *0.8 km*, to the

2.3 mile *3.7 km* point. The spring is on a small shelf to your left. The water has been channeled so it flows from a black plastic pipe. The spring is usually dependable but the Forest Service recommends purifying its water. From the place where the water comes out of the pipe you will see a thin river of green grass running down a long way, ultimately into Sycamore.

A few yards below the spring there is a large shelf of land, a beautiful idyllic spot.

You will also find markers for the **Kelsey-Winter Trail** coming through this large shelf of land. Dorsey Spring is located about midway between Kelsey Spring and Winter Cabin Spring on the Kelsey-Winter Trail. You can go north along Kelsey-Winter about 2.0 miles *3.2 km* to **Babe's Hole** and into the gorge of Sycamore Canyon via **Geronimo Spring** or you can go south about 2.0 miles *3.2 km* to **Winter Cabin** and into the Sycamore Canyon gorge via **Ott Lake**, so it is an ideal resting place in between.

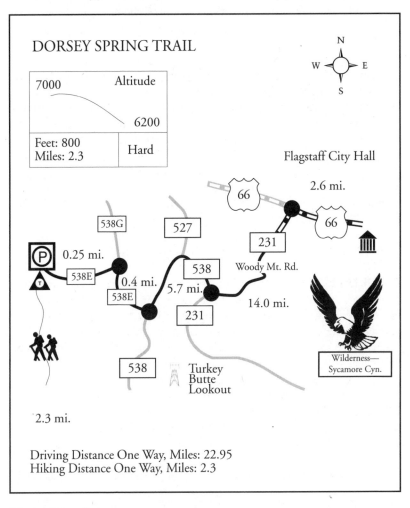

Mangum

DRY LAKE HILLS

General Information
Location Map E3
Humphreys Peak and Flagstaff West USGS Maps
Coconino Forest Service Map

Driving Distance One Way: 7.6 miles *12.2 km* (Time 30 minutes)
Access Road: All cars, Last 4 miles *6.4 km* good dirt road
Hiking Distance One Way: 1.75 miles *2.8 km* (Time 60 minutes)
How Strenuous: Moderate
Features: Views

NUTSHELL: Located 7.6 miles *12.2 km* north, this hike takes you through beautiful forests and meadows to a superb lookout point.

DIRECTIONS:
From Flagstaff City Hall Go:
    North on Humphreys Street a distance of 0.60 miles *1.0 km* to the stoplight at Columbus Ave. See Access Map, page 10. Turn left here. The street you will be on bears three names: Columbus, Ft. Valley Road and Highway 180. It goes around a big curve and heads north, taking you out of town. At 3.1 miles *5.0 km* (MP 218.6) the Schultz Pass Road (FR 420) branches off to the right. Take it. At 3.6 miles *5.8 km* it curves to the left at a junction. Go left here. The paving ends soon after the curve. At 7.6 miles *12.2 km* you will be well up in the mountains, where a sideroad drops off sharply to your right into a gully. Take this road, which is marked FR 789, down to a gate. You will have to park by the gate.

TRAILHEAD: No trail signs. You walk the road, FR 789.

DESCRIPTION: The old road (FR 789) passes through a lovely mixed forest of aspen, spruce, fir and pine. It is moist in this forest, so there are many flowers, ferns and other botanicals. At 0.90 miles *1.5 km* you will come out into a clearing where there is a broad meadow. This is the first of the Dry Lakes. In the spring it will hold water from snow melt but during the rest of the year it will live up to its name and be dry. At the entrance to this first meadow are a couple of fenced ponds that hold water year around.
    The first meadow was the site of the Brookbank Ranch, built in the late 1800s. Into the 1960s the old abandoned ranch house and some other structures were still there. In the late 60s and early 70s, however, many old cabins in the Peaks area were torn down by the Forest Service, including this one.
    At 1.0 miles *1.6 km* you will see a trail going off to your left. This con-

nects with the **Brookbank Trail**. We have seen mountain bikers take this. At 1.5 miles *2.4 km* you have reached the end of the first Dry Lake. Here the road branches left and right and the trail ahead seems blocked by a hump. If you walk over this hump and go straight ahead you will come to the second Dry Lake. It is a bit smaller than the first, but is worth a look.

A more interesting experience is to take the road to the left. It goes to a rocky outcrop that is a fine viewpoint from which to get views of Mt. Elden and East Flagstaff. This is the end of the line. Coming back you'll have prime views of the Peaks.

The best way to show someone where the Dry Lake Hills are is to take them to Macy's for a cup of coffee. A good idea anyway. When you're finished, go outside and have them look up Beaver Street. It forms a frame aiming right at the Dry Lake Hills. We have tried this several times and it always works. "Oh, so that's what those are."

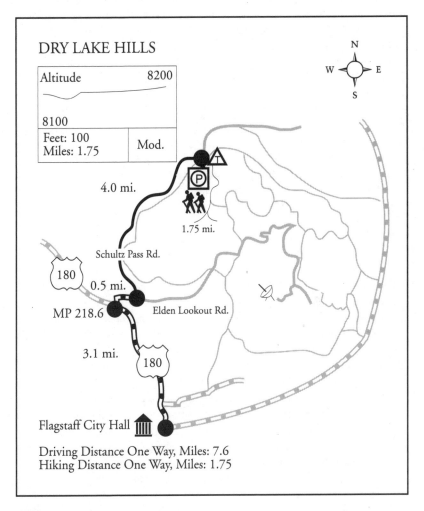

Mangum

EAST POCKET

General Information
Location Map F2
Wilson Mtn. USGS Map
Coconino Forest Service Map

Driving Distance One Way: 30.0 miles *48 km* (Time 1 hour)
Access Road: All cars, Last 27.4 miles *43.9 km* good dirt road
Hiking Distance One Way: 1.5 miles *2.4 km* (Time 1 hour)
How Strenuous: Moderate
Features: Beautiful forest, wonderful views over Oak Creek Canyon

NUTSHELL: You walk an old road out to the tip of a ridge projecting from a place on the Mogollon Rim known as East Pocket. From trail's end you have wonderful views to the south, over the Oak Creek Canyon and Sedona redrock country.

DIRECTIONS:
From Flagstaff City Hall Go:
    West one block on Route 66 (Santa Fe), then left (south) beneath the railroad overpass. See Access Map, page 10. At 0.50 miles *0.8 km* you will reach a Y intersection. The right fork is Route 66. Take it. You will soon leave town. At 2.6 miles *4.2 km* you will reach a road going to the left. This is the Woody Mountain Road, FR 231. Take it. It is paved about a mile and then turns into a cinder road. Stay on this road to the 30.0 mile *48 km* point, where you will see a gate below the entrance to the lookout tower. Pull off to the right on a jeep road.

TRAILHEAD: Nothing marked. Walk the closed road to the south.

DESCRIPTION: The little jeep road where you park is within sight of the gate blocking the end of FR 231 up to the fire tower. You can see the gate about twenty yards up the road. As you begin walking the road on which you pull off and park, it seems like a track that goes somewhere, but that is deceptive, as it ends in about 100 yards. At this point, bushwhack straight ahead. You will immediately see a distinct old road just below you. Get on this road, turn left, and follow it to the top of the ridge.
    You will reach a top in about 0.2 miles *0.32 km*. To your right here, the road is very near the rim and you can get some nice views into wild, broken canyon country. The road is now fairly level. At 0.4 miles *0.64 km* you will find a fork, where a primitive road goes off downhill to your left (east). This road goes to East Pocket Tank, and is shown on the USGS map. Avoid this road and stay up on the top. The hiking trail from this point to the end is a

minor road that seems to have been created for the purpose of allowing vehicles to set up an aerial photography marker. You will stay on the road all the way to its end. Look carefully, as there are places where it is faint, but it does exist. Generally it stays pretty close to the west edge of the ridge, and you will enjoy several nice viewpoints as you go.

The trail ends on a bare spot near the rip of the ridge. From here the views are spectacular. From this point, because the country is open, with low-growing plants, you can easily navigate to the very end of the ridge, for even better views.

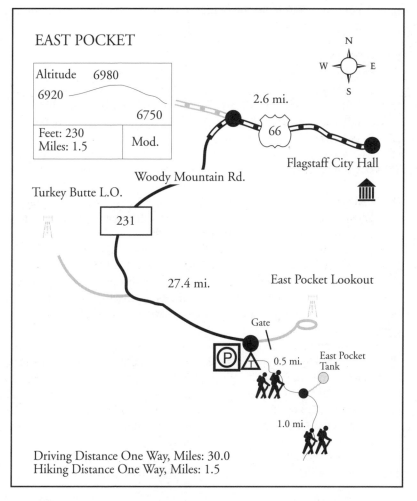

ELDEN LOOKOUT TRAIL #4

General Information
Location Map E3
Flagstaff East USGS Map
Coconino Forest Service Map

Driving Distance One Way: 5.2 miles *8.3 km* (Time 10 minutes)
Access Road: All cars, All paved
Hiking Distance One Way: 3.0 miles *4.8 km* (Time 2 hours)
How Strenuous: Hard
Features: Views

NUTSHELL: This marked and maintained trail runs from the base of Mt. Elden in East Flagstaff to the top of the mountain where a fire lookout tower is located.

DIRECTIONS:
From Flagstaff City Hall Go:
    East on Highway 89. See Access Map, pages 10-11. At 5.2 miles *8.3 km* (MP 419.5), just beyond the Flagstaff Mall, you will see a sign for the "Mt. Elden Trailhead" and a paved driveway to your left into a parking lot bounded by a pole fence. Pull in there and park.

TRAILHEAD: There is a sign with map at the gate in the parking lot.

DESCRIPTION: You will meet the **Fat Man's Loop Trail** branching to the right shortly after you begin. After that you will come to two fences that have maze-type gates. Go through them. You will see clearly by now that you are walking directly toward Mt. Elden. In about a quarter mile *0.4 km* you will reach the junction with the **Pipeline Trail**, which goes left. For about the first mile *1.6 km* you will pass through a pine forest. The trail rises as it approaches the mountain. At the top of this approach, which is the apex of the Fat Man's Loop, you will see a sign showing the Elden Lookout Trail going uphill.
    From this point to the top, about two miles *3.2 km*, the trail is very steep. There is hardly a level stretch anywhere. You will note that a lot of work has been done on this trail. In some places "stairs" have been built and in others cribbing has been used to hang the trail out over space. Mt. Elden is so steep and so rocky that constant maintenance is needed to keep this trail open. Every year it must be cleared of fallen trees, rock slides, etc. We appreciate the work the Forest Service does on this trail.
    The forest through which you pass on your way to the top is not heavy. This is due to the terrain and a 1978 forest fire. Consequently there are many

open spaces for great views. You look out north and east into East Flagstaff, Doney Park, the Sunset Crater area, and the Painted Desert.

The three mile *4.8 km* point at the top where the sign indicating the end of the trail is located is not the absolute top of Mt. Elden. You will find a sign indicating that the tower is 0.25 miles *0.4 km* away. If you have enough energy, by all means, make this final ascent, because the views at the top are as good as any in the Flagstaff area. If a ranger is in the tower you may be invited up. Go. You won't regret it.

We like this hike much better going down, not only because it's easier on the heart, but because the views are before you, unfolding. Using two cars, you park the first one at the bottom. Then everyone rides the second car to the top. You hike down and then drive back to the top to retrieve the second car.

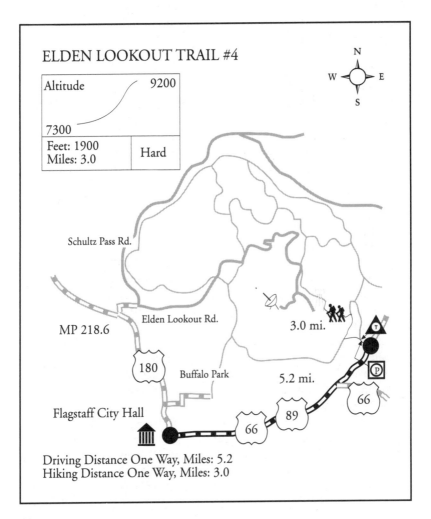

ELDEN LOOKOUT TRAIL #4

Altitude 9200

7300

Feet: 1900
Miles: 3.0   Hard

Schultz Pass Rd.

Elden Lookout Rd.

MP 218.6

180

Buffalo Park

3.0 mi.

5.2 mi.

66

Flagstaff City Hall

66   89

66

Driving Distance One Way, Miles: 5.2
Hiking Distance One Way, Miles: 3.0

Mangum

ELDEN PUEBLO

General Information
Location Map E3
Flagstaff East USGS Map
Coconino Forest Map

Driving Distance One Way: 6.4 miles *10. 24 km* (Time 10 minutes)
Access Road: All cars, All paved
Hiking Distance One Way: 0.10 miles *0.16 km* (Time 30 minutes)
How Strenuous: Easy
Features: Indian ruins located inside Flagstaff city limits

NUTSHELL: Interesting Indian ruins, presently being excavated. Located just north of Flagstaff, this is more of a sightseeing excursion than a hike, as you do very little walking.

DIRECTIONS:
From Flagstaff City Hall Go:
East, then north on Highway 89. See Access Map, pages 10-11. At 6.4 miles *10.24 km* (MP 420.7), you will see a sign, "Elden Pueblo Ruins" and a gravel drive going into the trees to your left just before the stoplight at the junction of Highway 89 and the Townsend-Winona Road. This is the entrance to the parking area for Elden Pueblo. Pull in there and park.

TRAILHEAD: There are no trail signs. A path starts at the south end of the parking lot. It is easy to find.

DESCRIPTION: From the parking lot there is a road going through a gate to your right (north). It does go to the ruin, but it is the long way around, intended for vehicles only, so that they can loop around and avoid driving right on the site of the ruins. You will find signs directing you to the pueblo site. The ruins are very near the highway and you will soon see them when you begin to walk the footpath. They are undergoing restoration but this is sporadic and there is no way of knowing on any particular day whether any-one will be there. If no one is present, you are welcome to help yourself and wander around. Unfortunately there are no self-guiding signs.
At times the Forest Service sponsors amateur digs at Elden Pueblo, when the public is invited to come out and work for a day under the guidance of professional archaeologists. Look for announcements in the Flagstaff news-paper or call the Elden Pueblo Project Manager, Northern Arizona Natural History Association, (520) 523-9642 for recorded information on these digs. It's your chance to find out what archaeology is really like.
Elden Pueblo was discovered in 1916 by Mary-Russel Ferrell Colton,

while horseback riding. The prominent federal archaeologist Jesse Fewkes conducted digs at the site in the early 1920s and sent carloads of artifacts from Elden Pueblo to the Smithsonian. The dismay of townspeople at seeing this wholesale loss of local relics was one of the main reasons that Mrs. Colton and her husband joined other townspeople and organized the Museum of Northern Arizona.

A look at this site shows you how much effort goes into excavation. You can appreciate better what has happened at some fully restored places such as Wupatki or Tuzigoot when you look at the work here. The more they dig at Elden Pueblo, the bigger the ruin seems and the present thought is that there may be an older ruin under the surface ruin.

In addition to the highly publicized Indian ruins such as Wupatki there are many smaller ruins like Elden Pueblo located northeast of Flagstaff.

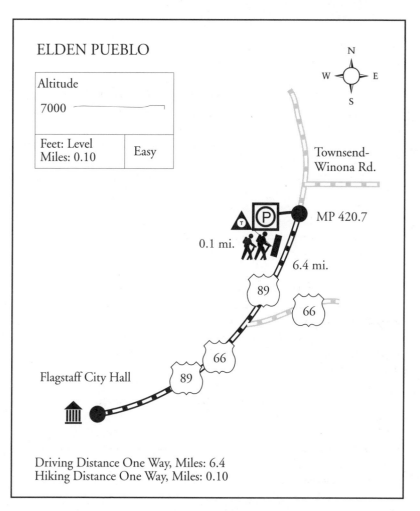

ELDEN PUEBLO

Altitude

7000

Feet: Level
Miles: 0.10 — Easy

Townsend-
Winona Rd.

MP 420.7

0.1 mi.

6.4 mi.

89

66

66

89

Flagstaff City Hall

Driving Distance One Way, Miles: 6.4
Hiking Distance One Way, Miles: 0.10

ELDEN SKYLINE TRAIL

General Information
Location Map E3
Humphreys Peak & Sunset Crater West USGS Maps
Coconino Forest Service Map

Driving Distance One Way: 9.4 miles *15 km* (Time 40 minutes)
Access Road: All cars, Last 5.8 miles *9.3 km* winding gravel road
Hiking Distance One Way: 1.0 miles *1.6 km* (Time 35 minutes)
How Strenuous: Moderate
Features: Unsurpassed views of Flagstaff

NUTSHELL: This trail starts at Sunset Park near the top of Mt. Elden and goes to a point just below the lookout tower.

DIRECTIONS:
From Flagstaff City Hall Go:
   North on Humphreys Street for 0.60 miles *1.0 km*. See Access Map, page 10. Turn left at the stoplight onto Columbus Avenue and follow it around a big curve to the north. You will see the street signs call this road Columbus Avenue at first, then Ft. Valley Road and then Highway 180. Stay on Highway 180 to the 3.1 miles *5.0 km* point (MP 218.6), where the Schultz Pass Road, FR 420, goes to the right. Follow this road. At the 3.6 miles *5.8 km* point it curves left. There you will see the unpaved Elden Lookout Road (FR 557) going straight. Take the right fork and follow FR 557 to the 9.4 mile *15 km* point, where you will park in an area off the right shoulder.

TRAILHEAD: Walk across the road, where you will see a footpath going uphill to the skyline. At the crest you will find signs.

DESCRIPTION: This trail is considered officially to be the last leg of the Sunset Trail. We feel that it is a much better experience to treat it as a separate trail, as the Sunset Trail is too long if you add this extension to it.
   The place where the trail starts is a junction of the **Sunset Trail** and the **Oldham Trail No. 2** and you will find signs for each of them here. Go to the right, on the Sunset Trail.
   This whole area on top of Mt. Elden shows the results of what a forest fire can do. Hundreds of acres of prime forest were burned away in 1978 in the catastrophic Radio Fire. The area is just now beginning to heal.
   Your trail will take you along the crest of Mt. Elden, climbing uphill a bit a first and then dipping. Almost all the way you will have tremendous views. You look down on East Flagstaff, the Doney Park area, and off toward the Sunset Crater area. On a clear day you can see the Painted Desert.

One of the first trees to come back after a forest fire is the aspen and you will find groves of young aspens along this trail. They have replaced the spruce that predominated here before the fire.

At about the three-quarter mile *1.2 km* point, the trail comes very close to the road going to the fire lookout, but then it veers away from it. At the 1.0 mile *1.6 km* point you will reach the place where this trail meets the **Elden Lookout Trail** coming up from East Flagstaff.

This is the end of the trail, but at this point you have two options: one is to take the Elden Lookout Trail up to the fire tower, a quarter mile *0.4 km* hike. The views from the tower are superb. If a ranger is in the tower you may be invited up. Go up if you get the chance. You won't soon forget what you see from there. The other option is to bushwhack out to the end of a rocky knob that is to your left at the junction. This is only about one-tenth of a mile *0.16 km* and takes you to an excellent viewpoint.

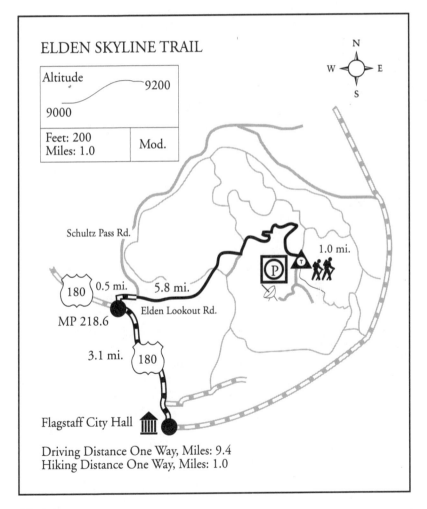

FAT MAN'S LOOP #25

General Information
Location Map E3
Flagstaff East USGS Map
Coconino Forest Service Map

Driving Distance One Way: 5.2 miles *8.3 km* (Time 10 minutes)
Access Road: All cars, All paved
Hiking Distance, Complete Loop: 2.4 miles *3.8 km* (Time 1.5 hours)
How Strenuous: Moderate
Features: Views

NUTSHELL: This maintained trail located in East Flagstaff at the base of Mt. Elden is designed to provide moderate exercise for a "fat man." It provides good scenery and views.

DIRECTIONS:
From Flagstaff City Hall Go:
   East, then north on Highway 89. See Access Map, pages 10-11. At 5.2 miles *8.3 km* (MP 419.5) just past the Flagstaff Mall, you will see a sign for the "Mt. Elden Trailhead" and a paved driveway to your left into a parking lot bounded by a pole fence. Pull in there and park.

TRAILHEAD: There are trail signs at the gate in the parking lot fence.

DESCRIPTION: The Forest Service has developed a trail system around the Mt. Elden\Dry Lake Hills areas in Flagstaff and this trail connects with others in that system. You will find trail information at the trailhead. Fat Man's Loop is a nice trail, well marked, The footing is good. As the name suggests, the trail makes a loop. It is not flat, as it climbs to a high point beyond midway and then descends.
   Start out on the main trail and watch for a fork at 0.15 miles *0.24 km*. There Fat Man's branches to the right. At 0.30 miles *0.48 km* you will come to a pole fence with a squeeze through opening designed to pass humans but not horses. At this point the trail, which up to now has been heading toward Mt. Elden, turns to the right and moves parallel to the base of the mountain. Just beyond this gate, a secondary trail intersects at right angles. Don't turn left or right here. Go straight. At 0.40 miles *0.64 km* you hit another trail junction. This is posted with a sign reading, "Fatman's Loop, Elden Lookout." You want to go left here, toward Mt. Elden. Soon after this, the trail winds around and under a giant old alligator-bark juniper tree, which is quite a sight. Since these trees live to be very old, this one must be ancient to have grown so large.

At 0.90 miles *1.44 km* you are high enough to get some views. To your right the open plain is Doney Park. To your left you see immense cliffs on Mt. Elden. These are made of columns of lava caused by huge volcanic outbursts two million years ago. All through this area you will see volcanic boulders, some of them big as a house and your trail will wind through a nifty crevice between boulders.

You reach the high point of the trail at 1.5 miles *2.4 km*, where there is another trail junction. The path to the right is the **Elden Lookout Trail**, which is not for fat men as it is a very steep climb. You take the trail to the left, from where it is all downhill back to the starting point.

At 2.0 miles *3.2 km* you will reach another junction where there is a sign reading, "**Pipeline Trail No. 42**, **Oldham Trail No. 1**, Buffalo Park 4." Just beyond this point is another pole fence with a squeeze through. From there you saunter back to your car.

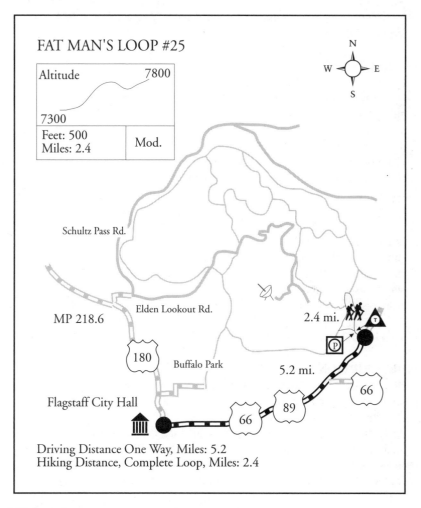

FOSSIL SPRINGS TRAIL

General Information
Location Map G4
Strawberry USGS Map
Coconino Forest Service Map

Driving Distance One Way: 82 miles *131 km* (Time 2 hours)
Access Road: All cars, Last 3.5 miles *5.6 km* good unpaved road
Hiking Distance One Way: 3.8 miles *6.1 km* (Time 2 hours)
How Strenuous: Hard
Features: Beautiful canyon, Views, Perennial spring-fed stream

NUTSHELL: Starting at a point on the top of the Mogollon Rim near Strawberry, you hike an old road to the bottom, where you will find spring-fed Fossil Creek, a beautiful riparian environment.

DIRECTIONS:
From Flagstaff City Hall Go:
    West and then south on Route 66. See Access Map on page 10. At 0.5 miles *0.8 km* go straight on Milton Road, where there is a stoplight. At 1.7 miles *2.7 km* turn right at Forest Meadows. Then turn left on Beulah which will connect onto Highway 89A. At the 2.4 miles *3.8 km* point (MP 401.6) you will see the turnoff to the Lake Mary Road to your left (south). Take it and follow the Lake Mary Road (also known as FH3) to the 56.6 mile *90.6 km* point, the junction with Highway 87 at Clint's Well. Turn right on Highway 87 and drive it to the 76.3 miles *122 km* point, MP 271, where you reach the hamlet of Strawberry. Turn right (west) on Route 708 (also known as Fossil Creek Road). The road is paved for 2.5 miles *4 km*, then becomes unpaved. Stay on FR 708 to the 81.1 mile *130 km* point, where you will see the signed road to the trailhead to your right. Turn off on this access road, which has some washouts, but can be driven by any car that has reasonable clearance. You will reach the loop parking area at 82 miles *131 km*.

TRAILHEAD: At the parking place. There is a sign.

DESCRIPTION: For the first 3.0 miles *4.8 km* of this trail you follow an old road, now closed to vehicles, down to the bottom of the canyon. You can see this road from the top. Because the road was designed for motor vehicles, the grades are fairly moderate.
    At the bottom of the canyon, you will reach the streambed. Here the old road disappears and the trail turns into a footpath. You walk parallel to the creek and then cross it on stepping stones. Usually the creek is not deep here. On the other side, you walk the final mile down to the utility hut. This is the

most beautiful part of the hike, as the stream gets bigger and bigger as more springs feed into it. The vegetation is lush and there are many side trails taking you to the water's edge.

Fossil Creek is one of the most reliable, abundant water sources in northern Arizona, and therefore has been used since 1916 to generate hydroelectric power. Originally the electric power went to Jerome, and was later expanded to go to Phoenix, providing the capital city with most of its power in the early days. Where the hike ends, you find the beginning of the water works. Water is channeled into a flume here and runs seven miles down to the Verde River, passing through generating plants at Irving and Childs on its way.

The creek gets its name, not because it contains fossils, but because the water contains high levels of calcium, which encrusts objects in the water with a stony shell, like a fossil.

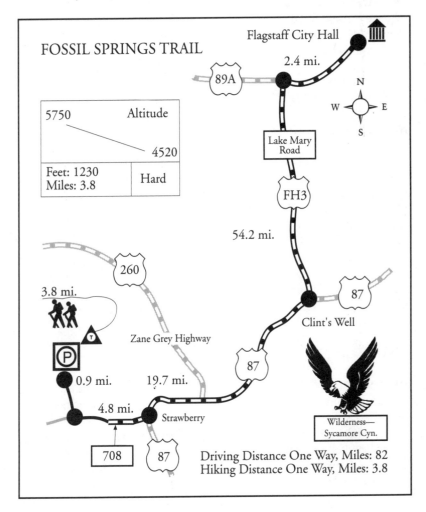

FOSSIL SPRINGS TRAIL

Flagstaff City Hall

2.4 mi.

89A

5750	Altitude
	4520
Feet: 1230 Miles: 3.8	Hard

Lake Mary Road

FH3

54.2 mi.

260

3.8 mi.

Zane Grey Highway

Clint's Well

87

87

0.9 mi. 19.7 mi.

4.8 mi.

Strawberry

708 87

Wilderness—
Sycamore Cyn.

Driving Distance One Way, Miles: 82
Hiking Distance One Way, Miles: 3.8

Mangum

GERONIMO SPRING

General Information
Location Map F2
Sycamore Point USGS Map
Coconino Forest Service Map

Driving Distance One Way: 24.1 miles *38.6 km* (Time 1 hour)
Access Road: High clearance needed for last 1.8 miles *2.9 km*
Hiking Distance One Way: 2.0 miles *3.2 km* (Time 1.5 hours)
How Strenuous: Hard, very steep
Features: Remote spring in the bottom of Sycamore Canyon

NUTSHELL: Located 24.1 miles *38.6 km* southwest of Flagstaff, this trail requires a strenuous descent to the bottom of Little LO Spring Canyon, a tributary of Sycamore Canyon. There are beautiful forests and cliffs, lots of good exploring at the bottom. **A personal favorite.**

DIRECTIONS:
From Flagstaff City Hall Go:
   West one block on Route 66 (Santa Fe), then left (south) beneath the railroad overpass. See Access Map, page 10. At 0.50 miles *0.8 km* you will reach a Y intersection. The right fork is named Route 66. Take it. You will soon leave town. At 2.6 miles *4.2 km* you will reach a road going to the left. This is the Woody Mountain Road, FR 231. Take it. It is paved about a mile and then turns into a cinder road. At 16.6 miles *26.6 km* you will intersect FR 538. Turn right onto FR 538 and follow it to the 22.3 mile *35.7 km* point, where it intersects FR 538E. Turn right on 538E. At 22.7 miles *36.3 km* you hit another intersection, where FR 538E forks to the left, going to Dorsey Spring Road. The road is rough beyond here. Keep straight, now on FR 538G, and follow it to its end at 23.7 miles *37.9 km*, where it meets FR 527A. Turn left onto the Kelsey Trail road, going to the 24.1 mile *38.6 km* point, the parking area. This last 0.4 mile *0.64 km* stretch is terrible, a real tire-eater.

TRAILHEAD: You will see a sign at the parking area.

DESCRIPTION: This trail shares the same right of way with the **Kelsey Spring** and **Babe's Hole** trails and you have to pass through them to reach Geronimo Spring. So you get a three-hikes-in-one experience.
   The parking lot is located on the edge of the rim, so the trail immediately plunges down into the canyon. It passes through a beautiful forest, which gets more beautiful and interesting as you go. Kelsey Spring is reached in 0.5 miles *0.8 km*, on a shelf of level land. Enjoy it and then continue down

the canyon until you reach Babe's Hole. At Babe's Hole several hill folds come together to make a small protected pocket, with a spring bubbling out into a small pool

From Babe's Hole go downhill 0.1 miles *0.16 km*, to a junction. The **Kelsey-Winter Trail** goes left, to **Dorsey Spring** and then **Winter Cabin Spring**, and is marked. The trail to Geronimo Spring goes to the right and is unmarked.

From this point it is 0.75 miles *1.2 km* to the bottom. The trail becomes very steep about half way down. You will emerge at a trail junction, where Little LO Spring Canyon meets Sycamore Canyon. Take the left fork to Geronimo Spring, only a few feet away at a small flat area. The trail to the right takes you up Little LO Spring Canyon. You will find a trail to the west going into the big canyon.

This is a really remote wilderness spot, offering great opportunities for exploration.

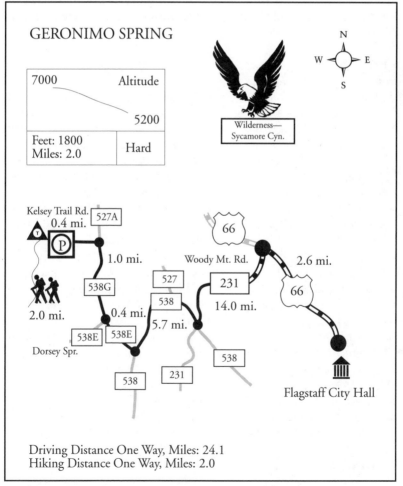

GERONIMO SPRING

N
W ← → E
S

7000   Altitude
         5200
Feet: 1800   Hard
Miles: 2.0

Wilderness—
Sycamore Cyn.

Kelsey Trail Rd.
0.4 mi.   527A
     P
       1.0 mi.   Woody Mt. Rd.
           66
           527   231   2.6 mi.
538G   538   14.0 mi.   66
2.0 mi.   0.4 mi.
          5.7 mi.
538E   538E
Dorsey Spr.
         538
       538   231
               Flagstaff City Hall

Driving Distance One Way, Miles: 24.1
Hiking Distance One Way, Miles: 2.0

Mangum

GOVERNMENT KNOLL

General Information
Location Map E2
Parks and Wing Mt. USGS Maps
Kaibab (Williams) Forest Service Map

Driving Distance One Way: 25.9 miles *41.5 km* (Time 45 minutes)
Access Road: All cars, Last 11 miles *17.6 km* medium gravel road
Hiking Distance One Way: 0.5 miles *0.8 km* (Time 30 minutes)
How Strenuous: Moderate
Features: Views

NUTSHELL: This cinder cone located at the north end of Government Prairie 25.9 miles *41.5 km* west of Flagstaff provides beautiful views of Kendrick Mountain and the San Francisco Peaks. It is easy to reach and to climb.

DIRECTIONS:
From Flagstaff City Hall Go:
    West a block on Route 66 (Santa Fe), then south, beneath the railroad overpass. See Access Map, page 10. At 0.50 miles *0.8 km* you will reach a Y intersection. The right fork is named Route 66. Take it. You will soon leave town, driving on a stretch of fabled Highway 66. At the 4.8 mile *7.7 km* point you will merge onto Interstate-40 West. Look for Exit 185, "Transwestern Rd., Bellemont" and take it. It is at the 10.8 mile *17.3 km* point. From the exit turn right and go to the frontage road, where you turn left onto FR 146. You are now following another stretch of U.S. 66. Stay on this to the 18 mile *28.8 km* point, where you will see FR 107 fork right. Take FR 107 and follow it to the 23.2 mile *37.1 km* point, just beyond a bare hill we call Rain Tank Hill (unnamed on government maps). Here you will find FR 793 to the right. It has no sign at the entrance and looks primitive but it is a decent road when it is dry. Turn right and follow FR 793. It will take you north across the prairie. At 23.9 miles *38.3 km* you will see a sign marked 793 and 81. Take the left fork here. There is a gate at 24.1 miles *38.6 km*. Go through it. At 24.3 miles *38.9 km* you will pass the **Beale Road on Government Prairie**. Look for markers showing the right of way of this historic road as you pass. You can also see the old wagon tracks. At 25.4 miles *40.6 km* you will come to Horseshoe Tank at the base of Government Knoll. The road splits here. Take the left fork and drive along the north side of the hill. When you come to the 25.9 mile *41.5 km* point you will see a V-shaped notch in the hill with boulders at the bottom of the V. Park there.

TRAILHEAD: There is no trail. You walk up the hill through the notch.

DESCRIPTION: These cinder hills are all extinct volcanoes. From a distance they look symmetrical like a perfect cone or anthill. As you explore them you will find that most of them have a low side with a V-shaped opening gouged out by lava flow. Such is the case with Government Knoll.

Once you climb past the notch you are on the inside of the crater. Walk uphill to your left (north) on a gentle slope that is a natural ramp to the top. The highest point of the hill is the north side.

The hike is not long or overly hard. All you can see until you crest out are the sides of the crater. Then you break over the top and are presented with a genuine "*Aha!*" panorama.

This hill is located at the north end of Government Prairie, close to Kendrick Mountain and the San Francisco Peaks and you have superlative views of them. Government Prairie is a fragile environment, and is now closed to off-road vehicles.

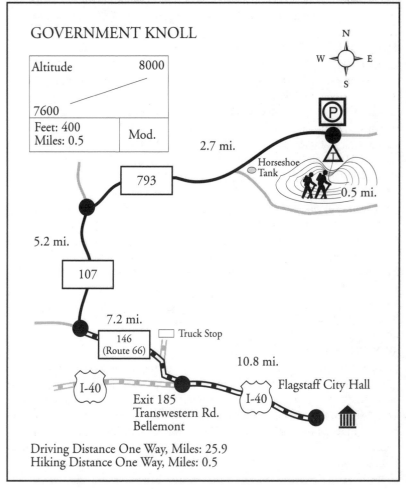

Mangum

GRAND FALLS

Driving Distance One Way: 38.8 miles *62.1 km* (Time 1 hour)
Access Road: All cars, Last 9.1 miles *14.6 km* medium gravel road
Hiking Distance One Way: 0.75 miles *1.2 km* (Time 45 minutes)
How Strenuous: Moderate
Features: Waterfall, Painted Desert Views, Peaks views

NUTSHELL: Located 38.8 miles *62.1 km* east of Flagstaff, Grand Falls is Arizona's biggest waterfall, with a drop higher than Niagara's. Admire it from the top and then hike down to the water.

DIRECTIONS:
From Flagstaff City Hall Go:
    East, then north on Highway 89. See Access Map, pages 10-11. At 6.5 miles *10.4 km* (MP 420.5) you will reach the last stoplight in town at the junction of the Townsend-Winona Road. Turn right here onto the Townsend-Winona Road and follow it to the 14.7 miles *23.5 km* point (MP 428.8) where it intersects Leupp Road. Turn left on the Leupp Road and take it to the 29.7 miles *47.5 km* point (MP 443.5), where Navajo Route 70 joins it to the left. You will see a sign for the Grand Falls Bible Church at the turn. From here you follow Navajo Route 70 to the 38.3 miles *61.3 km* point. The road surface is of cinders. These sometimes cause loose pockets where traction is not good. The road is very dusty and washboardy. At 38.3 miles *61.3 km* there is an unmarked turn uphill to the left. Take it (it's rough) and you will top out at 38.8 miles *62.1 km* where you will see some picnic shelters. Park here near the rim. If you drive all the way to the river, you have missed the uphill turn.

TRAILHEAD: 375 feet from the last picnic shelter.

DESCRIPTION: Take this trip when the river, the Little Colorado, is carrying lots of water, which means during spring snow melt in March and April. When you reach the parking area, park at the first cluster of shelters. Some shelters are picnic tables and others are viewpoints. From this place you will see other shelters downstream. You can drive to the last one, but the road to that point is really rough. We prefer to park the car at the top and walk the rest of the way. When you reach the last shelter, you will see a jeep road that appears to go right to the rim. This is the trailhead. It is unmarked.

The trail is crude and goes abruptly to the river bottom. Once there you can walk along the shore toward the falls and—depending on how muddy it is—you can get quite close to the falls. If you get close enough to be hit by spray you will find that the water is almost as much soil as liquid and when it dries on you, it leaves a film of dirt. The high dirt content of the water accounts for the color and thickness of the falls, which look exactly like cocoa. The falls spill over two major levels.

We have seen daredevils work their way around so that they can stand under the falls at their extreme end but this can be very dangerous and you should not try it unless you have a strong death wish.

The canyon walls at the bottom are interesting. The wall that the falls spill over is sandstone, whereas the wall on your side of the river is lava. Roden Crater erupted and poured this lava into the riverbed, damming the river and changing it to its present course.

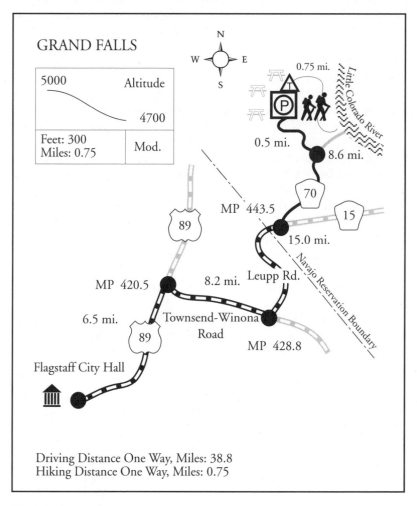

Mangum

GRANDVIEW TRAIL

General Information
Location Map B2
Grandview Point USGS Map
Kaibab (Tusayan) Forest Service Map

Driving Distance One Way: 89.1 miles *143 km* (Time 2 hours)
Access Road: All cars, All paved
Hiking Distance One Way: 3.5 miles 5.6 *km* (Time 6.5 hours total)
How Strenuous: Hard
Features: Best views, Historic mine, Uncrowded

NUTSHELL: This trail is seldom maintained and is not as heavily used as Bright Angel or South Kaibab. It offers superior views (living up to its name), plus the exploration of old mine works.

DIRECTIONS:
From Flagstaff City Hall Go:
   North on Humphreys Street 0.60 miles *1.0 km* to a stoplight. See Access Map, page 10. Go left on Columbus Avenue and follow the curve north. Street signs will show the street first as Ft. Valley Road, then Highway 180, a major road to the Grand Canyon. At 50.4 miles *80.7 km* (MP 265.8), you will intersect Highway 64, coming out of Williams, at Valle. Go right at this junction and follow the highway to the south entrance to the Grand Canyon National Park. You will have to pay an entrance fee. Go on to the Rim Drive at 79.8 miles *127.7 km*, where you turn right, away from Grand Canyon Village. You will motor along the East Rim Drive to the 88.5 mile *141.6 km* point, the entrance to Grandview Point. Turn left here and go down to the parking areas, another 0.6 miles *0.96 km*, and park.

TRAILHEAD: At the NE end of the lower parking area. It is posted.

DESCRIPTION: The Grandview Trail was constructed in 1892 by Pete Berry, to serve his Last Chance copper mine, the richest copper strike ever made in the Grand Canyon. The trail was designed so that mules could take sacks of ore to the rim, from where the ore would be transported to Flagstaff, then to a smelter at El Paso.
   Berry was working on a shoestring and mostly with hand tools and a little dynamite. Constructing this trail under these conditions was a major feat that will cause you to marvel as you see it.
   The trail starts with a series of switchbacks as it descends sharply down the face of a cliff. Here you will find many "stairsteps" and "cobblestone" areas. The footing is difficult due to the steepness of the trail and the pres-

ence of loose rock underfoot. You must move slowly and cautiously. The good news is that the scenery hits you—bam—right away and is constantly in view. After winding around a castle formation, the trail drops again very sharply. When it reaches the red rock, there are places where it was washed out and is now a mere thread, but you can always find the trail. As you move out toward Horseshoe Mesa, you think that the trail has leveled out, only to have it make the final drop to the mesa across a narrow ridge.

Some show the mileage on this hike as 2.0 miles *3.2 km*. We think this is inaccurate. If you go to Horseshoe Mesa and do some exploring there, you will hike at least 3.5 miles *5.6 km*. This hike is extremely steep and there is no water. This is a strenuous hike which should be undertaken only by those who are really fit and have adequate time and water.

A good hike is to go down 1.0 miles *1.6 km* (one hour) to the USGS marker, a disk set into a boulder at the right side of the trail. This gives a good taste of the trail without turning the hike into a death march.

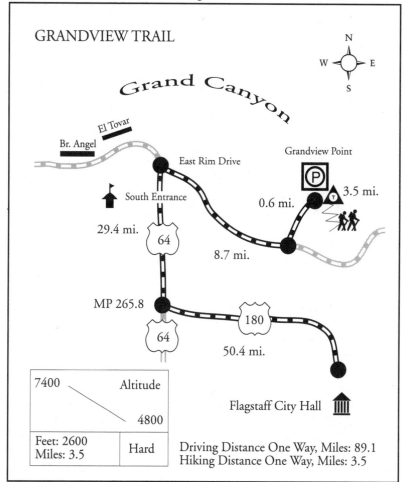

GRANDVIEW TRAIL

GRIFFITHS SPRING CANYON

General Information
Location Map F3
Mountainaire USGS Map
Coconino Forest Service Map

Driving Distance One Way: 7.5 miles *12.0 km* (Time 20 minutes)
Access Road: All cars, Last 0.3 miles *0.5 km* good dirt road
Hiking Distance One Way: 0.8 miles *1.3 km* (Time 30 minutes)
How Strenuous: Easy
Features: Beautiful canyon, Easy to reach trailhead

NUTSHELL: This small canyon is located just south of Flagstaff. Because water usually runs through the canyon all year, a rarity in Arizona, the streambed is a haven for wildlife and supports diverse plant life.

DIRECTIONS:
From Flagstaff City Hall Go:
   West on Route 66 (Santa Fe) one block then left (south) on Route 66 under the railroad overpass. At 0.5 miles *0.8 km*, go straight on Milton Road. See Access Map, page 10. At 1.7 miles *2.7 km* you reach the stoplight at Forest Meadows, where you turn right. At the next corner turn left on Beulah and follow it out of town. Beulah will connect onto Highway 89A which is the road to Oak Creek Canyon and Sedona. At 7.2 miles *11.5 km* (MP 396.8) on Highway 89A you will see an unmarked access road to your left. Take it. Just off the highway there is an unlocked gate. Go through it and stay on the dirt road to the 7.5 miles *12.0 km* point. Park.

TRAILHEAD: No trail signs. You will see the canyon floor down to your left. Walk into it on an old primitive road and go downstream (to the southeast).

DESCRIPTION: From the gate, you want to drive about 0.3 miles *0.5 km*, to a point where the road forks. The road is a bit rough but a passenger car can handle the road when it is dry. Park at the fork. The right fork just peters out in about 0.10 miles *0.16 km*. Walk the left fork, which goes down into the canyon.
   The canyon is narrow and there is usually a little stream running through it. There is no developed hiking trail but you will find a well-defined footpath along the side of the stream. You will cross the stream several times, which could be troublesome if it is carrying much water. In some areas the canyon walls are high Malpais (basaltic lava) cliffs cut and cracked into very attractive lines and angles. In other places the walls are low and open. The

forest is mostly pine but there are copses of oak and others of aspen.

On a hike in August we saw lots of flowers, among them potentillas, wild roses, asters, penstemons, Indian paintbrushes, lupines, evening primroses, linarias, cranesbills and many others. There was also an abundance of elk sign.

The hike ends on a jarring note at 0.8 miles *1.3 km* where the canyon is blocked by an earth fill which supports a road into the south end of Forest Highlands subdivision. There is a huge culvert underneath, but it is closed with a chain and No Trespassing sign. On the other side is Lindbergh Springs, which used to be a lovely place but now is disfigured by the road building. This is a pretty hike until you round the final bend.

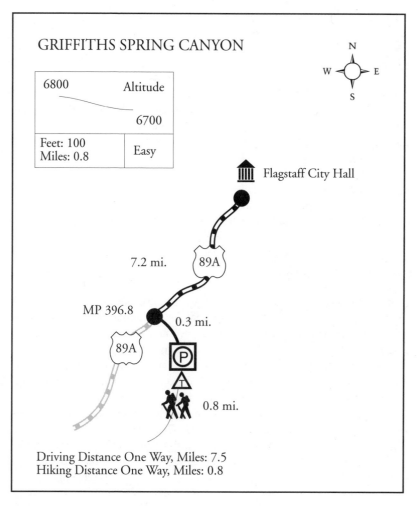

GRIFFITHS SPRING CANYON

N
W ← ⬥ → E
S

6800   Altitude
                6700

Feet: 100
Miles: 0.8   Easy

🏛 Flagstaff City Hall

7.2 mi.   89A

MP 396.8

89A   0.3 mi.

Ⓟ

0.8 mi.

Driving Distance One Way, Miles: 7.5
Hiking Distance One Way, Miles: 0.8

HEART TRAIL #103

General Information
Location Map E3
Flagstaff East & Sunset Crater West USGS Maps
Coconino Forest Service Map

Driving Distance One Way: 7.0 miles *11.2 km* (Time 15 minutes)
Access Road: All cars, Last 0.1 mile *0.16 km* good dirt road
Hiking Distance One Way: 3.85 miles *6.2 km* (Time 2.5 hours)
How Strenuous: Moderate to Hard
Features: Unusual red and white hills, Rock formations, Views

NUTSHELL: This trail, located just 7.0 miles *11.2 km* from City Hall, takes you up a red hill on the east face of Mt. Elden.

DIRECTIONS:
From Flagstaff City Hall Go:
   East, then north on Highway 89. See Access Map, pages 10-11. At 6.5 miles *10.4 km* (MP 420.7), you will see the stoplight at the junction of Highway 89 and the Townsend-Winona Road. Look for a dirt road (FR 9129) going into the trees to your left 0.40 miles *0.64 km* beyond the stoplight, at 6.9 miles *11.1 km* (MP 421.1). Take this dirt road to the parking area at the fence, at 7.0 miles *11.2 km.*

TRAILHEAD: There are lath-type trail signs. You will also see a sign through the fence saying, "Sandy Seep Vehicle Closure. This area closed to motor vehicles to protect the critical Sandy Seep deer winter range and to offer non-motorized recreation opportunities." Go through the opening in the fence and walk a few yards to your left, where you will pick up an old road. Follow the road.

DESCRIPTION: The road is easy to walk and makes a good hiking path because it has been closed to motor vehicles. At about one third of a mile *0.53 km* you will come to the back fence. The road turns right here. Keep following it. The road will wind through the forest and at about one mile *1.6 km* you will come to a hill. The road curves around it. At 1.5 miles *2.4 km* you will see a trail sign leave the road to the left. Get off the road and follow the footpath. Sandy Seep is to your right.
   You will walk into a ravine and then up to another closed road that leads to Mt. Elden. Note that the soil here is red. There are two redrock hills looking like importations from Sedona to your right and a red foothill projecting from the face of Mt. Elden. At 2.1 miles *3.4 km* you will reach the base of the red foothill, where there is a water tank. You will also see a plastic pipe

going up a canyon to tap a spring.

From this point the trail switchbacks up the red hill to the top of Mt. Elden. The trail is nicely laid out.

Sherry, with her photographer's eye, says this part of the trail is *visually exciting*. There are many bold and unusual lava dike formations, burnt trees like totems, vast views to the east, finger ridges running parallel to the hill you are climbing and other delights.

You will come to the top of Mt. Elden at a point on the **Sunset Trail** that is 0.56 miles *0.9 km* from its end, just above the Elden Lookout Road. If you are hardy, you could do the **Elden Skyline Trail** over to the lookout tower and then take the **Elden Lookout Trail** to the bottom.

This is a dandy two-car hike, parking one at the bottom and one at the top, then hiking down.

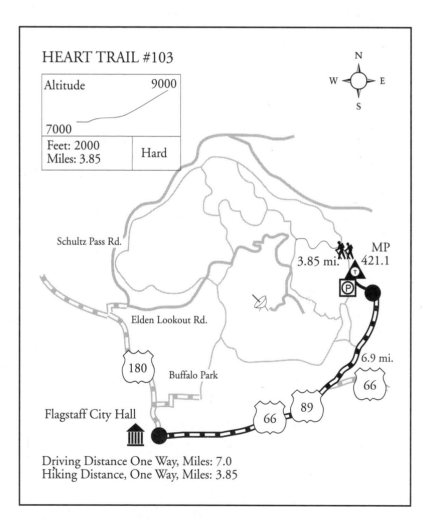

Mangum

HERMIT TRAIL

General Information
Location Map B2
Bright Angel USGS Map
Kaibab (Tusayan) Forest Service Map

Driving Distance One Way: 90 miles *144 km* (Time 2.25 hours)
Access Road: All cars, All paved except last 0.2 mile *0.32 km*
Hiking Distance One Way: 2.0 miles 3.2 *km* (Time 2 hours)
How Strenuous: Hard
Features: Magnificent views, Historic trail

NUTSHELL: This trail at the west end of the south rim of the Grand Canyon is not as heavily used as Bright Angel or South Kaibab, and has less distractions. It is not maintained, but is still a good trail. You will hike 2.0 miles *3.2 km* to the rest house at Santa Maria Spring.

DIRECTIONS:
From Flagstaff City Hall Go:
   North on Humphreys Street 0.60 miles *1.0 km* to a stoplight. See Access Map, page 10. Go left on Columbus Avenue and follow the curve north. Street signs will show the street first as Ft. Valley Road, then Highway 180. This is a major road to the Grand Canyon. At 50.6 miles *81 km* (MP 265.8), you will intersect Highway 64, coming out of Williams, at Valle. Go right at this junction and follow the highway to the south entrance to the Grand Canyon National Park at 75.1 miles *120 km*. You will have to pay an entrance fee. At 79.2 miles *127 km*, you reach the Rim Drive. Turn left, to Grand Canyon Village. You will reach the village area at the 82.1 mile *131.4 km* point. Keep going on the main road, past Bright Angel Lodge. In high season, you will have to park around here and take a shuttle bus to Hermit's Rest. Otherwise, you will drive there, to the 90 mile *144 km* point. You will see trail signs at Hermit's Rest.

TRAILHEAD: At the extreme end of the parking area. It is posted.

DESCRIPTION: The Santa Fe Railroad built the Hermit Trail in 1910 to avoid the tolls charged for the privately-owned Bright Angel Trail. The Santa Fe abandoned the trail in 1931 after the Bright Angel became public property, and the trail has been slightly maintained since.
   The Hermit is one of the few Grand Canyon trails created with professional engineering and with substantial capital. You will see examples of handwork all along the way, especially the "cobblestones."
   For a day hike, you do not need a permit nor do you need to advise the

Park Rangers, but please be prepared. Take water (one quart per person), wear suitable shoes and clothing, and allow enough time.

The footing—due to minimal maintenance—is so bad in most places that this trail is as slow going downhill as up, contrary to most Grand Canyon trails, which take twice as long to ascend as to descend. Views open up early and are a constant delight. At 1.2 miles *2 km*, you reach the Waldron Trailhead. The Dripping Springs Trailhead is next, at 1.5 miles *2.4 km*.

Down to this point, you have passed through white sandstones. From here, you enter the red Hermit Shale zone and will be in it to the end. The footing here is a mixture of good and bad, but it is very beautiful. As you round a bend, you will see the rest house in the distance.

At Santa Maria you will find a resting place built by the Santa Fe for its mule-ride guests decades ago. It makes a perfect stopping place for this day hike, with shade, a bench and water. The spring produces water year-around, but if you want to drink it, you should purify it.

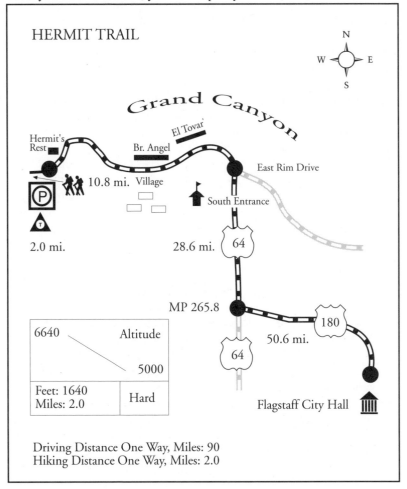

HERMIT TRAIL

Driving Distance One Way, Miles: 90
Hiking Distance One Way, Miles: 2.0

Mangum

HOG HILL TRAIL

General Information
Location Map F2
Sycamore Point USGS Map
Coconino Forest Service Map

Driving Distance One Way: 22.95 miles *36.7 km* (Time 60 minutes)
Access Road: High clearance for last 0.65 miles *1.0 km*
Hiking Distance One Way: 2.15 miles *3.5 km* (Time 1.50 hours)
How Strenuous: Hard
Features: Easy access to Winter Cabin via old road

NUTSHELL: This trail into Sycamore Canyon 23.0 miles *36.8 km* southwest of Flagstaff is unique among the upper canyon trails because it follows an old road rather than a footpath into the canyon.

DIRECTIONS:
From Flagstaff City Hall Go:
    West, then south beneath the railroad overpass on Route 66. See Access Map, page 10. At 0.50 miles *0.8 km* you will reach a Y intersection. The right fork is Route 66. Take it. You will soon leave town. At 2.6 miles *4.2 km* you will reach a road going to the left. This is the Woody Mountain Road, FR 231. Take it. It is paved about a mile *1.6 km* and then turns into a cinder road. At 16.6 miles *26.6 km* you will intersect FR 538. Turn right onto FR 538 and follow it to the 22.3 mile *35.7 km* point, where it intersects the Kelsey Spring Road, FR 538E. Turn right on 538E. The roads to this point are good, but beyond it they are rough. At 22.7 miles *36.3 km* you hit another intersection where FR 538E forks to the left. This is the Dorsey Spring Road. Turn left onto it and follow it to its end at 22.95 miles *36.7 km*, where you will find a parking lot.

TRAILHEAD: You will see a big sign at the parking area.

DESCRIPTION: You begin this hike by walking along the **Dorsey Spring Trail**. The beginning part of this trail is an old road that has been closed to vehicles. At 0.25 miles *0.4 km* you will see a sign saying, "Hog Hill Trailhead 1/2" and a road forking to the left. Take this road to the left and follow it to the 0.75 mile *1.2 km* point where you will reach a fence. The fence is officially the trailhead, although there is no marker or sign of any kind there except for Wilderness Area boundary signs.
    Go through the gate at the fence and continue to walk along the old road. The road becomes worse and worse as you go. There are no signs, markers or blazes along the way. We did find a few cairns. Pay attention and you

should have no trouble following the road.

At 0.85 miles *1.4 km* you will see the canyon rim nearby to your right. From here the road begins to descend steeply. It makes a decent hiking trail but you don't see how anyone could ever have driven it. The grade is very sharp and the surface consists of exposed rock all the way. You will never leave the road and go off onto a footpath.

The trail is not scenic. It passes through a typical pine forest and goes down the canyon in a businesslike way. At 2.0 miles *3.2 km* you will come to a side canyon.

We were here in October and saw many red leaves on the trees in the canyon. It turns out that they are maples. Originally the road crossed the canyon but washouts have erased it. The trail splits here. Take the right fork along the streambed. You will emerge in just a few yards onto a bare spot less than 0.1 mile *0.16 km* above Winter Cabin. You can see the cabin roof. The trail ends at 2.15 miles *3.5 km* at the cabin.

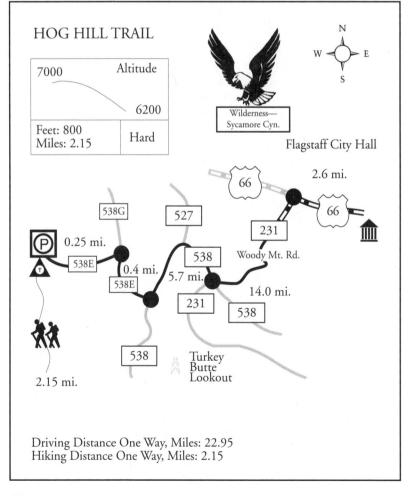

HOG HILL TRAIL

7000 Altitude 6200

Feet: 800
Miles: 2.15   Hard

Wilderness—
Sycamore Cyn.

Flagstaff City Hall

66   2.6 mi.

538G   527   231   66

0.25 mi.   538   Woody Mt. Rd.

538E   0.4 mi.   5.7 mi.

538E   231   14.0 mi.

538

2.15 mi.   538   Turkey Butte Lookout

Driving Distance One Way, Miles: 22.95
Hiking Distance One Way, Miles: 2.15

Mangum

HORSE CROSSING TRAIL #20

General Information
Location Map G4
Blue Ridge Reservoir USGS Map
Coconino Forest Service Map

Driving Distance One Way: 72.0 miles *115.2 km* (Time 1.5 hours)
Access Road: All cars, Last 2.0 miles *3.2 km* rough dirt road
Hiking Distance One Way: 1.5 miles *2.4 km* (Time 1 hour)
How Strenuous: Hard
Features: Views, Beautiful pristine stream, Remote canyon

NUTSHELL: This is one of the few trails into East Clear Creek, a remote canyon southeast of Flagstaff. The hike is steep but very beautiful.

DIRECTIONS:
From Flagstaff City Hall Go:

West, then south on Route 66 under the railroad overpass. See Access Map, page 10. As you go south, take Milton Road, leaving Route 66. At 1.7 miles *2.72 km* you will reach a stoplight at Forest Meadows Street. Turn right here onto Forest Meadows and go one block to Beulah. Turn left on Beulah and follow it south. Beulah merges onto Highway 89A. At 2.4 miles *3.84 km* (MP 401.6), turn left onto the Lake Mary Road. Follow the Lake Mary Road (also known as FH 3) to its end at the junction with State Route 87, 56.6 miles *90.56 km*. Turn left here on Highway 87, a paved road, and follow it to the 66 mile *105.6 km* point MP 299.9, where you turn right on FR 95, which is well posted. FR 95 is surfaced with gravel and is an all-weather road. Follow it to the 70 mile *112 km* point, where you turn left on FR 513B, which is a fairly rough dirt road, with ruts and rocks. Drive to the 72 mile *115.2 km* point, where you will see a sign for the Horse Crossing Trailhead to your right. Pull in and park in the little loop.

TRAILHEAD: There is a sign at the parking area. The trail starts behind the sign.

DESCRIPTION: Although Flagstaff is a green oasis surrounded by deserts, there are very few year-round streams in the region. Streamside hikes can be very rewarding, and we wanted to include some of them in this book.

From the trailhead, you have glimpses of the canyon. You will hike down 0.75 miles *1.2 km* to the bottom, a 500 foot drop. This descent is fairly mild and the trail is well laid out. There are cairns and blazes and the trail itself is distinct. At the bottom you will find East Clear Creek. You will see cairns here indicating a path to your left and to your right. The one to the right is the trail. The one to the left is a detour to a nice pool with a sandy beach. A perfect place to wade or swim.

To follow the trail, take the cairn to the right. The bottom is overgrown with willows and other plants, and finding the path can be difficult. Look for cairns. You will walk along the streambed for about 0.1 miles *0.16 km*, and then cross over the creek, which is split here, on stepping stones. In a few more yards, you cross the creek again. Once across, you will walk 0.15 miles *0.24 km* along the south bank. When you have come 1.0 miles *1.6 km* from the beginning, the trail lifts up out of the canyon. This point was not well marked, so look carefully. The trail itself, once you are on it, is easy to follow.

The climb up to the other rim is harder than the first, as you go 500 feet in 0.5 mile *0.8 km*. You will pass through a beautiful forest, with lots of firs and oaks, to the top, where the trail ends at a cairn by the side of a primitive road.

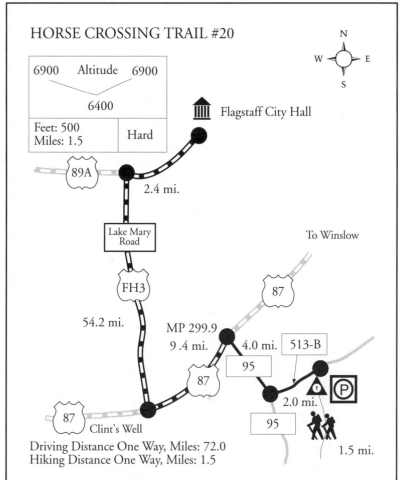

HOUSTON BROTHERS TRAIL #18

General Information
Location Map G4
Blue Ridge Reservoir, Dane Canyon USGS Maps
Coconino Forest Service Map

Driving Distance One Way: 77.2 miles *123.5 km* (Time 1.5 hours)
Access Road: All cars, Last 11.2 miles *18 km* good dirt roads
Hiking Distance One Way: 1.5 miles *2.4 km* (Time 1 hour)
How Strenuous: Easy
Features: Beautiful pristine stream, Historic cabins

NUTSHELL: This charming little trail is located in "The Rim" country. It starts at the historic Pinchot Cabin and proceeds south along Houston Draw to Aspen Spring, another cabin site.

DIRECTIONS:
From Flagstaff City Hall Go:

West, then south on Route 66. The street name will change to Milton Road as you go south. See Access Map, page 10. At 1.7 miles *2.72 km* you will reach a stoplight at Forest Meadows Street. Turn right here onto Forest Meadows and go one block to Beulah. Turn left on Beulah and follow it south. Beulah merges onto Highway 89A. At 2.4 miles *3.84 km* (MP 401.6), turn left onto the Lake Mary Road. Follow the Lake Mary Road (also known as FH 3) to its end at the junction with State Route 87, 56.6 miles *90.56 km*. Turn left here on Highway 87, a paved road, and follow it to the 66 mile *105.6 km* point (MP 299.9), where you turn right on FR 95, which is well posted. FR 95 is surfaced with gravel and is an all-weather road. Follow it to the 72.5 mile point *116 km*, down into the bottom of the canyon, where you will find a little bridge across East Clear Creek. This is a road junction. Take the right-hand road, which is still FR 95, and climb uphill on a winding road. On the top, FR 95 curves frequently as it winds around the canyons that cut the area. At 77.0 miles *123.2 km*, you will see FR 139A going to the left. Take it. (Just before this, you will see a sign for Houston Draw to your left). At 77.2 miles *123.5 km* you will see a primitive road to your left going downhill into the bottom of Houston Draw. Stop here and park. We recommend that you not try to drive to the bottom. Begin the hike from here.

TRAILHEAD: The official trailhead is down in Houston Draw, about thirty yards south of Pinchot Cabin.

DESCRIPTION: You walk down the primitive road to the bottom of Houston Draw, a beautiful place, green because of its perennial stream. Turn south and in 0.2 miles *0.32 km*, you will see Pinchot Cabin. Go over and inspect it. There is an interpretive sign about the cabin. Gifford Pinchot, regarded as the father of the Forest Service, visited the site and remarked upon its beauty, and the cabin was named for him. This place is a trail intersection, with markers for the Arizona, U-Bar and Cabin Loop Trails.

Follow the canyon south, toward the Mogollon Rim. Since the rim is uplifted, you will be walking uphill, but it is a gradual easy climb. Look for tree blazes, which are plentiful. The map shows what a blaze looks like.

The little canyon is very pretty, the trail is soft, and it has no steep grades. There are some attractive rock outcrops, aspens and other interesting sights. The trail goes 7.0 miles *11.2 km* to the Rim Road, FR 300, but that makes a long hike. As a pleasant day hike, we recommend stopping at Aspen Spring, where you will find a corral and the ruins of an old log cabin. Aspen Spring is 1.5 miles *2.4 km* from where you parked.

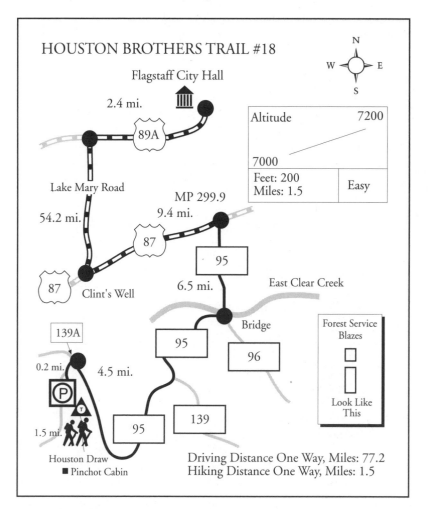

HUMPHREYS PEAK TRAIL

General Information
Location Map E3
Humphreys Peak USGS Map
Coconino Forest Service Map

Driving Distance One Way: 14.4 miles *23.0 km* (Time 30 minutes)
Access Road: All cars, All paved
Hiking Distance One Way: 4.5 miles *7.2 km* (Time 3 hours)
How Strenuous: Hard, Steep climb, High altitudes
Features: Highest point in Arizona, Alpine forests, Unsurpassed views

NUTSHELL: Starting from the Snow Bowl located about 15 miles *24 km* north of Flagstaff, this strenuous climb takes you to the top of the San Francisco Peaks, the highest point in Arizona.

DIRECTIONS:
From Flagstaff City Hall Go:
    North on Humphreys Street for 0.60 miles *1.0 km*. See Access Map, page 10. Turn left at the stoplight onto Columbus Avenue and follow it around a big curve to the north. You will see the street signs call this road Columbus at first, then Ft. Valley Road and then Highway 180. Stay on Highway 180 to the 7.3 miles *11.7 km* point (MP 223), where the road to the Snow Bowl branches off to the right. It is well posted. Follow the Snow Bowl road to the top at 13.9 miles *22.2 km*. You will encounter a parking area there. There is a trail sign showing Humphreys Peak Trail to the left. We call that place "Alternate Trailhead" on the map. If you know you will finish by 6:00 p.m., then drive beyond the first parking place to the highest parking area at the 14.4 miles *23.0 km* point and park there by the big chairlift, where the Skyride is run in the summer.

TRAILHEAD: There are two trailheads. Use the Alternate if you will not return by 6:00 p.m., as the road to the Skyride is blocked off then. Our primary trailhead is better if you return early.

DESCRIPTION: At 0.66 miles *1.05 km* both trails meet in the forest and thereafter are the same.
    The forest in the first couple of miles is a heavy one of fir, spruce and aspen. There are many fallen timbers, making a tangle on the floor. The trees are tall, shutting out most of the sun and allowing no views.
    As you go higher, the forest opens and you will encounter small meadows which permit views to the west. At about the 10,500 foot point the aspens begin to disappear. You can see from here into the Snow Bowl area.

What appear to be roads there are actually the ski runs cut through the trees. The major peak that you will see is Mt. Agassiz.

At 3.75 miles *6.0 km* the only trees are twisted and stunted bristlecone pines. There is no cover for the trail here and the footing is not very good. At 4.0 miles *6.4 km* you reach the rim where the Humphreys Trail joins the **Weatherford Trail** coming in from your right. You can look into the Inner Basin of the Peaks here and enjoy a splendid view. You can also see to the east for the first time on the hike.

The mountain top will be different from what you imagined. You are above timberline. It is bare and almost always windy and cold. The footing is terrible, being a mixture of loose gravel and rough jagged lava. You can't really walk along the crest but must walk below it. To get to the top of Mt. Humphreys take the path to the left. The top is 0.50 miles *0.8 km* away. The altitude and the roughness of the trail make the crest hike hard. Allow a half hour.

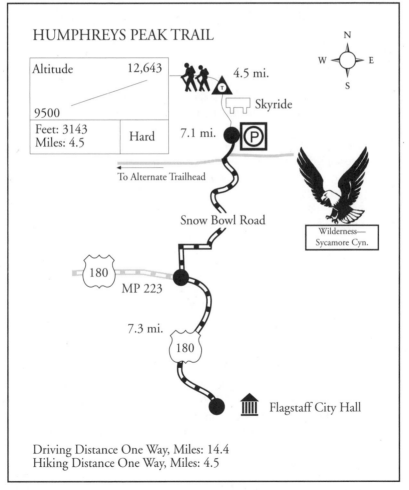

HUMPHREYS PEAK TRAIL

Altitude	12,643
9500	

| Feet: 3143 Miles: 4.5 | Hard |

4.5 mi.

Skyride

7.1 mi.

To Alternate Trailhead

Snow Bowl Road

Wilderness— Sycamore Cyn.

180

MP 223

7.3 mi.

180

Flagstaff City Hall

Driving Distance One Way, Miles: 14.4
Hiking Distance One Way, Miles: 4.5

Mangum

INNER BASIN TRAIL #29

General Information
Location Map E3
Humphreys Peak and Sunset Crater West USGS Maps
Coconino Forest Service Map

Driving Distance One Way: 21.6 miles *34.6 km* (Time 45 minutes)
Access Road: All cars, Last 4.5 miles *7.2 km* medium dirt road
Hiking Distance One Way: 2.0 miles *3.2 km* (Time 1 hour)
How Strenuous: Hard, Steep Climb, High altitudes
Features: High mountain, Alpine forests, Great views

NUTSHELL: The San Francisco Peaks located north of Flagstaff are an extinct volcanic crater with an opening to the east. This trail takes you up the valley formed by that eastern opening into the heart of the crater.

DIRECTIONS:
From Flagstaff City Hall Go:
East, then north on Highway 89. See Access Map, pages 10-11. At 17.1 miles *27.4 km* (MP 431.2)—just past the entrance to Sunset Crater—turn left onto FR 552 and take it to the 18.3 mile *29.3 km* point, where you will see a sign for Lockett Meadow. Go right. From here the road is a winding narrow gravel route which climbs up the face of the mountain. At 21.3 miles *34 km* you reach Lockett Meadow. There you will see a one-way road to your right into a campground. Take this and park in the Day Use Area at the 21.6 mile *34.6 km* point.

TRAILHEAD: To find the trailhead you must drive all the way back into the trees among the campsites. The trailhead is posted with a big sign to the left of a toilet.

DESCRIPTION: The trail is a road that is used by the City of Flagstaff for maintenance vehicles, because the Inner Basin of the Peaks is the city's watershed. This makes the trail wide and easy to walk. Even so, at these altitudes, the hike will be more strenuous than you would think, given its relatively short distance. You will be climbing constantly.

The Inner Basin of the Peaks has a tremendous amount of water because all the water from snow melting inside the crater gathers in the bowl. There are several springs in the basin. The early settlers of Flagstaff realized the importance of the basin as a water supply for the town and sewed up all the water rights. As a result most of the water is captured and channelled and you will see very little of it on the surface.

The vegetation here is very lush, as the basin is moist. You will pass through a beautiful forest of aspen, spruce and fir, with many ferns and other low growing plants.

At the 1.5 mile *2.4 km* point you will come to Jack Smith Spring where there are two green cabins. There is a faucet outside the larger cabin from which you can drink delicious cold spring water. The altitude at Jack Smith is 9400 feet.

You will find a hiker's log in an ammo can here and you are requested to enter your name and other information. The spring is a crossroads and you will see a sign showing FR 146 going to the left to what we call the **Tunnel Trail** and ending at the Schultz Pass Road 8.5 miles *13.6 km* away. To the right FR 146 goes about 5.25 miles *8.4 km* to a point on the north face of Mt. Humphreys. Along the way it intersects the **Bear Jaw Trail** at 3 miles *4.8 km* and the **Abineau Trail** at 5 miles *8.0 km*.

Instead of taking a fork, go straight ahead. At 2 miles *3.2 km* you will break out of the timber into a bare area. This is the Inner Basin.

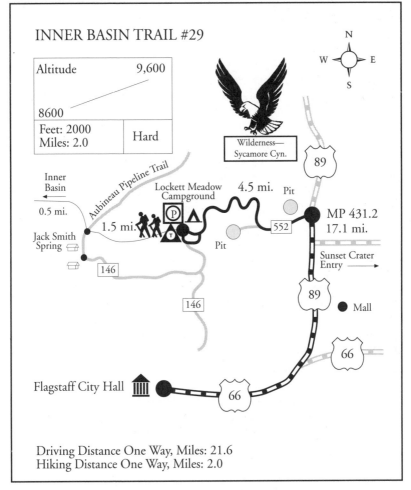

JAMES CANYON

General Information
Location Map F3
Mountainaire USGS Map
Coconino Forest Service Map

Driving Distance One Way: 13.6 miles *21.8 km* (Time 30 minutes)
Access Road: Last 2.8 miles *4.5 km* rough dirt road needs high clearance
Hiking Distance One Way: 1.5 miles *2.4 km* (Time 1.5 hours)
How Strenuous: Hard—for experienced hikers
Features: Beautiful canyon near Flagstaff

NUTSHELL: This hidden gem is only a few miles from town. It requires scrambling down into the canyon on a game trail and boulder hopping along the bottom, but the rewards are significant.

DIRECTIONS:
From Flagstaff City Hall Go:
    West, then south on Route 66 to Milton Road. See Access Map, page 10. Stay on Milton south and get onto Interstate-17 (toward Phoenix). Drive I-17 south for 10.8 miles *17.3 km* to the Kelly Canyon Exit 331. Go right (west) at the stop sign, where you will immediately get onto FR 631. Follow this main road. Several minor roads branch off, but the main road is obvious until you get to the pit at one mile. Go to the left around the pit (do not go down into it). From this point the road is not maintained and is very rough. The road is unmarked. Your destination is a barbed wire fence at 13.6 miles *21.8 km*. If the road is too rough to drive all the way, then park and walk the rest of the road to the fence.

TRAILHEAD: Do not go through the fence. Turn left and walk south along the fence, using it as your guide.

DESCRIPTION: As you begin this walk, you will be aware of the mighty canyon before you, even though you only get glimpses of it. From the starting point, hike 0.1 miles *0.16 km* to a point where there is a gap in the fence, with a gate that is usually down. Turn to the left here. You will see two ravines. Walk over to the one that is farthest to your left (east) and then begin walking south along its west rim.
    The ravine will immediately deepen and turn into a substantial canyon. You will soon encounter a distinct game trail headed toward the major canyon. Following it, you will reach the lip of James Canyon in another 0.1 miles *0.16 km*. The animals have, through generations of experience, figured how to get down into the canyon at one of its few entry points. Take advan-

tage of their knowledge.

From the canyon rim, you will have a very steep descent with tricky footing, but it's only 0.1 miles *0.16 km* to the bottom. Mark the place where you entered the canyon with a stack of rocks so that you won't miss it on the way back. Then turn left and walk along the streambed. Don't try this hike when there is a substantial amount of water running unless you are willing to wade/swim. You will find a few places where you can walk along the bank, but most of the way you will be walking the channel on fist-size rocks, which is hard on the feet. The canyon goes all the way to I-17.

The canyon will delight you, with massive textured walls, lush vegetation, and a get-away-from-it-all feeling.

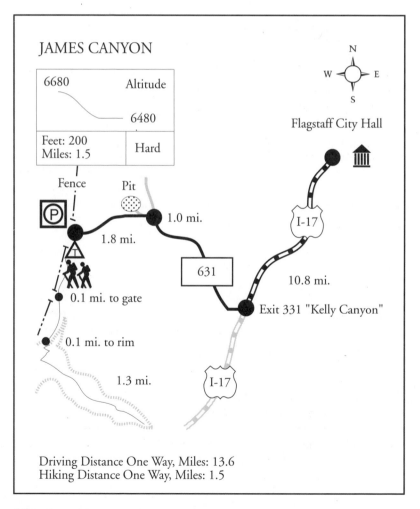

KACHINA TRAIL #150

General Information
Location Map E3
Humphreys Peak USGS Map
Coconino Forest Service Map

Driving Distance One Way: 14.1 miles *22.5 km* (Time 40 minutes)
Access Road: All cars, All paved
Hiking Distance One Way: 6.0 miles *9.6 km* (Time 3 hours)
How Strenuous: Moderate if done as recommended
Features: High mountains, Alpine forests, Excellent views

NUTSHELL: This mildly strenuous hike across the south face of the San Francisco Peaks a dozen miles north of Flagstaff displays the best the Peaks have to offer. **A personal favorite.**

DIRECTIONS:
From Flagstaff City Hall Go:
    North on Humphreys Street for 0.60 miles. See Access Map, page 10. Turn left at the stoplight onto Columbus Avenue and follow it around a big curve to the north. The street signs call this road Columbus at first, then Ft. Valley Road and then Highway 180. Stay on Highway 180 to the 7.3 miles *11.7 km* point (MP 223), where the road to the Snow Bowl branches off to the right. It is well posted. Follow the Snow Bowl road to the top at 13.9 miles *22.2 km* where you will see a trail sign and encounter a parking area. Turn right and drive 0.2 miles *0.32 km* to the end of this large graveled parking area and park.

TRAILHEAD: You will see a large sign announcing the trail at the end of the parking lot.

DESCRIPTION: This trail starts at the 9300 foot level and winds its way across the south face (Flagstaff side) of the Peaks, dropping to 8800 feet at trail's end. This is a very gradual hike for the Peaks where every trail tends to be very steep. Nevertheless, the high elevation may make this a tougher hike than the mileage would indicate.
    The trail starts in a lovely forest of fir, spruce and aspen. This is a good trail to take in the fall to see the changing aspen leaves.
    You will see some interesting basalt cliffs at 1.5 miles *2.4 km*. In places you will find clearings that give you views out over the countryside.
    Just beyond the 4.0 mile *6.4 km* point you will enter Friedlein Prairie, a beautiful meadow area, visible from Flagstaff. You will walk near the foot of the prairie, enjoying breathtaking views up the mountain, which seems

huge from this vantage point.

You will meet a trail coming up the prairie from your right in this area. There is a sign giving mileage for the Kachina Trail at the junction. Do not turn right here. Keep going straight.

The trail continues for 2.0 miles *3.2 km*, ending at an old road. This road is a portion of the historic Weatherford Road, and is now part of the **Weatherford Trail**. (Please note that we do not use the Schultz Pass access to the Weatherford Trail. We prefer to follow the old road.)

The Kachina Trail is hard if you must turn around at the end and go back 6.0 miles *9.6 km* uphill to the start. The best way to do this hike is to use two cars. Drive both up the Snow Bowl Road 2.4 miles *3.8 km* from Highway 180. Turn right on FR 522, the Friedlein Prairie Rd., and drive 4.0 miles *6.4 km,* where the entry to the Weatherford Trail is barricaded and signed. Then take one car to the top. On the hike, when you reach the end of the Kachina Trail, turn right and walk 0.33 miles *0.5 km* to your parked car.

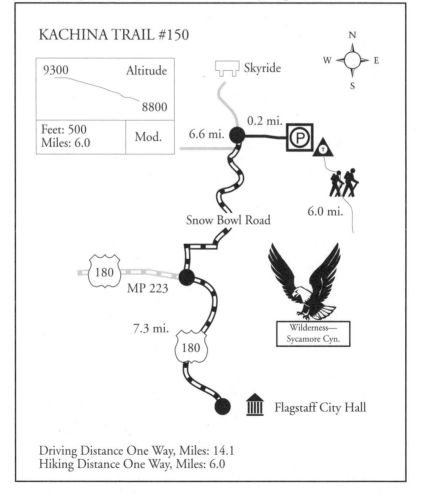

KACHINA TRAIL #150

9300   Altitude

8800

Feet: 500
Miles: 6.0   Mod.

Skyride

6.6 mi.

0.2 mi.

Snow Bowl Road

6.0 mi.

180
MP 223

7.3 mi.

180

Wilderness—
Sycamore Cyn.

Flagstaff City Hall

Driving Distance One Way, Miles: 14.1
Hiking Distance One Way, Miles: 6.0

Mangum

KELLY CANYON

General Information
Location Map F3
Mountainaire USGS Map
Coconino Forest Service Map

Driving Distance One Way: 11.7 miles *18.7 km* (Time 30 minutes)
Access Road: Last 0.7 miles *1.1 km* rough dirt road, needs high clearance
Hiking Distance One Way: 2.0 miles *3.2 km* (Time 1.5 hours)
How Strenuous: Moderate
Features: Beautiful little canyon near Flagstaff

NUTSHELL: Travelers on Interstate I-17 buzz right by this canyon south of Flagstaff without even noticing it, but it is a scenic jewel and makes a fine day hike.

DIRECTIONS:
From Flagstaff City Hall Go:
    West, then south on Route 66 to Milton Road. See Access Map, page 10. Stay on Milton south and get onto Interstate-17 (toward Phoenix). Drive I-17 south for 10.8 miles *17.3 km* to the Kelly Canyon Exit 331 and take the exit. At the stop sign, 11.0 miles *17.6 km*, reset your mileage meter to zero. Go right (west) at the stop sign, where you will immediately get onto FR 631. At the 0.3 mile *0.5 km* point, where FR 631 makes a curving turn to your left, you will see a primitive jeep track take off to the right, straight ahead, parallel to the highway. Turn off on this and drive it. Where the road splits, take the left fork that runs along the power line, and go to the 0.7 mile *1.1 km* point, where you will find an abandoned homestead in a clearing, complete with log cabin. Park here.

TRAILHEAD: There is no trailhead. Follow the big power line to get to Kelly Canyon.

DESCRIPTION: It is hard to tell the age of old cabins in the forest. We believe that the one you will see at the parking place was a real family home, not just a shack. The cabin is well built and nicely finished, with remnants of carpet on the floor. Our guess is that it was abandoned about the time that I-17 was built through this area, meaning the late 1950s or early 1960s. Before the highway was built, this would have been an idyllic setting, calm and peaceful, yet not far from town.
    Look toward the highway and you will see a power line. Walk up to it and use it as your guide, going north, toward Flagstaff. The line splits. Follow the big line. You will come to an unnamed small canyon in 0.16

miles *0.26 km*. Cross it and keep going. At 0.5 miles *0.8 km*, you will come to the second canyon, which is Kelly Canyon. The canyon is fairly shallow here (which is why the highway bridge was located nearby) and it is not difficult to get to the bottom. Once on the bottom, turn left and follow the canyon downstream. There is no trail, meaning you will have to rock hop, but the footing is pretty good.

Kelly Canyon has a nice comfortable feeling. As you get down into the lower part of the canyon, you reach a zone of redrock, with some nicely sculpted formations. Kelly Canyon is a tributary of Pumphouse Wash, and empties into it at the end of this hike. Pumphouse Wash begins in the Kachina Village area and runs into Oak Creek Canyon at the first bridge on the switchbacks as you drive down Highway 89A into Oak Creek. If you want to explore Pumphouse Wash, be sure to mark your entrance point so that you can find it on your way back.

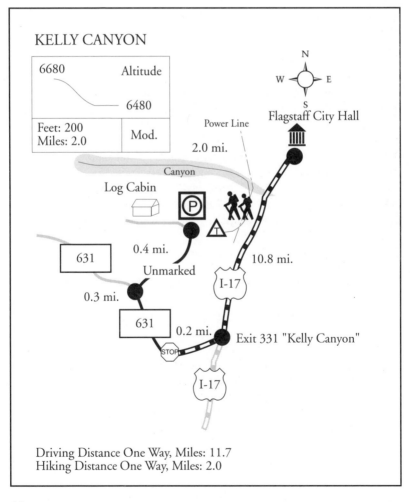

Mangum

KELSEY SPRING TRAIL

General Information
Location Map F2
Sycamore Point USGS Map
Coconino Forest Service Map

Driving Distance One Way: 24.1 miles *38.6 km* (Time 1 hour)
Access Road: High clearance needed for last 1.8 miles *2.9 km*
Hiking Distance One Way: 0.50 miles *0.8 km* (Time 30 minutes)
How Strenuous: Moderate
Features: Views, Sycamore Canyon access

NUTSHELL: Located about 25 miles *40 km* southwest of Flagstaff, this is a scenic trail in its own right as well as being an access trail into Sycamore Canyon.

DIRECTIONS:
From Flagstaff City Hall Go:
    West, then south on Route 66 beneath the railroad overpass. See Access Map, page 10. At 0.50 miles *0.8 km* you will reach a Y intersection. The right fork is Route 66. Take it. You will soon leave town. At 2.6 miles *4.2 km* you will reach a road going to the left. This is the Woody Mountain Road, FR 231. Take it. It is paved about a mile *1.6 km* and then turns into a cinder road. At 16.6 miles *26.6 km* you will intersect FR 538. Turn right onto FR 538 and follow it to the 22.3 mile *35.7 km* point, where it intersects FR 538E. Turn right on 538E. At 22.7 miles *36.3 km* you hit another intersection, where FR 538E forks to the left, going to Dorsey Spring Road. The road is rough beyond here. Keep straight, now on FR 538G, and follow it to its end at 23.7 miles *38 km*, where it meets FR 527A. Turn left onto the Kelsey Trail road, going to the 24.1 mile *38.6 km* point, the parking area. This last 0.4 mile *0.64 km* stretch is terrible, a real tire-eater.

TRAILHEAD: You will see a big sign at the parking area.

DESCRIPTION: The Kelsey Spring Trail is marked and maintained by the Forest Service and is in good condition. Start this hike by going to the rim of Sycamore Canyon rather than taking the main trail down into the canyon. You will see an unmarked but distinct footpath going to the rim to the left of the main trail. The main trail goes down into the canyon, whereas the rim trail stays on top. Sycamore Canyon deserves the overworked adjective "awesome" and the rim here is a great vantage point from which to see it. After you fill your eyes then go back to the main trail and make your descent.

The trail down is fairly steep but the footing is good and it passes through a beautiful forest. At 0.50 miles *0.8* you will reach a meadow onto which Kelsey Spring flows after running out of a concrete box. Take a look around and you will find the remains of an old cabin. There isn't much left, no standing walls, just some lumber and rubble. If you want to see an interesting cabin, try the nearby **Winter Cabin Trail.**

The shelf of land on which the spring is located is a veritable Shangri-La, a tranquil remote haven away from the cares of the world. Visit this place on a fine summer day when the spring is flowing, flowers are blooming and birds are singing and you won't want to come back out. It is idyllic.

From Kelsey Spring the trail goes on down another 0.7 miles *1.1 km* to **Babe's Hole**, then down another 0.8 miles *1.28 km* to **Geronimo Spring**, in the inner gorge of Sycamore Canyon.

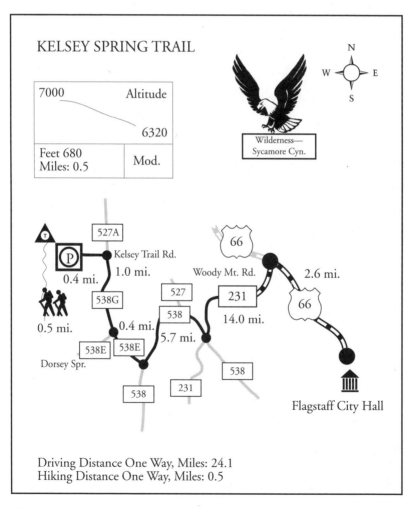

Driving Distance One Way, Miles: 24.1
Hiking Distance One Way, Miles: 0.5

Mangum

KELSEY-WINTER CABIN TRAIL

General Information
Location Map F2
Sycamore Point USGS Map
Coconino Forest Service Map

Driving Distance One Way: 24.1 miles *38.6 km* (Time 1 hour)
Access Road: High clearance needed for last 1.8 miles *2.9 km*
Hiking Distance One Way: 5.5 miles *8.8 km* (Time 3 hours)
How Strenuous: Hard
Features: Springs, Pristine forests, Views

NUTSHELL: This trail is located in Sycamore Canyon, 24.1 miles *38.64 km* southwest of Flagstaff. It takes you along the side of the canyon between Kelsey Spring and Winter Cabin.

DIRECTIONS:
From Flagstaff City Hall Go:
West, then south on Route 66 beneath the railroad overpass. See Access Map, page 10. At 0.50 miles *0.8 km* you will reach a Y intersection. The right fork is Route 66. Take it. You will soon leave town. At 2.6 miles *4.2 km* you will reach a road going to the left. This is the Woody Mountain Road, FR 231. Take it. It is paved about a mile and then turns into a cinder road. At 16.6 miles *26.6 km* you will intersect FR 538. Turn right onto FR 538 and follow it to the 22.3 mile *35.7 km* point, where it intersects FR 538E. Turn right on 538E. At 22.7 miles *36.3 km* you hit another intersection, where FR 538E forks to the left, going to Dorsey Spring Road. The road is rough beyond here. Keep straight, now on FR 538G, and follow it to its end at 23.7 miles *37.9 km*, where it meets FR 527A. Turn left onto the Kelsey Trail road, going to the 24.1 mile *38.6 km* point, the parking area. This last 0.4 mile *0.64 km* stretch is terrible, a real tire-eater.

TRAILHEAD: You will see a big sign at the parking area.

DESCRIPTION: From the parking area you hike down the **Kelsey Spring Trail**. You will reach Kelsey Spring at 0.5 miles *0.8 km*. Then go down the trail to **Babe's Hole** at 1.2 miles *2.0 km*. Go on down the trail to 1.3 miles *2.1 km*, where you reach a trail junction. The Kelsey-Winter Trail goes left, while the trail to **Geronimo Spring** goes right.

From this point, the trail moves along the side of the canyon within a one hundred foot band, with minor ups and downs. The first portion of the trail is in a forest, but at about the 1.7 mile *2.7 km* point you will reach a clear area. This is nice for variety and gives good views of Sycamore Canyon.

Then you enter into a wooded area again.

You will reach Dorsey Spring at 2.9 miles *4.6 km*. The trail turns left and goes uphill to the actual spring, getting there at 3.10 miles *5.0 km*. Before the spring, in a flat area, there is a sign showing the way to Winter Cabin.

The second leg of the trail from **Dorsey Spring** to **Winter Cabin** follows the same lateral course but is more interesting. There are more open spots, high cliffs on your left, a Thumb Butte on your right. There is about a half mile where you pass narrowly through scrub oak and locust, meaning thorns and sharp edged leaves. Bare arms and legs will be scratched here. You will reach Winter Cabin at 5.5 miles *8.8 km*.

You can reverse your course when you reach Winter Cabin and go back to the Kelsey Spring trailhead or you can hike 1.5 miles *2.4 km* up to the Winter Cabin trailhead (where you have thoughtfully parked a second car).

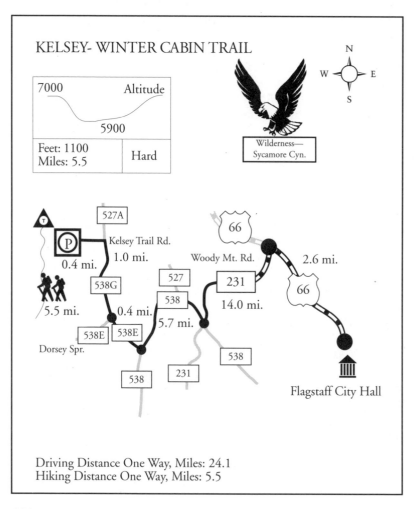

KELSEY- WINTER CABIN TRAIL

Driving Distance One Way, Miles: 24.1
Hiking Distance One Way, Miles: 5.5

KENDRICK MT. TRAIL #22

General Information
Location Map E2
Kendrick Peak and Wing Mt. USGS Maps
Coconino Forest Service Map

Driving Distance One Way: 21.2 miles *33.9 km* (Time 45 minutes)
Access Road: All cars, Last 6.7 miles *10.7 km* good gravel road
Hiking Distance One Way: 4.6 miles *7.36 km* (Time 3.0 hours)
How Strenuous: Hard
Features: Ten thousand foot peak, Views

NUTSHELL: Located 21.2 miles *33.9 km* north of Flagstaff, Kendrick Peak is next tallest to the San Francisco Peaks. This trail switchbacks to the summit where you get great views.

DIRECTIONS:
From Flagstaff City Hall Go:
    North on Humphreys Street for 0.60 miles *1.0 km*. See Access Map, page 10. Turn left at the stoplight onto Columbus Avenue and follow it around a big curve to the north. You will see the street signs call this road Columbus at first, then Ft. Valley Road and then Highway 180. Stay on Highway 180 to the 14.5 mile *23.2 km* point (MP 230), where an unpaved road takes off to the left. Turn left onto this road, FR 245, and follow it to the 17.6 mile *28.16 km* point where it intersects FR 171. Turn right on FR 171 and follow it to the 20.7 mile *33.12 km* point, where you turn right, then immediately right again on FR 190 and take it to the 21.2 mile *33.9 km* point. You will see a sign for the Kendrick Trail. Turn right on the drive to the trailhead. There is a parking area with a toilet.

TRAILHEAD: Well marked with a sign at the parking area.

DESCRIPTION: The Forest Service has developed nice facilities at the trailhead, with a good parking lot, trash dump and toilet.
    As you start this trail you will walk along a footpath to the 0.7 mile *1.12 km* point, where you join an old road, now closed. As is usual, hiking an old road is good news, for road builders of years ago had to hold a gentle grade so that the engines of the old cars could make it. This road is no exception.
    The forest for the first mile or so has been heavily logged and is not very attractive. As you go higher, you rise above the logging zone and get into very attractive woods of mixed conifers and large aspen groves.
    The trail follows an unending series of steep switchbacks. Stay on the trail. Cutting switchbacks causes erosion. There are several open spaces

from which to enjoy views across Government Prairie.

At 2.0 miles *3.2 km* the road ends and you follow a footpath. This is a good path, following the contours of the mountain intelligently and providing good footing. It was built as a working trail so that rangers could reach the fire lookout tower by horseback.

From a distance you will notice that Kendrick Peak has one definite sharp point, not a series of peaks like its neighbor, the San Francisco Peaks. You will reach a flat area just below the absolute peak at about 4.1 miles *6.56 km*. Here you will find the Old Lookout Cabin. It was built in the years 1911-1912 and is remarkably preserved considering the harsh winters it endures. The **Bull Basin Trail** terminates just behind the cabin.

From this flat there is one last climb to the tower, reached at 4.6 miles *7.36 km*. One nice thing about the Kendrick hike is that you never rise above timber line. At the base of the tower you can see over the trees, but when you climb it, you get tremendous views, some of the best in the region.

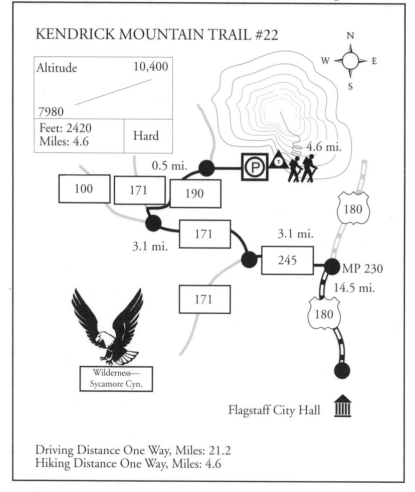

KENDRICK MOUNTAIN TRAIL #22

Driving Distance One Way, Miles: 21.2
Hiking Distance One Way, Miles: 4.6

Mangum

KEYHOLE SINK #114

General Information
Location Map E2
Sitgreaves Mtn. USGS Map
Coconino Forest Service Map

Driving Distance One Way: 22.6 miles *36.2 km* (Time 40 minutes)
Access Road: All cars, All paved
Hiking Distance One Way: 0.60 miles *1.0 km* (Time 20 minutes)
How Strenuous: Easy
Features: Hidden pond, Cliffs with Indian rock art

NUTSHELL: This easy hike is located in the Parks area, 22.6 miles *36.2 km* west of Flagstaff. It follows a little canyon into a picturesque rounded box. Water is dammed there by cliffs on which are scratched Indian rock art.

DIRECTIONS:
From Flagstaff City Hall Go:
   West a block on Route 66 (Santa Fe), then south, beneath the railroad overpass. See the Access Map on page 10. At 0.50 miles *0.8 km* you will reach a Y intersection. Take the right fork here, staying on Route 66. You will soon leave town. At the 4.8 mile *7.68 km* point you will merge onto Interstate-40 West. Continue west on I-40, to the 18.0 mile *28.8 km* point, where you take Exit 178, Parks Road. Turn right at the stop sign and travel to the 18.4 mile *29.4 km* point, where there is a second stop sign. Turn left here. You are now on a portion of an older alignment of Route 66 heading west. At the 19.0 mile *30.4 km* point you will see the Parks Store to your right. Keep going west to the 22.6 mile *36.2 km* point where you will see the entrance to the Oak Hill Snow Play Area to your left. Pull into the parking lot for the Oak Hill Snow Play Area and park there.

TRAILHEAD: Across Route 66, directly in line with the Oak Hill entrance.

DESCRIPTION: The Keyhole Sink Trail was opened in the summer of 1992. Across the highway from the parking lot, you will see a pole fence with a green metal gate. This is the start of the trail, and it is posted. The trail will follow a small canyon that winds around into a bottom, where you will see a stand of young aspen trees lining the floor of the canyon.
   You will walk a short distance along the canyon bottom until you come to a fence made of aspen logs. An interpretive sign is located at the gate, along with a Guest Register. Sign in and then go through the fence. Here the aspen grove stops and you will be looking into a charming little bowl where the canyon ends against basalt cliffs some thirty to forty feet high. The floor

of the bowl is covered with grass.

Walk toward the farthest, blackest cliff. In wet years there will be a pond of water at the base of the cliffs, because the cliff acts as a natural dam for all the water flowing into the canyon. We have visited this place when there was quite a lot of water in the pond, and we have also seen it bone dry.

As you face the cliff, look for rock art on the cliff faces to the left of the blackest face. There are two major panels of rock art. If you look carefully, you will see a few more figures scattered here and there. The panel shown on the interpretive sign is to your left as you face the end cliff.

This is a natural waterhole for game and you will see elk and deer sign around it. It would also be a trap for any game cornered against the cliffs.

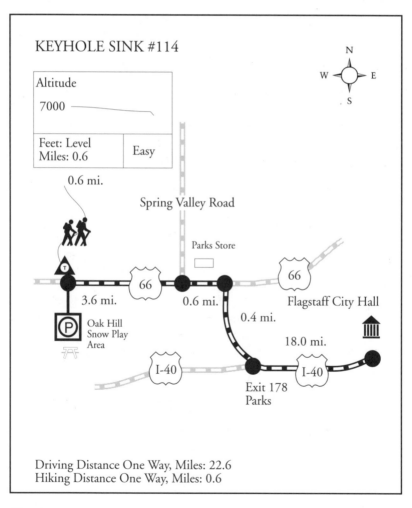

KEYHOLE SINK #114

Altitude	
7000	
Feet: Level Miles: 0.6	Easy

0.6 mi.

Spring Valley Road

Parks Store

66

66

Flagstaff City Hall

3.6 mi.

0.6 mi.

0.4 mi.

Oak Hill Snow Play Area

18.0 mi.

I-40

I-40

Exit 178 Parks

Driving Distance One Way, Miles: 22.6
Hiking Distance One Way, Miles: 0.6

Mangum

KINDER CROSSING TRAIL #19

General Information
Location Map G4
Blue Ridge Reservoir USGS Map
Coconino Forest Service Map

Driving Distance One Way: 71.0 miles *113.6 km* (Time 1.5 hours)
Access Road: All cars, Last 0.75 miles *1.2 km* rough dirt road
Hiking Distance One Way: 0.67 miles *1.1 km* (Time 1 hour)
How Strenuous: Moderate
Features: Beautiful pristine stream, Remote canyon

NUTSHELL: This is one of the few trails into East Clear Creek, a perennial stream in a remote canyon southeast of Flagstaff in the Mogollon Rim country.

DIRECTIONS:
From Flagstaff City Hall Go:
    West, then south on Route 66 under the railroad overpass. See Access Map, page 10. At 0.5 miles *0.8 km*, go straight, on Milton Road. At 1.7 miles *2.72 km* you will reach a stoplight at Forest Meadows Street. Turn right here onto Forest Meadows and go one block to Beulah. Turn left on Beulah and follow it south. Beulah merges onto Highway 89A. At 2.4 miles *3.84 km* (MP 401.6), turn left onto the Lake Mary Road. Follow the Lake Mary Road (also known as FH 3) to its end at the junction with State Route 87, 56.6 miles *90.6 km*. Turn left on Highway 87, a paved road, and follow it to the 66.0 mile *105.6 km* point MP 299.9, where you turn right on FR 95. FR 95 is surfaced with gravel and is an all-weather road. Follow it to the 70.25 mile *112.4 km* point, where you turn left on the access road. There is a sign for Kinder Crossing Trail here, but the road is not numbered. The road is easy to follow and is decent for about the first half mile *0.8 km*, but after that, it gets very rough. At 71.0 miles *113.6 km*, the road forward is blocked by a berm and the road swings downhill to the right to a parking loop. This last 0.1 miles *0.16 km* is almost impossibly rough and we recommend that you park at the berm and walk to the trailhead.

TRAILHEAD: We found no sign, but the trail was distinct and obvious. It is to your right as you face the canyon. Look for a couple of cut logs.

DESCRIPTION: The first 0.5 miles *0.8 km* is a gentle gradual descent into the canyon. At first, you walk along a nice soft path covered with pine needles. Then, as you get about half way down, you hike across exposed sandstone ledges. These are a little harder to walk on, but are not difficult. The last leg of the hike is a little steeper, but not bad.

The trail comes down to the water at a scenic pool at the foot of some impressive and colorful cliffs, where there is a nice gravel beach. This is a great spot for some photographs. If the water is high enough, you might even try a swim in the pool.

If you want to take the entire hike, you turn left (west) at the water and follow a path that is up some distance, away from the stream. Look for blazes in the trees. In 0.15 miles *0.24 km*, the trail crosses the stream on stepping stones on either side of a little sand bar, then goes up a side canyon, to reach the top at 1.5 miles *2.4 km*. Unless you are simply keen on hiking the entire trail in order to say that you have done it, we think you will be happier staying at the creek and doing some exploring in this very pretty canyon with its perennial stream.

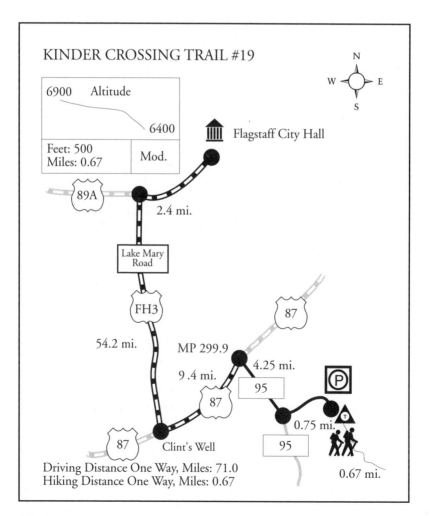

KINDER CROSSING TRAIL #19

6900   Altitude

6400

Feet: 500
Miles: 0.67   Mod.

Flagstaff City Hall

89A

2.4 mi.

Lake Mary Road

FH3

87

54.2 mi.

MP 299.9

4.25 mi.

9.4 mi.

95

87

0.75 mi.

87   Clint's Well

95

Driving Distance One Way, Miles: 71.0
Hiking Distance One Way, Miles: 0.67

0.67 mi.

Mangum

LAKEVIEW TRAIL #132

General Information
Location Map G3
Mormon Lake USGS Map
Coconino Forest Service Map

Driving Distance One Way: 28.2 miles *45.1 km* (Time. 35 minutes)
Access Road: All cars, Last 0.2 miles *0.32 km* good gravel road
Hiking Distance One Way: 1.25 miles *2.0 km* (Time 40 minutes)
How Strenuous: Moderate
Features: Beautiful forest, Excellent views

NUTSHELL: This hike gently climbs a ridge radiating south from Mormon Mountain. At the ridge top you are treated to sweeping views of Mormon Lake and the surrounding countryside.

DIRECTIONS:
From Flagstaff City Hall Go:
   West, then south on Route 66 under the railroad overpass. At 0.5 miles 0.8 km, get onto Milton Road. See Access Map, page 10. At 1.7 miles *2.72 km* you will reach a stoplight at Forest Meadows Street. Turn right here onto Forest Meadows and go one block to Beulah. Turn left on Beulah and follow it south. Beulah merges onto Highway 89A. At 2.4 miles *3.84 km* (MP 401.6), turn left onto the Lake Mary Road. Follow the Lake Mary Road to the 23.0 mile *36.8 km* point (MP 323.6), where you turn right onto the Mormon Lake Road. At 28 miles *44.8 km*, on the Mormon Lake Road, you will see a sign for the Lakeview Trail. Turn right here and follow the gravel road and signs to the 28.2 miles *45.1 km* point near the toilet at the campground.

TRAILHEAD: You will see a sign marking the trail to your left as you enter the campground.

DESCRIPTION: At the beginning of the trail you will encounter a little stream, a rarity in northern Arizona. There is a line of stepping stones across the stream, making it easy to cross. Once across, you will see the trail heading uphill to your right. In 0.1 miles *0.16 km* you will see the official trailhead sign for the Lakeview Trail. The trail is narrow but in good condition. It is well maintained. This is rocky soil, but the footing is pretty comfortable.
   The forest around Mormon Mountain is particularly beautiful. In addition to the ubiquitous Ponderosa pine, there is much oak and you will also see some aspen. Flowers and shrubs grow in profusion. Benches have been thoughtfully placed at the beginning, halfway and top of the trail. Since this

is a moderately easy hike, you can take your time. No need to hustle. Stop at the benches to catch your breath and enjoy the experience.

For nine-tenths of the hike, you cannot understand why the trail has been given the name Lakeview. Then, as you near the top, you can see why. The trail has been climbing gradually up a ridge. As you come to the top of the ridge, you find that its top is a lava cliff. Around the perimeter no pine trees grow, so you have unobstructed views.

You can walk around the ridge top and enjoy great views. As the name suggests, Mormon Lake is fully in view. Depending upon the wetness of the preceding winter, Mormon Lake will either be a substantial body of water or a great big pasture with a small pond in its center.

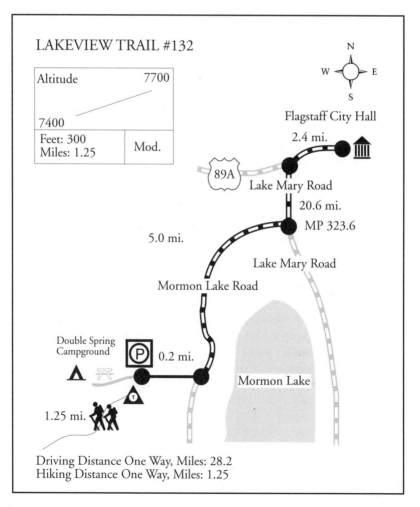

LAKEVIEW TRAIL #132

Altitude	7700
7400	
Feet: 300 Miles: 1.25	Mod.

N
W ← ○ → E
S

Flagstaff City Hall
2.4 mi.

89A   Lake Mary Road

20.6 mi.
MP 323.6

5.0 mi.

Lake Mary Road

Mormon Lake Road

Double Spring Campground

P 0.2 mi.

Mormon Lake

1.25 mi.

Driving Distance One Way, Miles: 28.2
Hiking Distance One Way, Miles: 1.25

Mangum

LAVA FLOW TRAIL

General Information
Location Map E4
Wupatki SW USGS Map
Coconino Forest Service Map

Driving Distance One Way: 22.1 miles *35.36 km* (Time 30 minutes)
Access Road: All cars, All paved
Hiking Distance, Complete Loop: 1.0 mile *1.6 km* (Time 45 minutes)
How Strenuous: Easy
Features: Views, Extinct volcanoes, Self-guided nature trail

NUTSHELL: This is an easy trail located in the Sunset Crater National Monument 22.1 miles *35.36 km* northeast of Flagstaff. It takes you on a fascinating self-guided nature walk through a volcanic field.

DIRECTIONS:
From Flagstaff City Hall Go:
   East, then north on Highway 89. See Access Map, pages 10-11. At 16.4 miles *26.24 km* (MP 430.3) you will reach the entrance to Sunset Crater National Monument. Turn right on the road into Sunset Crater. This road is also known as FR 545. At 18.4 miles *29.44 km* you will reach a ticket booth where you will have to pay admission. Just beyond that is the Visitor Center, which is worth a look. At 21.9 miles *35.0 km* you will see a road branching off to your right marked Lava Flow Trail Drive. Take it. It leads to a parking area at 22.1 miles *35.36 km.*

TRAILHEAD: You will see a sign at the parking area.

DESCRIPTION: This trail is designed as a self-guided walk with points of interest keyed to a guide booklet that is available from the dispenser located at the beginning of the trail. You can take a booklet free. If you decide to keep it, then you put fifty cents into the dispenser at the end of the trail. If you don't want to keep the booklet, then you return it to the dispenser.
   The trail is paved for a short distance. In fact the Forest Service has created a paved short version of the trail for wheelchair bound visitors—a nice gesture. On the main trail, once the paving ends, the trail surface is composed of black cinders. You would have no trouble walking the trail in street shoes but you would scuff them up plenty if you did. Jogging shoes or light trail shoes are excellent footgear for this hike.
   A hiker could hurry around the trail in thirty minutes but we recommend that you take your time. Use the booklet and read it at the stopping points that are described in the booklet. These points really are interesting and even

people who don't like museums or educational walks should find something to enjoy. These black cinder locations have a special feeling that some people respond to very positively. In winter you can sometimes see some startling special effects when white drifts of snow form stark contrasting patterns against the black cinders.

Until 1973 visitors could hike to the top of Sunset Crater. Because of the severe erosion that the multitudes of hikers were causing to the face of the crater, hiking Sunset Crater is now forbidden. The sides of the crater are covered with deep loose black cinders and are therefore unstable. They kept sloughing away from the trails. It is too bad people can't enjoy the experience anymore as we did when we were kids, but the closure was necessary.

One of the features of this trail is an ice cave, a lava tube such as you encounter on the **Lava River** and **Slate Lake Lava Cave** hikes, but it was closed in 1992 because it was collapsing.

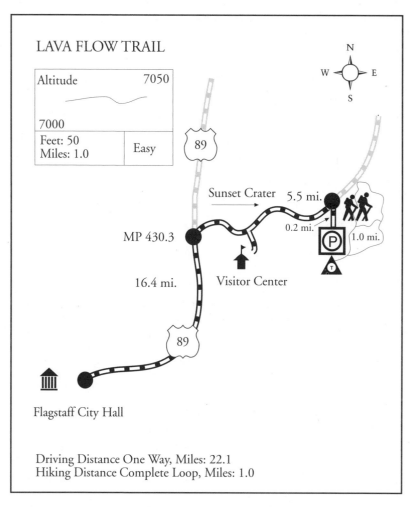

LAVA FLOW TRAIL

Altitude 7050

7000
Feet: 50
Miles: 1.0   Easy

89

Sunset Crater 5.5 mi.

0.2 mi.

MP 430.3

1.0 mi.

16.4 mi.   Visitor Center

89

Flagstaff City Hall

Driving Distance One Way, Miles: 22.1
Hiking Distance Complete Loop, Miles: 1.0

Mangum

LAVA RIVER CAVE

General Information
Location Map E2
Wing Mountain USGS Map
Coconino Forest Service Map

Driving Distance One Way: 18.85 miles *30.2 km* (Time 40 minutes)
Access Road: All cars, Last 4.35 miles *6.96 km* good gravel road
Hiking Distance One Way: 0.70 miles *1.12 km* (Time 1 hour)
How Strenuous: Moderate
Features: Unusual underground lava tube

NUTSHELL: This underground lava tube located 19 miles *30.4 km* northwest of Flagstaff is a unique experience. .

DIRECTIONS:
From Flagstaff City Hall Go:
    North on Humphreys Street for 0.60 miles *1.0 km*. See Access Map, page 10. Turn left at the stoplight onto Columbus Avenue and follow it around a big curve to the north. You will see the street signs call this road Columbus at first, then Ft. Valley Road and then Highway 180. Stay on Highway 180 to the 14.5 miles *23.2 km* point (MP 230), where an unpaved road takes off to the left. Turn left onto this road, FR 245, and follow it to the 17.6 mile *28.16 km* point where it intersects FR 171. Turn left onto FR 171 and follow it to the 18.6 mile *29.76 km* point, where it intersects FR 171B. Turn left on 171B and follow it to the 18.85 mile *30.2 km* point where you will find the outer parking area.

TRAILHEAD: Look for a large ring of stones circling a pit. There is an interpretive sign at the cave entrrance.

DESCRIPTION: Even if you know nothing about volcanos it is obvious that this part of Northern Arizona is an ancient volcanic field. Craters and cinder cones dot the landscape everywhere. The mighty San Francisco Peaks themselves are a huge volcanic crater.
    Lava tubes are formed when the outer portion of a river of lava cools while the interior is still hot and flowing. Under the right conditions the outer skin will form a hard shell and the inner core will flow right on through like water going through a straw, leaving an empty tube.
    That's what you will find on this trip. The Forest Service has made an attractive entrance down into the tube using native stone to form a natural stairway. You have to duck to get into the opening but then the tube deepens so that you can stand upright. The height of the tube is not uniform, how-

Kendrick Peak from Wild Bill Hill

Front Cover: *The San Francisco Peaks from White Horse Hills*

Government Prairie From Wild Bill Hill

Pictograph at Veit Spring

Secret Canyon

Wupatki Ruin

Doney Crater

Grand Falls

Tunnel Road

Lockett Meadow

Dry Lake Hills

South Rim of The Grand Canyon

ever, and there are low and high places along the way. The tube goes on for about 0.70 mile *1.12 km*. The coldest spot is near the entrance and you may find ice there. The cave was discovered in 1915 by lumberjacks who were logging nearby.

You must come properly prepared for this hike. It can be dangerous if you are unprepared. Once you get a short way past the daylight coming in from the entrance you are in absolute darkness. The floor, ceiling and walls are all extremely rough and uneven and you have to watch your step. It is also cold. This means that every member of your party should dress warmly and carry lights. We recommend that each person have two good flashlights equipped with fresh batteries.

We have heard a horror story of a hiker who went into Lava River Cave with one flashlight. He got into the cave about halfway and then dropped and broke his light. When this happened he freaked out, panicked and bashed himself up considerably trying to rush back to the entrance.

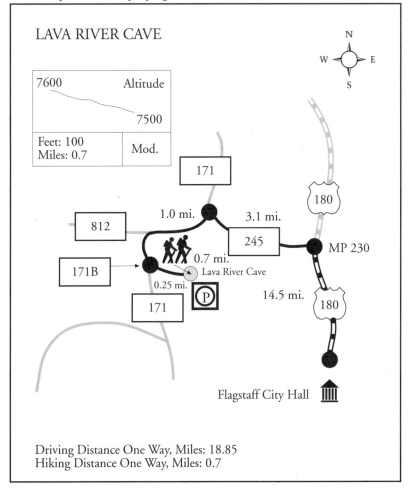

LEDGES TRAIL #138

General Information
Location Map G3
Mormon Lake USGS Map
Coconino Forest Service Map

Driving Distance One Way: 27.0 miles *43.2 km* (Time 30 minutes)
Access Road: All cars, All paved except last 0.3 miles *0.48 km*
Hiking Distance, Complete Loop: 1.5 miles *2.4 km* (Time 45 minutes)
How Strenuous: Moderate
Features: Views

NUTSHELL: This is a nice trail at the base of Mormon Mountain, 27.0 miles *43.2 km* southeast of Flagstaff. It takes you through a pine forest to The Ledges, a ragged basalt cliff, from where you have fine views of Mormon Lake.

DIRECTIONS:
From Flagstaff City Hall Go:
West, then south on Route 66 under the railroad overpass. See Access Map, page 10. At 0.5 miles *0.8 km*, get onto Milton Road. At 1.7 miles *2.72 km* you will reach a stoplight at Forest Meadows Street. Turn right here onto Forest Meadows and go one block to Beulah. Turn left on Beulah and follow it south. Beulah merges onto Highway 89A. At 2.4 miles *3.84 km* (MP 401.6), turn left onto the Lake Mary Road. Follow the Lake Mary Road to the 23.0 mile *36.8 km* point (MP 323.6), where you turn right onto the Mormon Lake Road. At 26.7 miles *42.7 km*, on the Mormon Lake Road, you will see a sign marked "Dairy Springs Amphitheater." Turn right here and follow the gravel road and signs to the 27.0 miles *43.2 km* point, at the back of the Dairy Springs Campground.

TRAILHEAD: There is a large sign at the parking lot marking the trailhead.

DESCRIPTION: This area is used for cross-country skiing in the winter and you will see signs and triangles nailed to trees along the way marking the various ski trails. The triangles for the Ledges Trail are silver.
From its start the trail gradually ascends a hill. The sides of the trail here are lined with rocks. You will see some houses below you toward Mormon Lake. At about 0.25 miles *0.4 km* you begin to see the lake and it will be in sight most of the way from this point.
Mormon Lake is a natural lake. It was originally called Mormon Dairy Lake because of the Mormon pioneers who ran a dairy here for several

years. Later, the name of the lake was shortened to Mormon Lake. Dairy Springs is another legacy from that time.

The trail goes through a forest of pine, oak and spruce. It reaches its apex at 0.75 miles *1.2 km* and then begins to descend. At 0.90 miles *1.44 km* you come onto the ledges for which the trail is named. Few things grow in this bare rock, so this is a good viewpoint. After the ledges the trail goes down-hill toward the Mormon Lake Road.

At about 1.0 miles *1.6 km* you will come to a group of homes. These are summer homes and if you are making the hike in the summer you may be greeted by inquisitive dogs or children. Many paths through this area make following the main trail difficult. No worries. Just keep working your way downhill toward the highway, which you can see plainly. When you reach the highway, go right (west) and you will return to the driveway entrance in about 0.20 miles *0.32 km*, from where it is about 0.1 mile *0.16 km* back to your car.

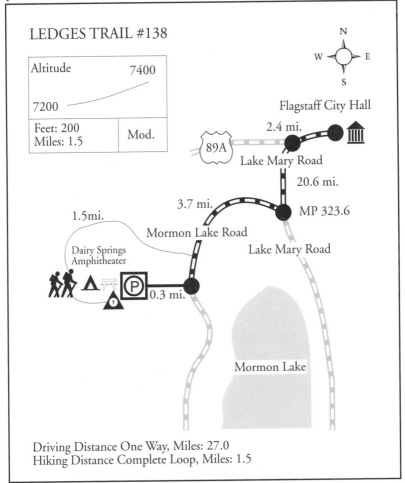

LITTLE ELDEN SPRINGS

General Information
Location Map E3
Sunset Crater West USGS Map
Coconino Forest Service Map

Driving Distance One Way: 11.3 miles *18.1 km* (Time 30 minutes)
Access Road: All cars, Last 2.1 miles *3.36 km* good gravel road
Hiking Distance One Way: 3.5 miles *5.6 km* (Time 2.0 hours)
How Strenuous: Moderate
Features: Beautiful spring, Cliffs, Views

NUTSHELL: Starting at Little Elden Springs 11.3 miles *18.1 km* north of
Flagstaff, this trail takes you south around the base of Little Elden Mt. into
a scenic bowl.

DIRECTIONS:
From Flagstaff City Hall Go:
    East, then north on Highway 89. See Access Map, pages 10-11. At 6.5
miles *10.4 km* you will pass the last stoplight in town at the Winona-
Townsend Road. Continue on Highway 89 to the 9.2 mile *14.7 km* point (MP
423.3) where a gravel road (FR 556) takes off to the left. Turn in on this.
You will see a sign identifying it as the Elden Spring Road. Drive FR 556 to
the 11.3 miles *18.1 km* point, where you will see a sign for the Horsecamp.
The spring is to your left. If you have high clearance, you can drive up near
it and park.

TRAILHEAD: There are no trail signs, but you will see the trail running
along outside the fence. Go up and visit the spring—it is only a few yards
away. When you come back, turn right (east) as you go through the squeeze-
through gate and follow the fence about 40 yards to its end. There you will
go through a take-down gate and head southeast.

DESCRIPTION: Little Elden is not a freestanding mountain but is the
north wing of Mt. Elden. The fire lookout tower is on the south wing. In
between the wings there is an arc which forms a fascinating basin filled with
unusual features. This trail takes you to that basin. Since the earlier editions
of this book, the Forest Service has marked this trail and it is now much easier to follow.
    The trail starts at Schultz Tank, about three miles north. See the **Little
Elden Springs-Horsecamp** hike for details. This part of the trail is a distinct
trail on its own. It is pitifully bare because of the terrible Radio Fire that
raged through here in 1978, but the bareness does give you open views.

The face of Little Elden looks like a huge rock pile full of eye-catching formations, lines, crevices and mystery. Is that a cave you see or only a seam? The rock is a light rust color. For about the first mile you will walk along close to the base of the mountain, then swing away from it.

The trail serpentines to the base of a hill at 1.6 miles *2.56 km*, where you will find the soil is deep sand. This is Sandy Seep. The seep itself is a depression which sometimes holds water. You will walk next to it. In this area you will see a lot of red and white sandstone, quite a change from the volcanic rock that covers so much of Flagstaff.

At 2.0 miles *3.2 km*, you will intersect the Heart Trail, which turns to the right (west), the end of this hike. If you have two cars, you can park one at the Sandy Seep entry (see **Heart Trail** map), then start the hike as written. You would then go straight ahead, and end the hike at the Sandy Seep entry, 1.5 miles *2.4 km* away.

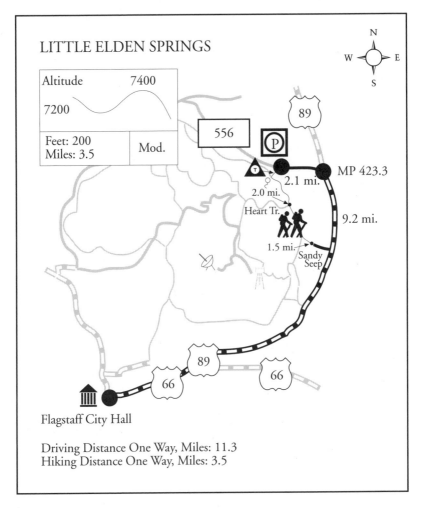

Driving Distance One Way, Miles: 11.3
Hiking Distance One Way, Miles: 3.5

Mangum

LITTLE ELDEN SPRINGS—HORSECAMP

General Information
Location Map E3
Sunset Crater West USGS Map
Coconino Forest Service Map

Driving Distance One Way: 11.7 miles *18.7 km* (Time 30 minutes)
Access Road: All cars, Last 2.5 miles *4.0 km* good gravel road
Hiking Distance One Way: 3.0 miles *4.8 km* (Time 1.5 hours)
How Strenuous: Moderate
Features: Alpine forests, Views

NUTSHELL: Starting above Little Elden Spring 11.7 miles *18.7 km* north of Flagstaff, this trail takes you northwest around the base of Little Elden Mountain and the Dry Lake Hills to Schultz Tank, a large pond.

DIRECTIONS:
From Flagstaff City Hall Go:
    East, then north on Highway 89. See Access Map, pages 10-11. At 6.5 miles *10.4 km* you will pass the last stoplight in town at the Winona-Townsend Road. Continue on Highway 89 to the 9.2 mile *14.72 km* point (MP 423.3) where a gravel road (FR 556) takes off to the left. Turn in on this. You will see a sign identifying it as Elden Spring Road. Drive this to the 11.7 miles *18.7 km* point, where you will see a parking apron and pole fence to your right. Do not turn off into the Horsecamp itself. Stay on the Elden Springs Road, FR 556.

TRAILHEAD: You will see a small gap in the middle of the pole fence at the parking area. Go through there, away from the road, and you will find the trail marker. Turn left and walk uphill.

DESCRIPTION: Horsecamp is a wonderful idea. As you drove up FR 556, you passed the entrance to the camp about 0.3 miles *0.48 km* below the trail-head. The camp has sixteen sites, all intended for people with horses, and everything in the camp is designed for horse use. Horse lovers should appreciate this. The Horsecamp Trail was designed primarily for the use of horse riders, but it makes a good hiking trail and is open to bike use as well.
    The first leg of this hike takes you through a pine forest that has been recently logged. This means that the forest is thin and not pretty, but you get some views. You walk along following the base of Little Elden for a short distance. You can see clearly the notch between Mt. Elden and the Dry Lake Hills. Thereafter you hike along the base of the Dry Lake Hills.
    You are never very far from FR 556 and there are times when you can

see it plainly—and hear traffic on it. Too bad, as this detracts from the peace of the forest.

At the 7800 foot level you leave the bare pine forest and enter into a more interesting mixed forest of pines, firs and aspens. This has not been logged and is much more attractive. At about 7900 feet you will come into a small canyon on the north face of the hill and seems to get lots of moisture. The growth is heavy here. Where the trail crosses the bottom a spring (sometimes) flows.

About a half mile from the end, the trail winds around Schultz Tank, a sizable pond, (always staying outside the fence) and winds up at the **Sunset Trail** parking area.

TIP: We find this a very refreshing hike if you take two cars. Park the first one at the trailhead. Drive the second one 2.1 miles *3.36 km* to intersect FR 420, then go left 0.75 miles *1.2 km* to the Sunset Trailhead. Park, and hike downhill all the way from there.

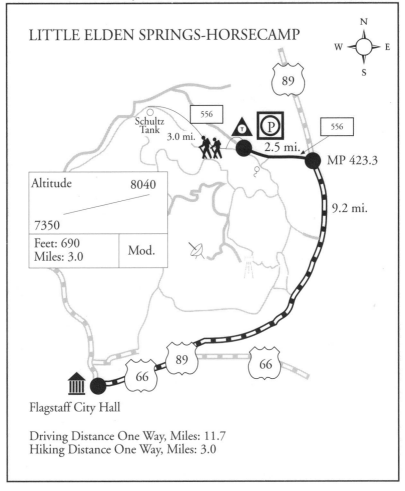

LITTLE ELDEN SPRINGS-HORSECAMP

Schultz Tank   3.0 mi.

556

89

556

2.5 mi.

MP 423.3

9.2 mi.

Altitude   8040

7350

Feet: 690
Miles: 3.0   Mod.

66   89   66

Flagstaff City Hall

Driving Distance One Way, Miles: 11.7
Hiking Distance One Way, Miles: 3.0

Mangum

LITTLE ROUND MOUNTAIN

General Information
Location Map F2
Loy Butte, Sycamore Pt., Wilson Mt. USGS Maps
Coconino Forest Service Map

Driving Distance One Way: 30.5 miles *48.8 km* (Time 1.5 hours)
Access Road: High clearance, Last 6.7 miles *10.72 km* difficult roads
Hiking Distance One Way: 1.5 miles *2.4 km* (Time 1 hour)
How Strenuous: Moderate
Features: Glorious views off the Mogollon Rim into redrock country

NUTSHELL: Located 30.5 miles *48.8 km* southwest of Flagstaff, this little-known trip takes you to a superb viewpoint on the Mogollon Rim.

DIRECTIONS:
From Flagstaff City Hall Go:
    West, then south on Route 66 beneath the railroad overpass. At 0.50 miles *0.8 km* you will reach a Y intersection. See Access Map, page 10. The right fork is Route 66. Take it. You will soon leave town. At 2.6 miles *4.16 km* you will reach a road going to the left. This is the Woody Mountain Road, FR 231. Take it. It is paved about a mile and then turns into a cinder road. Take FR 231 to the 23.2 mile *37.12 km* point, where you will reach a junction. Go left here, still on FR 231. At the 23.8 miles *38.08 km* point you turn right onto FR 539, a dirt road going uphill. You will see a big steel pole gate there. You follow FR 539 to its end, but it is poorly marked, so follow directions carefully. At 25.1 miles *40.16 km* you come to a junction. Go left here (you will see a pole gate to your right). At 25.8 miles *41.28 km* you reach another fork where there is a marker for FR 6249 to the right. Go left here. At 26.5 miles *42.4 km* you will reach a tank marked Rattle (not Rattle*snake*) Tank; take the left fork here. At 27.1 miles *43.36 km* there is another fork, where you go right (don't take the road with the pole gate marked FR 6273). At 27.6 miles *44.16 km* you will reach Rattlesnake Tank, where you go left. At 28.3 miles *45.28 km* you reach a fork where you go right. At 28.6 miles *45.76 km* you will hit another fork, where you go right. At 29.0 miles *46.4 km* there is a junction. You will see an unnamed tank and a fence to your right. Turn left here. At 30.3 miles *48.5 km* you will see Li'l Round Tank below to your left at a fork. Go left here. At 30.5 miles *48.8 km* you will reach the Little Round Mountain sign, where you park.

TRAILHEAD: At the Little Round Mountain sign where you park.

DESCRIPTION: Before you take the hike, drive on to the end of the road, through the camping areas on out to the very end, another 0.15 miles *0.24 km.* Here you will emerge onto a lookout that is sublime, one of our favorite viewpoints. You are looking from the Mogollon Rim into the Sedona redrock country, which is very beautiful.

From the promontory, drive back to the trailhead and begin the hike. The trail is baffling. It starts out fine, well marked and easy to follow, looking like a major hiking trail. It goes downhill and up through a thick beautiful forest. At 1.0 mile *1.6 km,* just as you come to the top of the first upgrade, you will see a trail going to the left. It does not look like the main trail, but it is. Take it. It leads you to the rim and then seems to end indecisively. From there just work your way around the rim enjoying the views to your heart's content and then return the way you came.

The other fork of the trail tops out on a mesa and then mysteriously terminates with no apparent rhyme or reason in a place that isn't even scenic.

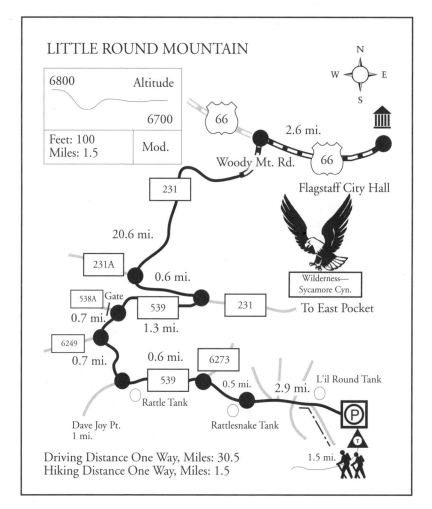

Mangum

LITTLE SPRING

General Information
Location Map E3
Humphreys Peak and White Horse Hills USGS Maps
Coconino Forest Service Map

Driving Distance One Way: 22.66 miles *36.26 km* (Time 40 minutes)
Access Road: All cars—2.4 miles *3.84 km* good gravel road, 0.66 miles *1.1 km* rough dirt road
Hiking Distance One Way: 0.75 miles *1.2 km* (Time 1.0 hours)
How Strenuous: Moderate
Features: Beautiful alpine forest, Meadow with lake, Peak views

NUTSHELL: A steep climb through lovely alpine forests takes you to an aspen ringed lake.

DIRECTIONS:
From Flagstaff City Hall Go:
   North on Humphreys Street for 0.60 miles *1.0 km*. See Access Map, page 10. Turn left at the stoplight onto Columbus Avenue and follow it around a big curve to the north. You will see the street signs call this road Columbus at first, then Ft. Valley Road and then Highway 180. Stay on Highway 180 to the 19.6 miles *31.36 km* point (MP 235.1), where the unpaved upper Hart Prairie Road branches off to the right. Turn right onto this road, which is also identified as FR 151, and follow it to the 22.0 miles *35.2 km* point. There FR 418B branches to the left, going to Little Spring. Take FR 418B and follow it 0.66 miles *1.1 km*, to the 22.66 mile *36.26 km* point, where the road makes a loop in a meadow. Park at the "top of the keyhole" where the road starts to loop back. You will see Little Spring off to your right, marked by the greenery that thrives on its water. Park anywhere in the clearing.

TRAILHEAD: Behind the spring you will see an old road going uphill with a barricade across it. This is the trail.

DESCRIPTION: The water at Little Spring made the land valuable for ranching, and the clearing was a natural place to set up a ranch house. For many years there were a couple of cabins at Little Spring, but now you can see only faint remnants of them.
   Little Spring played an important role in Flagstaff's early days, as it was a stop on the famous Flagstaff-Grand Canyon Stage Coach line because of its dependable water.
   The clearing is a beautiful place for a picnic. This is a great place to bring the family. They can see a very attractive forest and do some exploring.

The spring itself isn't much to see. It has been captured and pours through a metal pipe into a small pool that is always swarming with gnats. On the uphill side of the spring you will see a barricade with signs telling you that the portion behind the barricade is part of the Bismarck Lake Elk Preserve. This hike ends at Bismarck Lake.

You will walk up through a beautiful forest of aspen and spruce. This north slope of the mountain seems to get plenty of water. The forest floor is covered with ferns, and on a hike in August we saw mushrooms everywhere.

The first 0.35 miles *0.56 km* of the trail is a bit of a struggle because it is so steep. At this point you will come across an old road. Go to the right (south) here. Soon you will enter a more level area where there is a narrow open park leading toward a large park. From the 0.5 mile *0.8 km* point you will be in sight of the San Francisco Peaks, which look enormous from here.

The trail ends at Bismarck Lake. Calling this small pond a lake seems like a misnomer, but remember, this is dry Arizona.

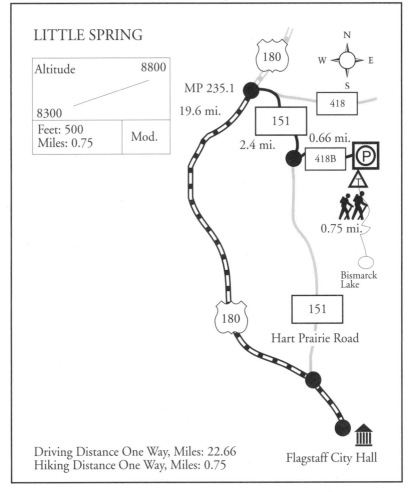

LITTLE SPRING

Altitude 8800
8300
Feet: 500
Miles: 0.75
Mod.

Driving Distance One Way, Miles: 22.66
Hiking Distance One Way, Miles: 0.75

Flagstaff City Hall

Mangum

LOCKETT MEADOW LOOP

General Information
Location Map E3
Humphreys Peak and Sunset Crater West USGS Maps
Coconino Forest Service Map

Driving Distance One Way: 21.6 miles *34.6 km* (Time 45 minutes)
Access Road: All cars, Last 4.5 miles *7.2 km* medium dirt road
Hiking Distance Complete Loop: 4.2 miles *6.7 km* (Time 2.5 hours)
How Strenuous: Hard, Due to Steep Climb, High altitudes
Features: Alpine valley, Dense aspen forests, Clear views

NUTSHELL: This hike displays almost all the features of the San Francisco
Peaks: alpine forests of aspen and fir, a deep scenic valley, and sweeping
views. You hike old roads all the way.

DIRECTIONS:
From Flagstaff City Hall Go:
   East, then north on Highway 89. See Access Map, pages 10-11. At 17.1
miles *27.4 km* (MP 431.2)—just past the entrance to Sunset Crater—turn left
onto FR 552 and take it to the 18.3 mile *29.3 km* point, where you will see
a sign for Lockett Meadow. Go right. From here the road is a winding narrow gravel route which climbs up the face of the mountain. At 21.3 miles *34
km* you reach Lockett Meadow. There you will see a one-way road to your
right into a campground. Take this and park in the Day Use Area at the 21.6
mile *34.6 km* point.

TRAILHEAD: Drive all the way back into the trees among the campsites.
The trailhead is posted with a big sign to the left of a toilet.

DESCRIPTION: This hike has three distinct legs.
   First Leg: Hike up the Inner Basin Trail to Jack Smith cabin, a distance
of 1.5 miles *2.4 km*. This takes you up a deep valley toward the Inner Basin
along a closed maintenance road. You will pass through beautiful forests to
reach a couple of old green cabins, at a trail junction marked by signs. This
leg is an 800 foot climb.
   Second Leg: Hike FR 146 for 1.4 miles *2.24 km*. From the cabins, you
turn to the left (east) on FR 146, going past the corrugated metal shed. FR
146 is used, but is closed to traffic except for City of Flagstaff maintenance
trucks, so it is in good condition and makes a fine hiking road. You will pass
through thick stands of aspens here, an ideal place to see the changing leaves
in October. This leg is on a gentle downhill grade. You will come to a steel
gate at the end of this leg, where the road makes a big curve to your right.

Go left here, just beyond the gate, downhill, through a barbed wire gate, to get onto an old disused, unmarked road.

Third Leg: Hike the old unused road back down to Lockett Meadow. This leg is downhill through open country and gives you great views. You look right down on Sunset Crater and the extensive volcanic field around it. At 3.65 miles *5.8 km*, you will come to an old road surfaced with gray gravel. Turn left here. Shortly you will intersect another unmarked gray road. Turn left here also. From here you will make a steep descent back down to the Lockett Meadow Road. Turn left, walking the wrong way on the one-way road and follow it back to the parking place.

Note: USGS and Forest Service maps are inaccurate in their depiction of the roads on the third leg of this hike. We took this hike in October, 1994, and our map shows how the roads look now.

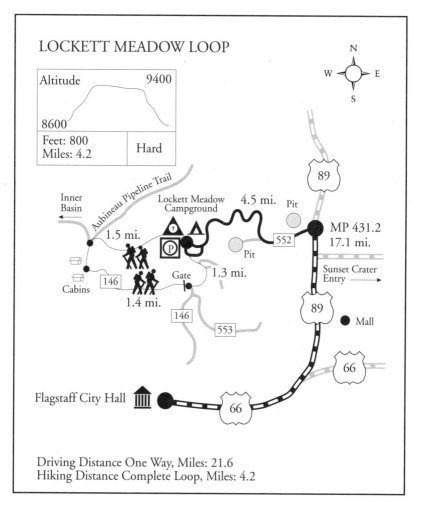

Mangum

LONESOME POCKET TRAIL #61

General Information
Location Map F2
May Tank Pocket & White Horse Lake USGS Maps
Coconino Forest Service Map

Driving Distance One Way: 52.6 miles *84.2 km* (Time 1.75 hours)
Access Road: All cars, Last 10.5 miles *17 km* decent gravel roads
Hiking Distance One Way: 5.0 miles *8.0 km* (Time 3.0 hours)
How Strenuous: Hard
Features: Views

NUTSHELL: A long drive through remote country takes you to seldom seen viewpoints on the Mogollon Rim west of Sycamore Canyon. You descend an old livestock trail to the bottom of the Rim.

DIRECTIONS:
From Flagstaff City Hall Go:
West, then south on Route 66 under the railroad overpass. See Access Map, page 10. Turn right at 0.5 miles *0.8 km* and follow Route 66 out of town. It merges with I-40 west in 5.0 miles *8.0 km*. Stay on I-40 West to the 30.3 mile *48.5 km* point, Williams Exit #165. Take that exit and at the stop sign go left to Williams. Go into downtown Williams on Route 66 (Railroad Avenue) and turn left at Fourth Street, 32.9 miles *52.6 km*, which will take you out of town. Beyond town, the road is called FR 173 (the Perkinsville Road). At 42.1 miles *67.4 km* turn left (east) onto unpaved FR 354. Take FR 354 to the 49.3 mile *78.9 km* point, where you will see FR 354 turn to your right (west). FR 105 starts here. Take FR 105 to the 50.9 mile *81.4 km* point, where it intersects FR 125. Turn right (south) on FR 125 and follow it to its end at 52.6 miles *84.2 km*, where you park.

TRAILHEAD: From the parking place, FR 7125 goes south. A lath-type marker indicates that the road is to be used only by hikers, bikers and horse riders.

DESCRIPTION: You will hike an old jeep road. To your right (west) is Wagner Hill. Starting in a thick pinon-juniper forest, the road goes along terrain that is fairly flat, with a few ups and downs, in a southerly direction. The forest thins as you come out onto a mesa where you begin to see canyons all around you. You are walking toward the outer edge of the Mogollon Rim.
At 1.4 miles *2.3 km* you reach the rim. The road curves to the left (east) here. There is a great lookout at this place, to which you may want to detour. You will pass through a gate at 2.3 miles *3.7 km*. At 2.4 miles *3.8 km* the

road forks. Take the right fork, which brings you right to the rim. At 2.6 miles *4.2 km*, look for a triple-trunk juniper with a blaze. This is the start of the trail to the bottom of the rim. You will see a footpath plunging steeply between two barbed wire fences. You will now descend 1340 feet in 2.4 miles *3.8 km* to a ranch house (clearly visible from the start down) at Henderson Flat. The trail is very rocky and not maintained. All the way down, you will enjoy sweeping views across the Verde Valley to the Black Hills and beyond.

We recommend using two cars. From 4th Street in Williams, take both cars to the end of the paving on the Perkinsville Road, 24.5 miles *39.2 km*. Follow the unpaved Perkinsville Road to the 29.8 miles *47.7 km*, point where you will see a sign for Henderson Flat pointing to your left. This is FR 181. Drive FR 181 to the 37.55 mile *60 km* point, and park at the ranch house, where you will see trailhead signs. Then take one of the cars back up to the top.

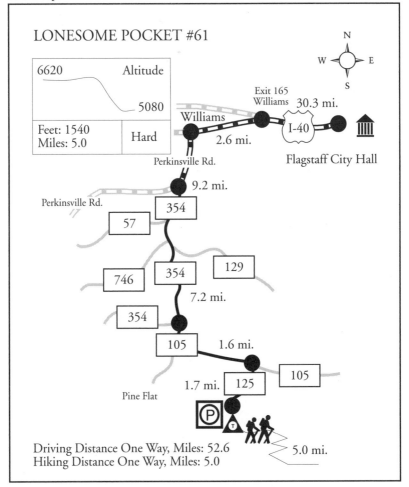

LONESOME POCKET #61

6620	Altitude
	5080
Feet: 1540 Miles: 5.0	Hard

N
W E
S

Exit 165
Williams 30.3 mi.
Williams I-40
2.6 mi.
Perkinsville Rd.
Flagstaff City Hall

Perkinsville Rd. 9.2 mi.
354
57
746 354 129
7.2 mi.
354
105 1.6 mi.
1.7 mi. 125 105
Pine Flat

Driving Distance One Way, Miles: 52.6
Hiking Distance One Way, Miles: 5.0
5.0 mi.

Mangum

LOST BURRITO TRAIL

General Information
Location Map E3
Humphreys Peak & Flagstaff West USGS Maps
Coconino Forest Service Map

Driving Distance One Way: 3.9 miles *6.24 km* (Time 20 minutes)
Access Road: All cars, Last 0.25 miles *0.4 km* medium unpaved road
Hiking Distance One Way: 1.8 miles *2.9 km* (Time 1.5 hours)
How Strenuous: Hard, steep slippery trail at the top
Features: Nice forest, Good views of Flagstaff

NUTSHELL: This trail branches off from the **Rocky Ridge Trail** and climbs to the southern edge of the Dry Lake Hills.

DIRECTIONS:
From Flagstaff City Hall Go:
    North on Humphreys Street for 0.60 miles *1.0 km*. See Access Map, page 10. Turn left at the stoplight onto Columbus Avenue and follow it around a big curve to the north. You will see the street signs call this road Columbus Avenue at first, then Ft. Valley Road and then Highway 180. Stay on Highway 180 to the 3.1 miles *5.0 km* point (MP 218.6), where the Schultz Pass Road, FR 420, goes to the right. Follow the Schultz Pass Road. As it starts around a curve to the left, at the 3.6 miles *5.76 km* point, you will see the unpaved Elden Lookout Road going straight. Ignore this and stay on the paved road. The paving will end soon and the road will become gravel. At the 3.9 miles *6.24 km* point, you will see a gate, which closes the road in winter. Just beyond the gate is FR 9128Y which goes downhill to your right. Take this. At the bottom turn left and follow the road a few yards to a fence, where you park.

TRAILHEAD: You will see a wooden sign for the Rocky Ridge Trail in the fence opening to your right.

DESCRIPTION: This trail starts at the same place that the **Schultz Creek Trail** ends. There are two distinct openings in the fence, one for the Schultz Creek Trail and the other for Rocky Ridge.
    Walk the Rocky Ridge Trail for 0.5 miles *0.8 km*. This trail climbs, but not too steeply, and then becomes more level. The Rocky Ridge is a maintained and posted trail. The Lost Burrito Trail is not. When you reach the 0.5 mile *0.8 km* point, look carefully to your left for a trail going uphill into the woods. It is not marked, but it is the only side trail you will encounter in the area, so if you are alert, you will see it.

Although the trail seems faint at its beginning, you will find as you hike it that it is not a mere game trail. It was constructed with some care in the past. You will see that rocks have been rolled aside and that the path of the trail is lined with rocks in many places. Erosion controls have been installed. There is even a little bench on the left side of the trail 0.2 miles *0.32 km* from its beginning. The trail climbs steadily, but the grade is not too steep at first.

You will come to a Y fork at about 1.0 mile *1.6 km*. Turn right here, going uphill. From this point, the trail becomes much steeper, and difficult to climb because of loose rock underfoot. After this hard pull to the top, you will emerge onto the rim of a bowl, where there is a bare meadow surrounded by hills. This is the second (most southerly) of the Dry Lakes, and is a pretty sight. You can continue to the north, where you will enter into the second Dry Lakes, which has connections to the Schultz Pass Road and Brookbank Trail. See the entry for **Dry Lake Hills** for more information.

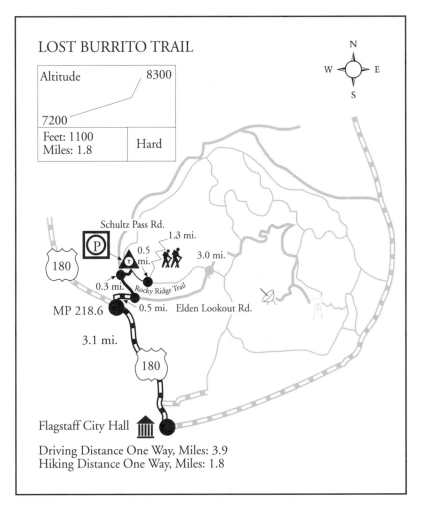

LOST BURRITO TRAIL

Altitude 8300
7200
Feet: 1100
Miles: 1.8
Hard

Schultz Pass Rd.
1.3 mi.
0.5 mi.
3.0 mi.
180
0.3 mi. *Rocky Ridge Trail*
MP 218.6
0.5 mi. Elden Lookout Rd.
3.1 mi.
180
Flagstaff City Hall

Driving Distance One Way, Miles: 3.9
Hiking Distance One Way, Miles: 1.8

Mangum

MARSHALL LAKE

<hr>

General Information
Location Map F3-F4
Flagstaff East, Lower Lake Mary USGS Maps
Coconino Forest Service Map

Driving Distance One Way: 14.45 miles *23.2 km* (Time 25 minutes)
Access Road: All cars, Last 1.2 miles *1.9 km* good unpaved road
Hiking Distance One Way: 5.8 miles *9.28 km* (Time 3 hours)
How Strenuous: Moderate
Features: Easy to reach, Beautiful canyon with cliffs and caves

NUTSHELL: Best as a two-car shuttle. This trail is a leg of The Arizona Trail. It starts on Anderson Mesa at scenic Marshall Lake, then crosses the mesa to descend into Walnut Canyon where you have good views, climbing out at Sandys Canyon to your second car.

DIRECTIONS:
From Flagstaff City Hall Go:
    West, then south on Route 66 under the railroad overpass. See Access Map, page 10. At 0.50 miles *0.8 km* you will reach a stoplight at a Y inter-section. Leave Route 66 here and go straight on Milton Road. At 1.70 miles *2.72 km* you reach the stoplight at Forest Meadows, where you turn right. At the next corner turn left on Beulah and follow it out of town. Beulah will connect onto Highway 89A. At the 2.4 miles *3.84 km* point (MP 401.6) you will see the turnoff to the Lake Mary Road to your left at the last stoplight in town. Turn and follow the Lake Mary Road to the 7.9 mile point *12.6 km* (MP 338.4)—just across a cattle guard—where you will see an unpaved road to your left with a big steel gate. Turn in here and go about 0.2 miles *0.32 km* to the parking lot for the **Sandys Canyon** Trailhead. Leave your second car here and have all hikers get into the first car. Back out on the Lake Mary Road, reset your odometer, turn left, and drive 4.1 miles *6.56 km* (MP 334.3) where you will see the paved Marshall Lake road to your left going uphill. Turn left and take it to the 5.35 mile *8.6 km* point, where you will see a gravel road to your left, FR 128. Turn left and take FR 128 to the 6.35 miles *10.2 km* point, where the road forks at Marshall Lake. Take the left fork and follow it to the 6.55 mile *10.5 km* point and park.

TRAILHEAD: At the parking place. Look sharp, for the road in this area goes on past the trailhead. All you have to guide you is a small wooden sign.

DESCRIPTION: The trail heads west across Anderson Mesa through a typ-ical pine forest. You will be on fairly level ground for the first part of the hike. At the 3.0 mile *4.8 km* point you cross two jeep roads and begin to descend into a canyon. At 3.5 miles *5.6 km* you will catch views of the San Francisco Peaks. Walnut Canyon will come into view, and you will walk along its rim northerly. There is a good viewpoint at the top of the canyon. At this place you are just about due south of your second car, but in order to get down into the canyon and back up the other side, you must loop around to the north. Walnut Canyon is quite impressive from here.

At 4.0 miles *6.4 km,* you begin the steep hike to the canyon bottom, passing beautiful cliffs. These have strong crossbedding lines and a rosy hue that shows in late afternoon light. You reach the canyon bottom at 4.5 miles *7.2 km* where you intersect the Sandys Canyon Trail. Turn left (south) on the Sandys Canyon Trail. In 0.50 *0.8 km* miles you come to a side canyon where you climb 200 feet to the top in 0.2 miles *0.32 km.* From the top, walk south along the rim to the parking place for the second car, which is 0.6 miles *1.0 km* away.

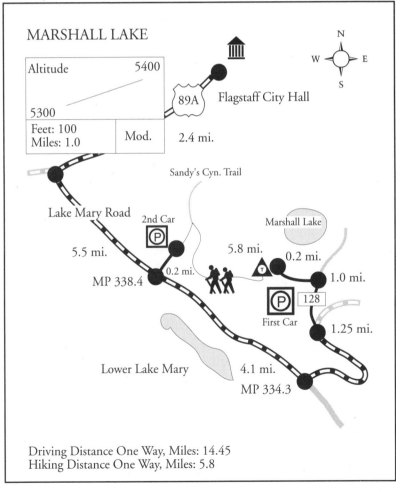

Mangum

MAXWELL TRAIL #37

General Information
Location Map G4
Calloway Butte USGS Map
Coconino Forest Service Map

Driving Distance One Way: 57.8 miles *92.5 km* (Time 1.5 hours)
Access Road: All cars, Last 8.9 miles *14.24 km* good gravel road
Hiking Distance One Way: 0.80 miles *1.3 km* (Time 45 minutes)
How Strenuous: Hard
Features: Views, Beautiful pristine stream, Remote canyon

NUTSHELL: This is one of the few trails into West Clear Creek, a remote canyon 57.8 miles *92.5 km* southeast of Flagstaff. The hike is short but steep and very beautiful.

DIRECTIONS:
From Flagstaff City Hall Go:
    West, then south on Route 66 under the railroad overpass. See Access Map, pages 10-11. At 0.5 miles *0.8 km*, leave Route 66 and go straight on Milton Road. At 1.7 miles *2.72 km* you will reach a stoplight at Forest Meadows Street. Turn right onto Forest Meadows and go one block to Beulah. Turn left on Beulah and follow it south. Beulah merges onto Highway 89A. At 2.4 miles *3.84 km* (MP 401.6), turn left onto the Lake Mary Road. Follow the Lake Mary Road to the 48.9 mile *78.2 km* point (MP 297.7), where you turn right onto a gravel road, FR 81. Follow FR 81 to the 52.0 mile *83.2 km* point, where you reach a fork. Take the left fork, on FR 81E. Drive to the 55.8 mile *89.28 km* point, another fork. You will see a sign for the Maxwell Trail at the fork. Go left, to the 57.8 mile *92.5 km* point. Here you will find some campsites and a parking area. The road goes another 0.25 miles *0.4 km* but the last stretch is very rough. You may want to park at 57.8 miles *92.5 km* and walk the rest of the road.

TRAILHEAD: There is a sign at the parking area at the end of the road.

DESCRIPTION: West Clear Creek is a tributary of the Verde River. Its headwaters are on the uplands of the Mogollon Rim, where this hike takes place. Located in a remote area, West Clear Creek canyon cuts a course running from east to west. At its low end it joins the Verde River near Camp Verde.
    Getting to the trailhead you will drive through a pine forest that has plenty of open parks. These make good grazing areas for cattle and have been used for ranching ever since settlement of the country began in the late

1800s. The area has been thoroughly logged too, including some of the wild back country along FR 81.

When you get to the trailhead you can get glimpses into the canyon. These tell you that it is very steep. The walls of the canyon are a buff colored sandstone with pink tints. It looks a lot like **Walnut Canyon** near Flagstaff.

The trail takes you by a serpentine route to the canyon bottom where there is an unspoiled stream, living up to its name, Clear Creek. Along the way you walk right in the shadow of enormous cliffs.

The canyon at the bottom is rather narrow and there appear to be no developed trails along the streambed. It is possible to do some hiking at the bottom but this means boulder hopping and wading.

You will be enthralled by the quiet beauty of this canyon, especially at creekside, but look out for poison ivy and keep an eye out for snakes.

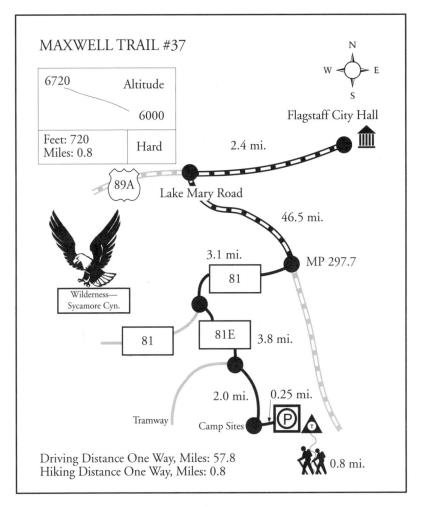

Mangum

METEOR CRATER

General Information
Location Map F5
Meteor Crater USGS Map
Coconino Forest Service Map

Driving Distance One Way: 43.9 miles *70.24 km* (Time 1 hour)
Access Road: All cars, All paved
Hiking Distance, Complete Loop: 2.5 miles *4.0 km* (Time 1.25 hours)
How Strenuous: Moderate
Features: Trip around rim of world-famed attraction

NUTSHELL: You hike around the rim of Meteor Crater, located 43.9 miles *70.24 km* east of Flagstaff, getting a good view of the inside of the crater and the surrounding countryside.

DIRECTIONS:
From Flagstaff City Hall Go:
   East, then north on Highway 89. See Access Map, pages 10-11. At 4.0 miles *6.4 km* you will see a sign to your right marking the entrance to Interstate-40. Take this entrance and at 4.2 miles *6.7 km* turn left on the Interstate-40 East Exit. This will place you on I-40 headed east. At 37.9 miles *60.64 km* (MP 233.6) you will reach the Meteor Crater turn, Exit 233. Turn right on this and follow the paved road to Meteor Crater. You will reach the parking lot at the Visitor Center at 43.9 miles *70.24 km.*

TRAILHEAD: You must go through the Visitor Center to gain access to this trail.

DESCRIPTION: Although Meteor Crater has all the appearance of a National Park or Monument, it is privately owned. You have to pay an admission fee to get in.
   When you arrive at the parking place you will find steps leading you into the ticket office where there is a snack bar and curio store. If you pay the admission fee, you can then go up to the next level where the museum and entrance to the crater is located.
   Take a few minutes and tour the museum. Until you see the exhibits, it is easy to underestimate the tremendous force generated by the meteorite hitting the ground. The museum highlights the use of the crater to prepare American astronauts for their landing on the moon in the Apollo flights in the 1960s.
   When you leave the museum and go outside to the crater you will see three areas to your left. The middle one is a platform cantilevered out over

the edge with several lensless "telescopes" aimed at points of interest. Below that there is a covered viewpoint. Above it there is a high platform with a real telescope. The trail starts at the high platform.

From the trailhead you simply walk around the rim of the crater. You can see the trail clearly. There are eight markers showing points of interest. Due to the roughness of the terrain, the trail does not absolutely stay on top of the rim at all times, but dips around obstacles.

It is interesting to see the crater from different angles as you circumnavigate it, and you will observe signs of old mining and ranching activity as you make the circle. You are totally exposed to the sun on this trail. There is no shade. There is a lot of white rock and soil that reflects sun back at you. The altitude is about 5700 feet, fairly low for northern Arizona. These all add up to one thing: this can be a very hot hike. Formerly hikers could go down to the crater's floor, but this is now forbidden.

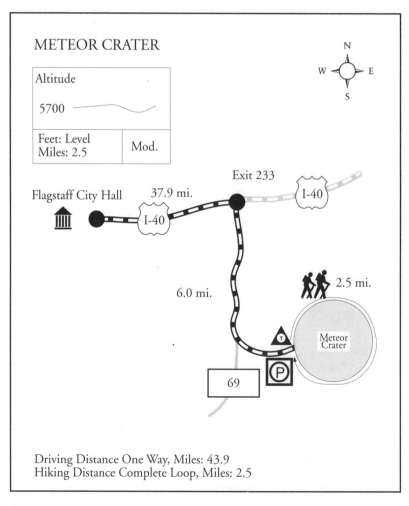

Driving Distance One Way, Miles: 43.9
Hiking Distance Complete Loop, Miles: 2.5

Mangum

MORMON MOUNTAIN #58

General Information
Location Map G3
Mormon Lake USGS Map
Coconino Forest Service Map

Driving Distance One Way: 27.0 miles *43.2 km* (Time 30 minutes)
Access Road: All cars, Last 0.3 miles *0.48 km* good gravel road
Hiking Distance One Way: 2.25 miles *3.6 km* (Time 75 minutes)
How Strenuous: Moderate
Features: Beautiful forest

NUTSHELL: This hike takes you to the top of the dominant mountain on the landscape 27.0 miles *43.2 km* southeast of Flagstaff.

DIRECTIONS:
From Flagstaff City Hall Go:
    West, then south on Route 66 under the railroad overpass. At 0.5 miles *0.8 km*, leave Route 66 and go straight on Milton Road. See Access Map, page 10. At 1.7 miles *2.72 km* you will reach a stoplight at Forest Meadows Street. Turn right here onto Forest Meadows and go one block to Beulah. Turn left on Beulah and follow it south. Beulah merges onto Highway 89A. At 2.4 miles *3.84 km* (MP 401.6), turn left onto the Lake Mary Road. Follow the Lake Mary Road to the 23.0 mile *36.8 km* point (MP 323.6), where you turn right onto the Mormon Lake Road. At 26.7 miles *42.7 km*, on the Mormon Lake Road, you will see a sign marked "Dairy Springs Amphitheater." Turn right here and follow the gravel road and signs to the 27.0 miles *43.2 km* point, at the back of the Dairy Springs Campground.

TRAILHEAD: There is a large sign at the parking lot marking the trailhead.

DESCRIPTION: This area is used for cross-country skiing in the winter and you will see signs and triangles nailed to trees along the way marking the various ski trails. This is also the trailhead for **The Ledges** hike, which you will find described in this book.
    This trail is gentle and wide at the start. The path of the ski trail is marked by graphics and metal triangles nailed to trees. White triangles mark the path you want to follow on this hike. The trail climbs through a lovely forest of pine, oak and fir, with some aspen located near the top. From the 0.5 mile *0.8 km* point to the 1.0 mile *1.6 km* point the grade is very steep but the rest of the trail is not particularly steep for a mountain trail.
    Just before you reach the top, you pass through a very attractive old

growth forest, but the top is disappointing, as it has been logged. As with many mountains, reaching the top is deceptive. You come to a point where you clearly stop climbing and level out on what appears to be a crest only to find that it is merely a fold or a bench. This happens on this hike. You will not reach a point where you can definitely say to yourself, *"This is the top."*

One of the attractions of a mountain hike is being rewarded with great views at the summit of the mountain. Unfortunately that does not happen here because the trees are so tall and thick that they block your view. We stopped at the 2.25 mile *3.6 km* point but the path goes on, over to the fire tower and radio-TV transmitters that are located on this mountain. These towers and transmitters are eyesores and are out of sight if you stop at the 2.25 mile *3.6 km* point.

You will see a sign at the area where we recommend stopping that is marked *1.5 miles* to the start. The sign is short by 0.75 miles *1.2 km*.

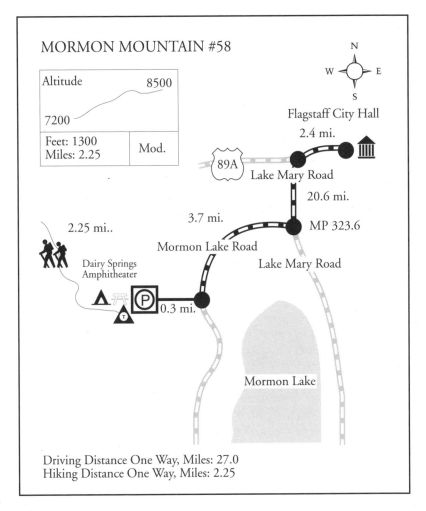

MORMON MOUNTAIN #58

Altitude 8500

7200

Feet: 1300
Miles: 2.25 — Mod.

N
W — E
S

Flagstaff City Hall
2.4 mi.

89A
Lake Mary Road

20.6 mi.

3.7 mi.

Mormon Lake Road

MP 323.6

Lake Mary Road

2.25 mi..

Dairy Springs
Amphitheater

0.3 mi.

Mormon Lake

Driving Distance One Way, Miles: 27.0
Hiking Distance One Way, Miles: 2.25

MUSEUM NATURE TRAIL

General Information
Location Map F3
Flagstaff West USGS Map
Coconino Forest Service Map

Driving Distance One Way: 2.9 miles *4.64 km* (Time 15 minutes)
Access Road: All cars, All paved
Hiking Distance Complete Loop: 0.5 miles *0.8 km* (Time 30 minutes)
How Strenuous: Easy
Features: Beautiful and informative nature trail

NUTSHELL: This nature trail is located adjacent to the Museum of Northern Arizona, 2.9 miles *4.64 km* north of Flagstaff. It takes you down into a pretty canyon and along a streambed where many plants of the area grow and are identified.

DIRECTIONS:
From Flagstaff City Hall Go:
    North on Humphreys Street a distance of 0.6 miles *1.0 km* to the stop sign at Columbus. See Access Map, page 10. Turn left here onto Columbus, which becomes Ft. Valley Road and Highway 180 as it goes north. At the 2.9 mile *4.64 km* point (MP 218.5) you will be at the entrance to The Museum of Northern Arizona. Turn left into its lot.

TRAILHEAD: To the left of the main entrance to the museum. It is marked as the *Rio de Flag Nature Trail*.

DESCRIPTION: If you have not visited The Museum of Northern Arizona, then by all means do so, as it is well worth seeing. These people really know their business and have a number of fascinating displays. It is a very good place to learn about northern Arizona. You will have to pay an admission fee at the door. This is the place to ask for a copy of the *Rio de Flag Nature Trail Guide*, a free booklet identifying the sights along the nature trail.
    At the beginning, you walk along the rim of a canyon. Below is the Rio de Flag, an intermittent stream that comes from the San Francisco Peaks, courses through Flagstaff and joins the Little Colorado River. The walls of the canyon here are about twenty feet high.
    At various points along the trail you will find numbered markers. These are keyed into the brochure. Plants and other objects of interest are identified. You might want to pay attention, because point #14 is poison ivy. At 0.1 mile *0.16 km* the trail dips down into the canyon and follows the streambed.

The streambed is overgrown with Arroyo Willows through most of the area. There is a little spring hidden in the willows, which flows in wet years and causes a stream to run along the bottom, an attractive feature.

You hike along to the north; then the trail meanders across the stream, crosses it on a plank bridge, and loops back to the south. At point # 24, a fallen tree, the trail splits. You can go to your left across the creek and climb back to the top, returning to the starting point the way you came along the rim portion of the trail. Taken this way the trail is about 0.4 miles *0.64 km* long. It is more interesting to take the right fork instead, on a short spur called The Aspen Trail. This takes you up a flight of semi-steps to the top and over to a side canyon where a stand of aspens grows, a lovely spot.

From here the trail returns to the canyon floor and loops back to the trail junction, from where you go back to the trailhead on the first leg of the trail. Done this way, the hike is about 0.5 miles *0.8 km* long.

MUSEUM NATURE TRAIL

N
W   E
S

7100   Altitude

7050

Feet: 50
Miles: 0.5   Easy

180

Rio de Flag

Museum   Humphreys Street

MP 218.5

180   2.3 mi.

Columbus

0.5 mi.   Columbus/Ft. Valley

Humphreys Street

0.6 mi.

Flagstaff City Hall

Route 66

Driving Distance One Way, Miles: 2.9
Hiking Distance Complete Loop, Miles: 0.5

Mangum

O'LEARY PEAK

General Information
Location Map E4
O'Leary Peak & Sunset Crater West USGS Maps
Coconino Forest Service Map

Driving Distance One Way: 22.0 miles *35.2 km* (Time 30 minutes)
Access Road: All cars, Last 3.9 miles *6.24 km* medium condition dirt road
Hiking Distance One Way: 1.5 miles *2.4 km* (Time 1 hour)
How Strenuous: Hard
Features: Views, Volcanic field

NUTSHELL: This trail takes you to the top of a peak located about 22.0 miles *35.2 km* northeast of Flagstaff. The peak dominates the Sunset Crater area and gives great views as a reward for a fairly strenuous climb.

DIRECTIONS:
From Flagstaff City Hall Go:
East, then north on Highway 89. See Access Map, pages 10-11. At 16.4 miles *26.24 km* (MP 430.3) you will reach the entrance to Sunset Crater National Monument. Turn right on the road into Sunset Crater. This road is also known as FR 545. At 18.1 miles *29 km* you will reach a dirt road going to your left marked FR 545A. Turn onto FR 545A and follow it. You will soon come to O'Leary Peak and begin to climb it. The road was built to service a fire lookout tower located on the top, so it is wide and in good condition. At the 22.0 miles *35.2 km* point you will reach a gate. Park there.

TRAILHEAD: You will not see any trail signs. Walk up the road to the top.

DESCRIPTION: The gate is located at a saddle and is a good place to stop and begin this hike. You could drive all the way to the top if the gate is open, but what's the fun of that? The gate is open when a fire ranger is in the lookout tower. This means, roughly speaking, during the summer when fire danger is high. Except in bad weather the road may be driveable any time of year.

As you walk up the road you will find that it winds around the mountain. Because of this you get to see out in all directions as you go. You will have great views. At first you will see into the Sunset Crater National Monument and then into the Bonito Lava Flow, which is part of the monument. Both of these are very interesting.

At the top you will find the fire lookout tower. If the ranger is present, ask to go up. Most of these people are very cordial and enjoy a bit of company as a break from their lonely vigils. The views from the tower are truly splendid. If you are interested in volcanoes, this is a must. O'Leary Peak itself is an extinct volcano. You will see out over a huge volcanic field running for many miles north and east of the San Francisco Peaks. You will also have grand views of the Painted Desert.

The walkway to the fire tower is a strange one. Corrugated metal sections looking something like treads for a giant Caterpillar tractor have been joined together to make a deckway. This gives good footing when it is dry but we wouldn't want to walk it while it is wet. We certainly wouldn't want to be on it when lightning was flashing. The metal plates would be a powerful attractor of thunderbolts. Fire towers themselves are well grounded and you need not fear being struck while you are in one, though their metal skin will glow and sizzle and scare the hell out of you.

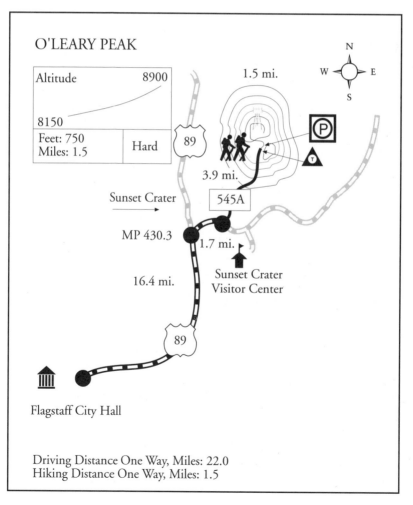

O'LEARY PEAK

Altitude	8900
8150	
Feet: 750 Miles: 1.5	Hard

1.5 mi.

89

3.9 mi.

Sunset Crater

545A

MP 430.3

1.7 mi.

16.4 mi.

Sunset Crater Visitor Center

89

Flagstaff City Hall

Driving Distance One Way, Miles: 22.0
Hiking Distance One Way, Miles: 1.5

OAK CREEK VISTA

General Information
Location Map F3
Mountainaire USGS Map
Coconino Forest Service Map

Driving Distance One Way: 13.7 miles *21.92 km* (Time 20 minutes)
Access Road: All cars, All paved
Hiking Distance, Complete Loop: 0.20 miles *0.32 km* (Time 30 minutes)
How Strenuous: Easy
Features: Sightseeing spot, Signs explaining flora and fauna

NUTSHELL: More of a stroll than a hike, this easy trail is located 13.7 miles *21.92 km* south of Flagstaff on the rim of Oak Creek Canyon.

DIRECTIONS:
From Flagstaff City Hall Go:
West, then south on Route 66 under the railroad overpass. At 0.5 miles *0.8 km*, leave Route 66 and go straight ahead on Milton Road. See Access Map, page 10. At 1.7 miles *2.72 km* you reach the intersection of Forest Meadows, where there is a traffic light. Here you turn right. You will see a sign for Highway 89A, which is the road you want. At the next corner turn left on Beulah and follow it out of town. Beulah will connect onto Highway 89A which is the road to Oak Creek Canyon and Sedona. At 13.7 miles *21.92 km* (MP 390) you will see the road to Oak Creek Vista to your left. Pull in on that road and park. It is paved and there are many parking spaces.

TRAILHEAD: The trail is paved. Pick it up from the parking lot at any point. It makes a loop, so you can join it anywhere you like and come back to where you started.

DESCRIPTION: The Forest Service has made an attractive viewpoint out of the old highway alignment, which used to go through here. On a busy weekend when the weather is good, you will find Native Americans selling jewelry on blankets they have laid out along the sides of the path.
The path follows around a bend in the canyon rim. Several standpoints have been established along the rim with signs at each point. The signs explain the history, biology, zoology and geology of the area. You will get some impressive views into the canyon depths from these standpoints.
The canyon is very deep below this part of the rim, probably one thousand feet or more. The area directly below the viewpoints is actually Pumphouse Wash, a tributary of Oak Creek Canyon, rather than Oak Creek Canyon itself. You will pass over Pumphouse Wash when you drive down

through Oak Creek Canyon. It is spanned by the first big bridge you come to, just below the Sterling Springs Fish Hatchery.

At the canyon rim, the rock you see is a thick cap of gray basalt (lava) at the top with white or buff sandstone cliffs below the gray. The redrock for which Sedona is famous occurs in lower strata. The basalt cliff faces here are favorite spots for rope climbers. Look for them on the cliff faces to the east (on your left) on the same wall of the canyon you are standing on.

An interesting sight is Highway 89A corkscrewing around the toe of a fin as it works its way downhill and comes out onto the floor of Oak Creek Canyon.

This is a very gentle and satisfying walk, an easy stroll for Aunt Maude or other visiting relatives. Kids even seem to like it. It gives an appreciation of the size and depth of Oak Creek Canyon.

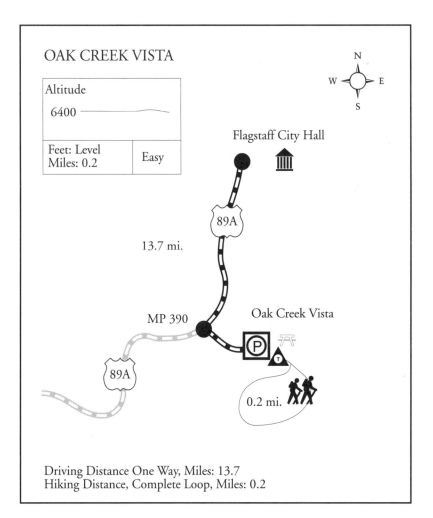

OAK CREEK VISTA

Altitude

6400

Feet: Level
Miles: 0.2

Easy

N
W E
S

Flagstaff City Hall

89A

13.7 mi.

MP 390

Oak Creek Vista

89A

0.2 mi.

Driving Distance One Way, Miles: 13.7
Hiking Distance, Complete Loop, Miles: 0.2

Mangum

OLD LOWELL OBSERVATORY ROAD

General Information
Location Map F3
Flagstaff West USGS Map
Coconino Forest Service Map

Driving Distance One Way: 1.0 mile *1.6 km* (Time 5 minutes)
Access Road: All cars, All paved
Hiking Distance One Way: 1.5 miles *2.4 km* (Time 45 minutes)
How Strenuous: Moderate
Features: Beautiful forest, Nicely maintained trail, Extremely easy access

NUTSHELL: This urban trail located in west Flagstaff is a moderate, pleasant walk to the top of Observatory Mesa, a long ridge that forms the western boundary of the town.

DIRECTIONS:
From Flagstaff City Hall Go:
West on Route 66 a block, where Route 66 curves left. See Access Map, page 10. Go straight on Santa Fe Avenue—do not turn left under the overpass. At 0.50 miles *0.8 km*, turn right on Toltec Street. At 1.0 miles *1.6 km* you will see the trail by a stone hut to your left. There is no parking to the left. Turn right into a paved parking lot near the ball fields. Park there.

TRAILHEAD: The trail is unmistakable. It is a graded and graveled path marked by boulders and signs.

DESCRIPTION: This trail is part of the City of Flagstaff Urban Trail System.
As you walk the trail, look to your left at the last line of boulders just before you start up a small side canyon. The dirt road that you will see there is the original road. Then you will walk up a little canyon that is pleasant and peaceful with a nice stand of big old pine trees, then top out on the mesa.
At 0.50 miles *0.8 km* you will reach a fence marking private property. The trail turns left at the fence and goes up the shoulder of Mars Hill. At 0.7 miles *1.12 km* you reach a point where the old road to Lowell Observatory turns left. There are signs here. Go straight ahead. You will climb some more, to the 0.8 mile *1.28 km* point, where you top out. From there the trail is level to the end. The trail terminates at a road junction at 1.5 miles *2.4 km*, on top of Observatory Mesa.
The old road you follow for the first 0.7 miles *1.12 km* was built by the Town of Flagstaff about 1894 as part of the town's inducements to get Dr. Percival Lowell to locate his observatory in Flagstaff. Lowell was checking

out several sites and had narrowed the list to a few contenders. Tucson was another hot prospect. Lowell sent scientist A. E. Douglass, who later was famed for developing the science of dendrochronology (tree ring dating), to investigate Flagstaff. The town fathers wined and dined Douglass and made such a favorable impression on him that he told Lowell Flagstaff was the place. The boosters promised Lowell that he could have his choice of ten acres of land free anywhere in the town and that the town would also build a road to the site for him. Lowell picked land at the top of the hill and the town obligingly built this road. The road has been relocated twice since then.

Lowell Observatory has been a magnificent asset for Flagstaff, crowned by the discovery there of the planet Pluto in 1930 by Clyde Tombaugh, who was working out some of Lowell's old theories. Lowell died in 1916 in his mansion at the observatory (since torn down).

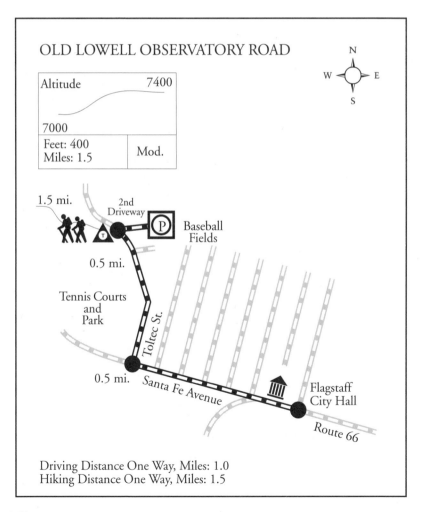

Mangum

OLD MUNDS HIGHWAY

General Information
Location Map G3
Stoneman Lake USGS Map
Coconino Forest Service Map

Driving Distance One Way: 29.5 miles *47.2 km* (Time 45 minutes)
Access Road: All cars, Last 2.4 miles *3.84 km* good gravel road
Hiking Distance One Way: 4.0 miles *6.4 km* (Time 2.0 hours)
How Strenuous: Moderate
Features: Historic road, Interesting canyons, Views

NUTSHELL: This hike follows a closed portion of a road that linked the Verde Valley to Flagstaff.

DIRECTIONS:
From Flagstaff City Hall Go:
    West, then south on Route 66, then take Milton Road south to get onto I-17. See Access Map, page 10. Drive I-17 to the 27.1 miles *43.4 km* point, Exit 315, Rocky Park (MP 315.9). Take Exit 315 and make a left turn at the stop sign and go east. You will reach a T intersection. The gravel road to the left (north) is marked FR 127. Take the other fork, the one to your right. It is unmarked here, but it is FR 80, heading south. Follow FR 80 for 2.4 miles *3.84 km*, where it meets FR 239 coming in from your left (east). Park at this place.

TRAILHEAD: Where FR 80 meets FR 239 as described above.

DESCRIPTION: There is a gate across FR 80, with a sign reading: "Rattlesnake Quiet Area. Open to foot/horse/bicycle travel only from 8/15 to 12/31 to provide a non-motorized hunting/hiking/riding experience."
    We believe that this is the old Munds Highway that connected to the 1912 Blue Grade Road, which leads from the Stoneman Lake road to the Verde Valley.
    You will walk through a pine forest for about 0.8 miles *1.3 km*. The land slopes gently downward so that the walking is easy. Beyond the forest, you emerge into a zone where junipers predominate and the country opens up. You have sweeping views to the south from here. The road then drops through an open meadow, where it comes very close to I-17, which is on your right (west). It appears that during the construction of I-17 there was a crusher and materials operation in this open park. Walk over toward the highway and you will have a good view of the Sedona area.
    The road continues dropping through a juniper-piñon forest, following

the eastern edge of an unnamed canyon. You will see the larger Rattlesnake Canyon beyond it. At the 2.5 mile *4.0 km* point, you will reach a low wide ford across the side canyon, a pretty spot with lots of foliage.

Beyond this point, the road climbs, soon coming out into another open area. You continue to head south until you reach the place where the side canyon meets Rattlesnake Canyon. Here the road swings left (east), running parallel to the big canyon. You will cross Rattlesnake at a shallow point, then make a gentle climb.

The hike ends where the old road joins the modern paved Stoneman Lake Road. If you want to do a two-car shuttle, park the second car at a point on the Stoneman Lake Road that is 5.1 miles *8.2 km* from the Stoneman Lake Exit on I-17. See the map.

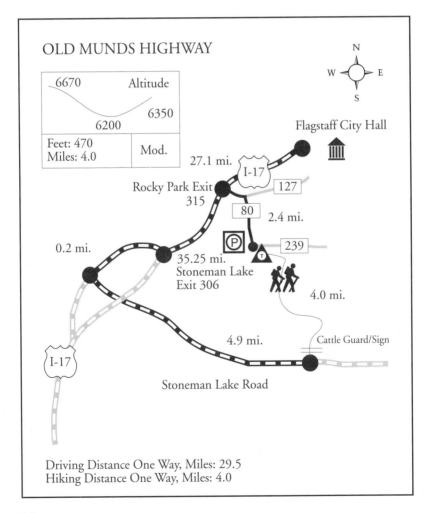

OLD MUNDS HIGHWAY

6670 Altitude
6350
6200

Feet: 470
Miles: 4.0   Mod.

Flagstaff City Hall

27.1 mi.
I-17
Rocky Park Exit
315
127
80   2.4 mi.
239
0.2 mi.
35.25 mi.
Stoneman Lake
Exit 306
4.0 mi.
I-17
4.9 mi.   Cattle Guard/Sign
Stoneman Lake Road

Driving Distance One Way, Miles: 29.5
Hiking Distance One Way, Miles: 4.0

Mangum

OLDHAM TRAIL NO. 1(#1)

General Information
Location Map E3
Flagstaff East and Flagstaff West USGS Maps
Coconino Forest Service Map

Driving Distance One Way: 2.3 miles *3.7 km* (Time 10 minutes)
Access Road: All cars, All paved
Hiking Distance One Way: 3.3 miles *5.28 km* (Time 1 hour 45 minutes)
How Strenuous: Moderate
Features: Views

NUTSHELL: This trail is part of a trail system developed by the Forest Service around Mt. Elden. Located just north of Flagstaff, this moderate hike takes you through a beautiful forest.

DIRECTIONS:
From Flagstaff City Hall Go:

North on Humphreys Street to the stoplight at 0.60 miles *1.0 km.* See Access Map, page 10. Turn right here onto Columbus Avenue and go one block east to the next stop sign, which is at Beaver Street. Turn left onto Beaver Street and go up the hill. At the 1.0 mile *1.6 km* point you will reach Forest Avenue. Turn right on Forest and follow it over a hill. On top of the hill, at 1.9 miles *3.04 km*, you will find Gemini Drive. Turn left onto it and at 2.3 miles *3.7 km* you will come to Buffalo Park. Park in the parking lot at Buffalo Park.

TRAILHEAD: There are trail signs and a map at the gate.

DESCRIPTION: The Forest Service has developed a trail system around the Mt. Elden\Dry Lake Hills areas in Flagstaff and this trail connects with others in that system. You will find trail information at the trailhead.

Buffalo Park is an open plain extending back about a half mile *0.8 km* from the gate. In the 1960s it was run as a sort of living zoo but failed due to lack of funds. You can see some vestiges of this operation near the entrance, where a welcoming arch and buffalo statue survive. Lately the City of Flagstaff has turned the area into a public park for joggers and walkers.

Oldham Trail No. 1 starts at the fence at the rear of the park. To reach it, stay on the main footpath from the gate, which is wide and gravelled, until you reach the natural gas substation and the back fence, at 0.5 miles *0.8 km.* Here the footpath goes through the fence, narrows and becomes The Oldham Trail.

The trail was originally developed by an old timer named Earl Oldham, who worked as a ranger for the Forest Service, was a member of the Coconino County Board of Supervisors and did some sheep ranching on the side. Busy fellow.

At. 1.25 miles *2.0 km* you will reach the junction of the Oldham Trail and the **Pipeline Trail**. The two trails are marked. If you just want a simple leisurely stroll, this is a good place to turn back. Up to this point the trail is gentle with little change in altitude. From here, the trail begins to climb.

After you have passed through Buffalo Park, you will be in a nice pine forest. Later the forest becomes more interesting as you hike through stands of oak, aspen, fir and spruce. Lava cliffs and groups of boulders big as box-cars that have tumbled from the cliffs are also interesting.

At 2.25 miles *3.6 km* you intersect a trail to the left. This is the **Rocky Ridge Trail**. The Oldham Trail ends at 3.3 miles *5.28 km*, where it meets the Elden Lookout Road, FR 557. Just before the road you will pass spectacular basalt cliffs loved by rock climbers.

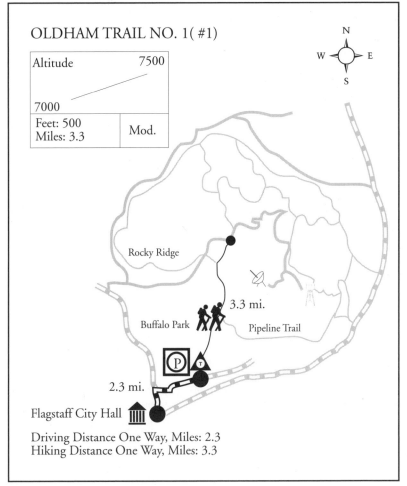

OLDHAM TRAIL NO. 1(#1)

Altitude	7500
7000	
Feet: 500 Miles: 3.3	Mod.

Rocky Ridge

3.3 mi.

Buffalo Park

Pipeline Trail

2.3 mi.

Flagstaff City Hall

Driving Distance One Way, Miles: 2.3
Hiking Distance One Way, Miles: 3.3

Mangum

OLDHAM TRAIL NO. 2

General Information
Location Map E3
Humphreys Peak & Sunset Crater West USGS Maps
Coconino Forest Service Map

Driving Distance One Way: 7.1 miles *11.36 km* (Time 30 minutes)
Access Road: All cars, Last 3.5 miles *5.6 km* medium unpaved road
Hiking Distance One Way: 1.75 miles *2.8 km* (Time 1 hour)
How Strenuous: Hard
Features: Views, Forests

NUTSHELL: This is a marked and maintained trail that starts at a point on the Elden Lookout Road near the top of Mt. Elden north of Flagstaff and climbs to Sunset Park.

DIRECTIONS:
From Flagstaff City Hall Go:
North on Humphreys Street for 0.60 miles *1.0 km*. See Access Map, page 10. Turn left at the stoplight onto Columbus Avenue and follow it around a big curve to the north. You will see the street signs call this road Columbus Avenue at first, then Ft. Valley Road and then Highway 180. Stay on Highway 180 to the 3.1 miles *5.0 km* point (MP 218.6), where the Schultz Pass Road, FR 420, goes to the right. Follow this road. At the 3.6 miles *5.76 km* point it curves left where you will see the unpaved Elden Lookout Road (FR 557) going straight. Take the right fork and follow FR 557 to the 7.1 mile *11.36 km* point, where you will park in an area off the left shoulder.

TRAILHEAD: Across the road from the parking place.

DESCRIPTION: This trail is part of the Dry Lake Hills/Mt. Elden trail system, so it is marked and maintained. You will follow an old road for the first 0.75 miles *1.2 km*. The climb on this stretch of the trail is gradual and doesn't really prepare you for the steep climb that is to follow. This part of the trail takes you through a dense spruce forest. Some of the trees have so much moss on their sides that you'd think you were in a rain forest.

The old road ends where it bumps up against the flank of Mt. Elden. From there a footpath climbs the mountain. This second part of the trail is very steep, really a hard climb. It also passes through a heavy forest. The trees are so thick that you don't get many views even though you are climbing high enough to have excellent vantage points.

Near the end of the trail you will come out into an open meadow called Oldham Park. You will cross it and reach the Elden Lookout Road at a place that is 2.3 miles *3.68 km* up the road from where you parked. This is officially the end of the trail, but you will miss a splendid view if you stop here. Go across the road up to the skyline where you will see two trail signs. This place is Sunset Park. You can walk along the crest in either direction to enjoy the views.

The views from the top are excellent due to the Radio Fire that burned away many acres of timber in 1978. This was a terrible fire and we remember it well. Started by a teenager's campfire on a dry, windy June day, the fire roared up a canyon, burst over the top and raged out of control for days. At night Mt. Elden looked like a huge heap of glowing embers.

Our text depicts the trail as planned by the Forest Service. However, we think that this is a much better hike if you use two cars. Park one at the 7.1 mile *11.36 km* point and take the other one to the top and park it at the 9.4 miles *15.0 km* point. Then you start the hike from the top.

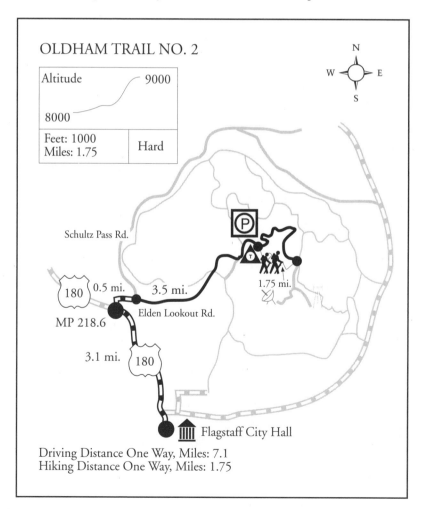

OLDHAM TRAIL NO. 2

Altitude — 9000

8000

| Feet: 1000 Miles: 1.75 | Hard |

Schultz Pass Rd.

180 0.5 mi. 3.5 mi.

1.75 mi.

MP 218.6 Elden Lookout Rd.

3.1 mi. 180

Flagstaff City Hall

Driving Distance One Way, Miles: 7.1
Hiking Distance One Way, Miles: 1.75

Mangum

168

OTT LAKE

General Information
Location Map F2
Sycamore Point USGS Map
Coconino Forest Service Map

Driving Distance One Way: 26.3 miles *42 km* (Time 1 hour)
Access Road: All cars, Last 22.7 miles *36.3 km* dirt roads, rough spots
Hiking Distance One Way: 2.5 miles *4.0 km* (Time 1.5 hours)
How Strenuous: Moderate
Features: Views, Sycamore Canyon access, Cabin

NUTSHELL: Located 26.3 miles *42 km* southwest of Flagstaff, Ott Lake is located in a hidden pocket adjacent to an access trail into Sycamore Canyon. There is an interesting cabin in an idyllic glade in the middle of this hike.

DIRECTIONS:
From Flagstaff City Hall Go:
    West, then south on Route 66 beneath the railroad overpass. See Access Map, page 10. At 0.50 miles *0.8 km* turn right on Route 66. At 2.6 miles *4.16 km* you will reach the Woody Mountain Road, FR 231, going to the left. Take it. It is paved 1.0 miles *1.6 km* and then turns into a cinder road. At 16.6 miles *26.56 km* you will intersect FR 538. Turn right onto FR 538 and follow it to the 22.3 mile *35.7 km* point, a T junction. Turn left, still on FR 538, and drive to the 25.7 mile *41.1 km* point, where it intersects FR 538H. Turn right on FR 538H and go to its end at 26.3 miles *42 km*. FR 538H is rather rough. Park at the end of the road.

TRAILHEAD: You will see a sign for the **Winter Cabin Trail** at the parking area.

DESCRIPTION: For the first leg of this hike, you will take the trail to Winter Cabin. This drops 600 feet, but the trail is engineered so that the grade is moderate. The trail is wide, easy to follow, and passes through a pleasant forest.
    Forest Service signs show the distance to Winter Cabin as 1.5 miles *2.4 km*. Our measurement was 1.1 miles *1.8 km*. The cabin is an old log cowboy relic with a corrugated metal roof, and is still in good condition. It is hard to tell how the place got its name, Winter Cabin, because one can't imagine cowboys surviving the winter here. Heavy snows fall in this area and once the snow season begins in the autumn, this place would be totally cut off from the outside world.
    There are trail signs at the cabin, showing the distance to Ott Lake as 1.5

Flagstaff Hikes

miles *2.4 km*. Take the Ott Lake Trail, going left (southwest). This trail seems to move more sideways than downhill, though it drops 300 feet, most of it toward its end. At the halfway point you will break out of the forest into an open area, giving splendid views of wild, rugged country. At 1.2 miles *1.9 km* you will reach to the fork to Ott Lake. The sign was down when we were here, leaving only the post. The trail goes uphill to your right (NW), to a gap between two hills, where you can see pine trees. You will hike 0.2 miles *0.32 km,* coming down into a hidden scenic basin. The lake is usually dry.

The main trail goes another 2.0 miles *3.2 km* into the bottom of Sycamore Canyon, a long steep haul—too much for a pleasant day hike.

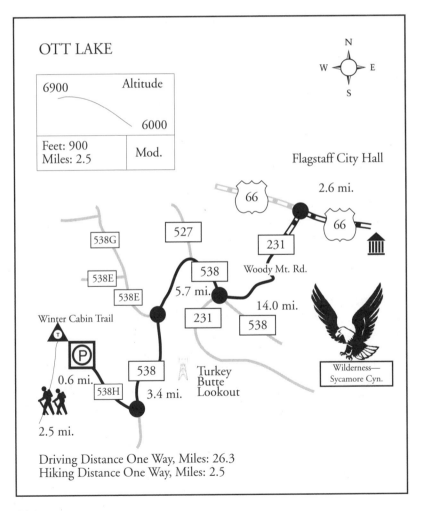

OVERLAND ROAD

General Information
Location Map E2
Bill Williams Mountain USGS Map
Kaibab (Williams District) Forest Service Map

Driving Distance One Way: 40.7 miles *65 km* (Time 60 minutes)
Access Road: All cars, Last 0.3 miles *0.48 km* good gravel road
Hiking Distance One Way: 6.0 miles *9.6 km* (Time 3.0 hours)
How Strenuous: Moderate
Features: Historic road, Cabin ruins

NUTSHELL: This hike takes you over a portion of the 1863 Overland Road, south of Williams.

DIRECTIONS:
From Flagstaff City Hall Go:
    West, then south on Route 66 under the railroad overpass. See Access Map, page 10. Follow Route 66 when it turns right at the second stoplight. In about five miles *8.0 km* you will merge onto I-40 West and stay on it to the 30.3 miles *48.5 km* point, the Williams Exit, #165. Take that exit and at the stop sign go left to Williams. Go into town on Railroad Avenue to the 32.9 mile point *52.6 km* where you will find Fourth Street. Turn left on Fourth Street. As it leaves town its name changes to the Perkinsville Road (FR 173). Stay on this road to the 40.4 miles *64.6 km* point, where you turn left onto FR 139. Take FR 139 to the 40.7 mile *65 km* point, where you will see a 4 x 4 post on the right side of the road with the burro symbol burned into it. Park there.

TRAILHEAD: The burro post is at the mouth of an old road. Hike the road.

DESCRIPTION: Gold was discovered in Prescott in 1863 and with the ensuing gold rush there came a clamor for a north-south road. The sensible way to approach this was to use the 1859 Beale Road as far as possible and then branch off of it to the south. This was done and the resulting road was called the Overland Road. After the railroad arrived in 1882, few people used the Overland Road and it was abandoned.
    For the first 0.85 miles *1.36 km* of this hike you will walk along a newer road that was laid on top of the Overland Road. You will find that the path is marked with posts, cairns and blazes. Every quarter of a mile there is a brass cap. You will pass Deadhorse Tank and go across a meadow and up the shoulder of a hill. The increase in elevation is gradual and most of the time thereafter the trail hugs the 7000 foot contour line.

At 3.1 miles *4.96 km* you will come to a clearing where you will find the ruins of a cabin. This was a way station called Big Spring. The spring forms a pool in the canyon behind the cabin. The trail swerves to the head of the canyon, crosses it and then comes back and begins a gradual descent.

At 4.75 miles *7.6 km* you will come upon a big meadow with an old barn, a cabin made of railroad ties and a pond. This place is the historic Whiting Ranch. There is a modern camp called Boys' Ranch nearby. From the Whiting Ranch you walk to the end of the meadow, where the trail intersects FR 109. We stop the trail here because this makes a nice day hike. We recommend doing this as a two-car hike, parking one at the beginning and one at the end.

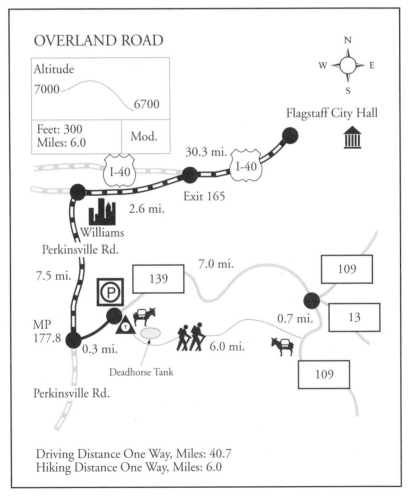

PIPELINE TRAIL

General Information
Location Map F3
Flagstaff East and Flagstaff West USGS Maps
Coconino Forest Service Map

Driving Distance One Way: 2.3 miles *3.7 km* (Time 10 minutes)
Access Road: All cars, All paved
Hiking Distance One Way: 4.0 miles *6.4 km* (Time 2 hours)
How Strenuous: Moderate
Features: Views

NUTSHELL: This trail is part of a trail system developed by the Forest Service around Mt. Elden. Located just north of Flagstaff, this moderate hike takes you around the base of Mt. Elden to connect with the Elden Lookout trailhead in East Flagstaff.

DIRECTIONS:
From Flagstaff City Hall Go:
   North on Humphreys Street to the stoplight at 0.60 miles *1.0 km*. See Access Map, page 10. Turn right here onto Columbus Avenue and go one block east to the next stop sign, which is at Beaver Street. Turn left onto Beaver Street and go up the hill. At the 1.0 mile *1.6 km* point you will reach Forest Avenue. Turn right on Forest and follow it over a hill. On top of the hill, at 1.9 miles *3.0 km*, you will find Gemini Drive. Turn left onto it and at 2.3 miles *3.7 km* you will come to Buffalo Park. Park in the parking lot at the park.

TRAILHEAD: There are trail signs and a map at the gate in the parking lot fence.

DESCRIPTION: The Forest Service has developed a trail system around the Dry Lake Hills\Mt. Elden areas in Flagstaff and this trail connects with others in that system. You will find trail information at the trailhead.
   Buffalo Park is an open plain extending back about a half mile *0.8 km* from the gate. In the 1960s it was run as a sort of living zoo but failed due to lack of funds. You can see some vestiges of this operation near the entrance, where a welcoming arch and buffalo statue survive. Lately the City of Flagstaff has turned the area into a public park for joggers and walkers.
   Start by taking the main jogging path which goes straight back to the fence at the rear of the park. It is wide and graveled, until you reach the natural gas substation and the rear fence, at 0.50 miles *0.8 km*. Here the trail goes through the fence, narrows and becomes the **Oldham Trail No. 1**.

Hike the Oldham Trail No. 1 to the 1.25 miles *2.0 km* point where you will reach the junction of the Oldham Trail and the **Pipeline Trail**. The two trails are marked. Turn right here onto the Pipeline Trail.

Although the trail comes very close to some houses as you get into East Flagstaff, it feels quite remote in places. At about the 1.75 mile *2.8 km* point there is a side trail going to the left. Someone has painted "Satan's Cave" on a boulder there. It is a short jaunt over to the cave and worth taking a look.

The Pipeline Trail comes close to many interesting boulder formations, with intriguing caves and crannies. Mt. Elden is essentially a giant lava pile and the lava did some interesting things as it settled and cooled.

The trail terminates at a place where it links with the **Elden Lookout Trail** in East Flagstaff. A good way to do this hike is to use a two-car shuttle. Park one car at Buffalo Park and the other at the Elden Lookout trailhead parking lot in East Flagstaff.

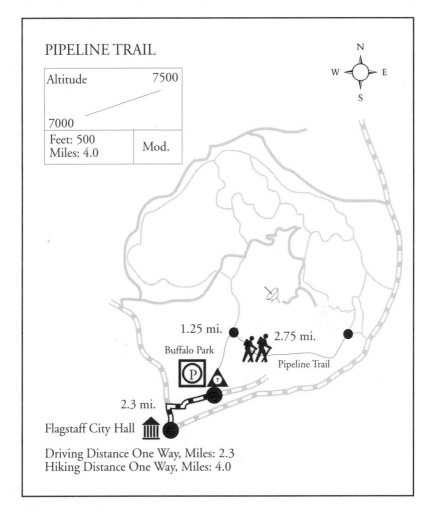

Mangum

PIVOT ROCK CANYON/WILDCAT SPRING

General Information
Location Map G4
Pine, Calloway Butte USGS Maps
Coconino Forest Service Map

Driving Distance One Way: 65.7 miles *105.12 km* (Time 1.25 hours)
Access Road: All cars, Last 3.35 miles *5.36 km* good dirt road
Hiking Distance One Way: **Pivot Rock**: 1.5 mi. *2.4 km* (1 hour), **Wildcat**:
   1.4 mi. *2.24 km* (1 hour)
How Strenuous: Both hikes are Easy
Features: Beautiful pristine stream, Rain forest, Remote canyon

NUTSHELL: Starting from the same point, both hikes take you along hidden canyons located in the Mogollon Rim area, just south of Clint's Well. You follow little streams through lush canyons.

DIRECTIONS:
From Flagstaff City Hall Go:
   West, then south on Route 66, under the railroad overpass. At 0.5 miles *0.8 km*, go straight on Milton Road. See Access Map, page 10. At 1.7 miles *2.72 km* you will reach a stoplight at Forest Meadows Street. Turn right here onto Forest Meadows and go one block to Beulah. Turn left on Beulah and follow it south. Beulah merges onto Highway 89A. At 2.4 miles *3.84 km* (MP 401.6), turn left onto the Lake Mary Road. Follow the Lake Mary Road (also known as FH 3) to its end at the junction with State Route 87, 56.6 miles *90.6 km*. Turn right here on Highway 87, a paved road, and follow it to the 62.35 mile *99.76 km* point (MP 284.7), where you turn right on FR 616, which is posted. FR 616 is surfaced with gravel and is a good road. Follow it to the 65.7 mile *105.12 km* point, where you will see a little campground downhill to your right. Turn down into this and park.

TRAILHEAD: Pivot Rock: At the far end the campground, notice a blocked road. This is the entrance to the trail. **Wildcat**: Just before you drive down into the campground, there is a closed road to your left. This closed road is the Wildcat Spring trail .

DESCRIPTION: Pivot Rock: You hike along a closed road through a green and wonderful canyon. The road ends and a foot path goes down to creek level. There is water in the creek most of the time. At the end of a mile *1.6 km*, the plant life thins out. You will reach the end of the hike at 1.5 miles *2.4 km*, where you will find the ruins of a log cabin on a bench of land.
   We have seen many cabin sites, but this has to rate as one of the finest.

The trail continues, but becomes less interesting. We followed it down to the 2.5 mile *4.0 km* point, before deciding that ending the hike at the cabin was perfect.

Wildcat Spring: As you enter this little canyon, you will be walking on a closed road. In 0.15 miles, *0.24 km*, you will reach a fork. Go downhill on the lower, dimmer road. You will soon see another road going uphill to your right. Stay down on the canyon bottom, where you will pick up a foot path at stream level.

For the next 0.5 miles *0.8 km*, you will walk through a beautiful little rain forest—yes, it's possible, even in dry Arizona. At the 0.7 mile *1.12 km* point, the foot path merges with the old road and you will walk the road to the end. You will reach Wildcat Spring at the 1.4 mile *2.24 km* point. There was a sign for the spring when we made the hike. It is to your left, uphill a bit, and is channeled into a concrete box.

The spring is the place to stop, though the road goes a bit farther.

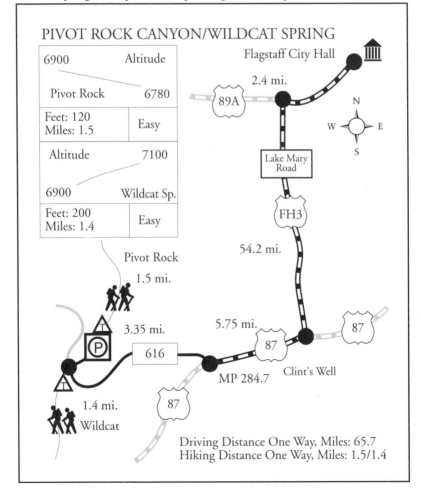

Mangum

PUMPKIN TRAIL #39

General Information
Location Map E2
Kendrick Peak, Moritz Ridge and Wing Mt. USGS Maps
Coconino Forest Service Map

Driving Distance One Way: 25.7 miles *41.12 km* (Time 1 hour)
Access Road: All cars, Last 11.2 miles *17.92 km* good gravel road
Hiking Distance One Way: 5.5 miles *8.8 km* (Time 4.0 hours)
How Strenuous: Hard
Features: Ten thousand foot peak, Views

NUTSHELL: Located 25.7 miles *41.12 km* north of Flagstaff, Kendrick Peak is next tallest to the San Francisco Peaks. This trail switchbacks to the summit where you get great views.

DIRECTIONS:
From Flagstaff City Hall Go:
   North on Humphreys Street for 0.60 miles *1.0 km*. See Access Map, page 10. Turn left at the stoplight onto Columbus Avenue and follow it around a big curve to the north. You will see the street signs call this road Columbus at first, then Ft. Valley Road and then Highway 180. Stay on Highway 180 to the 14.5 miles *23.2 km* point (MP 230), where an unpaved road takes off to the left. Turn left onto this road, FR 245, and follow it to the 17.6 mile *28.16 km* point where it intersects FR 171. Turn right on FR 171 and follow it to the 24.8 mile *39.7 km* point, where you will see a sign for the Pumpkin Trail. Turn right on the drive to the trailhead, which you will reach at 25.7 miles *41.12 km*. Park in the parking area.

TRAILHEAD: Well marked with a sign at the parking area.

DESCRIPTION: Unlike the nearby **Kendrick Mt. Trail,** which was made to provide access to a fire lookout tower by the Forest Service and was consequently engineered and built with an eye to making best use of the terrain, the Pumpkin Trail seems to have been built by and for sheepherders and just grew like topsy. It is rough and has some very sharp grades.
   From the parking lot you will climb along the side of a canyon for 1.0 miles *1.6 km* to a fence. Here you will turn right and begin going up a ridge. At 1.4 miles *2.24 km* you will meet the **Connector Trail** coming over from the **Bull Basin Trail.**
   Not far from this intersection you will climb into a more interesting forest, with many varieties of conifers and lots of aspens. The trail gets very rocky and rough in this stretch. At about 3.0 miles *4.8 km* you will find

breaks in the forests punctuated by meadows. The meadows provide good viewpoints, though the footing can be hard due to the fact that the grass in the meadows hides the rocks along the trail.

From the 4.0 mile *6.4 km* point the trail gets really steep and is hard going. You will reach the ruins of a log cabin at 5.0 miles *8.0 km* located at the edge of the biggest meadow. The slope of this meadow falls away so steeply that they must have issued spiked shoes to the sheep.

Beyond this meadow the trail becomes primitive and even harder, clawing its way to the top just below the base of the lookout tower at 5.5 miles *8.8 km*. Go on up to the tower for its superlative views.

This is a much harder trail than the Kendrick Mt. Trail or Bull Basin Trail. We think Bull Basin is the best of the three trails to the top, with the Kendrick Mountain Trail being next best.

A ranch near the trailhead is named Pumpkin Center, and there was a time when pumpkins were grown there.

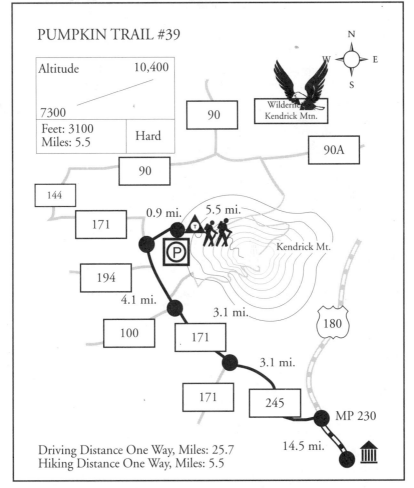

Mangum

RED BUTTE

General Information
Location Map C2
Red Butte USGS Map
Kaibab (Tusayan) Forest Service Map

Driving Distance One Way: 63.6 miles *102 km* (Time 90 minutes)
Access Road: All cars, Last 2.7 miles *4.3 km* good dirt road
Hiking Distance One Way: 1.2 miles *1.92 km* (Time 45 minutes)
How Strenuous: Moderate
Features: Unusual formation, Views of Grand Canyon country

NUTSHELL: This mountain stands alone near the Grand Canyon. A good trail makes a moderate climb worthwhile to enjoy the view.

DIRECTIONS:
From Flagstaff City Hall Go:
    North on Humphreys Street 0.60 miles *1.0 km* to a stoplight. See Access Map, page 10. Go left on Columbus Avenue and follow the curve north. Street signs will show the street first as Ft. Valley Road, then Highway 180. This is a major road to the Grand Canyon. At 50.4 miles *80.64 km* (MP 265.8), you will intersect Highway 64, coming out of Williams, at a place called Valle. Go right at this junction. At 60.9 miles *97.44 km* (MP 224), you will see a dirt road to the right. Turn right here. On our last trip there were no signs. At 62.3 miles *99.7 km*, you turn left. At 63.2 miles *101.1 km*, you go right. At 63.6 miles *102 km* you will be at the parking lot.

TRAILHEAD: This is a marked, maintained trail with signs.

DESCRIPTION: Although it is a small mountain for Northern Arizona, Red Butte dominates its area. Geologists speculate that because it had a thicker lava cap than the surrounding lands had, everything else eroded away, leaving Red Butte at the original ground level.
    On the south side of Red Butte you can see some red cliffs with white cliffs above them, capped by gray lava rock. These strata form interesting layers. The red stone is the Moenkopi formation, which abounds in Flagstaff. The county courthouse in Flagstaff was built of the stone in the 1890s, as were many other landmark Flagstaff buildings of that era. There was even a lively turn-of-the-century sandstone quarrying industry in Flagstaff to exploit the stone.
    The trail was built in 1976-77 and is well designed. Rather than trying to go straight up the mountain, it zigzags. The climb is fairly gradual at first, then gets steep going to the top. The trail takes you to the edge of the red

cliffs and then veers away from them.

The area at the top is small, about four acres, and bald, so that there are good views all around. Unfortunately, you can't see into the Grand Canyon.—you can only see the cliffs of the North Rim and the line of the South Rim. The best views are to the East, where you see the San Francisco Peaks and a long line of lesser mountains and hills. The land around Red Butte is a flat plain and the vegetation on it is sparse. You can see signs of cattle ranching activity. Decades ago when the sheep raising business was at its zenith, there would be many hundreds of sheep quartered on this plateau.

There is a fire lookout on top, and you can climb it and walk along its deck for the best views. Twenty minutes spent looking at the landscape from there is a better geology lesson than many hours in the classroom.

There is a helicopter landing pad at the top if you are a member of the jet set.

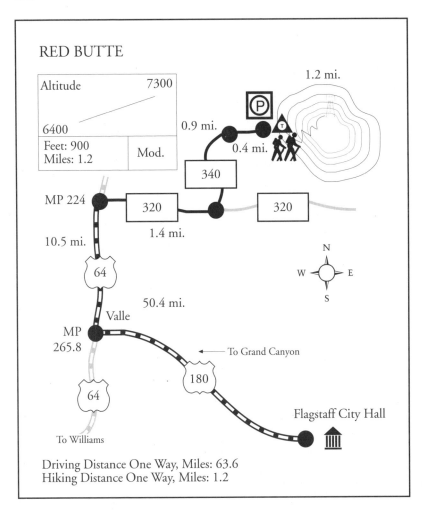

RED MOUNTAIN

General Information
Location Map D2
Ebert Mountain USGS Map
Coconino Forest Service Map

Driving Distance One Way: 31.7 miles *50.72 km* (Time 40 minutes)
Access Road: All cars, Last 0.3 miles *0.48 km* good gravel road
Hiking Distance One Way: 1.25 miles *2.0 km* (Time 40 minutes)
How Strenuous: Moderate
Features: Unique experience—you go into the heart of a cutaway volcano

NUTSHELL: Located 31.7 miles *50.72 km* north of Flagstaff, this moderate hike takes you into the heart of Red Mountain to enjoy its otherworldly sculptures and formations. **A personal favorite.**

DIRECTIONS:
From Flagstaff City Hall Go:
   North on Humphreys Street for 0.60 miles *1.0 km*. See Access Map, page 10. Turn left at the stoplight onto Columbus Avenue and follow it around a big curve to the north. You will see the street signs call this road Columbus at first, then Ft. Valley Road and then Highway 180. Stay on Highway 180 to the 31.4 miles *50.24 km* point (MP 247), where an unpaved road, FR 9032V, takes off to the left. You will see a sign reading, "Red Mountain Geological Area." Turn left onto FR 9032V and follow it to the 31.7 mile *50.72 km* point, where there is a parking lot.

TRAILHEAD: The trailhead is the gate at the parking lot.

DESCRIPTION: The Forest Service has done some nice work on this trail. When we first did this hike in 1985 there was no trail and hikers had to thread their way through a maze of bad roads. The trail is now well maintained and easy to follow. Look for white plastic diamonds nailed to trees; these mark the path.
   Your objective will have been in sight for miles. Red Mountain looks just like hundreds of other cinder hills in the area north of Flagstaff except for one thing: its east face is sheared off cleanly, as if someone had done a cross-section of it to expose its red innards. Geologists tell us that all red cinder hills are like this in their interior.
   This is juniper country and the land is pretty flat. It is an easy walk though the trail rises constantly. At 0.75 miles *1.2 km* the trail leaves the old road it has been following and goes into the bed of a wash. This makes for fine walking as the bed is hard sand, and it makes a perfect entrance into Red

Mountain. As you come nearer, the streambed becomes the bottom of a V flanked by high black cinder shoulders. Then you see some strange black lava formations forming a sort of gate at the entrance to the insides of the mountain. The area has an Easter Island appearance of mystery.

At the 1.2 mile *1.92 km* point, you will see a rock dam full of silt. You can climb up the dam (our route) or go up the black cinders to your right. Once on top, you are in a basin surrounded by weird hoodoos. You don't see black lava on the inside. The prevailing color is red. You will also see an unexpected mustard colored rock in the lower formations. The place is like a mini-Bryce Canyon.

Once on the inside, the trail disappears. No worries. You can explore all around, enjoying the colors, shapes, play of light and other features that make this place so special. You feel cut off from the world. Everywhere you look there is something to delight your eye.

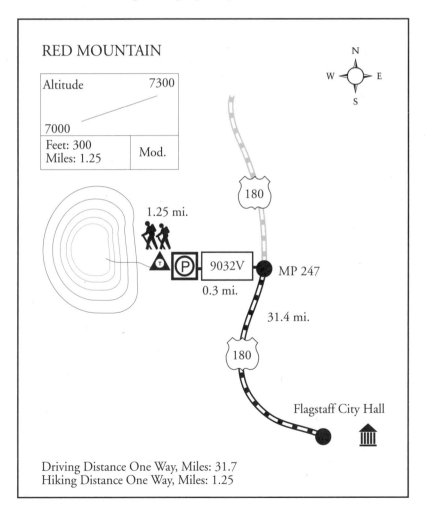

RED MOUNTAIN

Altitude	7300
7000	
Feet: 300 Miles: 1.25	Mod.

N
W ← → E
S

180

1.25 mi.

9032V — MP 247

0.3 mi.

31.4 mi.

180

Flagstaff City Hall

Driving Distance One Way, Miles: 31.7
Hiking Distance One Way, Miles: 1.25

Mangum

RIO DE FLAG TRAIL

General Information
Location Map F3
Flagstaff West USGS Map
Coconino Forest Service Map

Driving Distance One Way: 1.2 miles *1.92 km* (Time 5 minutes)
Access Road: All cars, All paved
Hiking Distance One Way: 1.2 miles *1.92 km* (Time 30 minutes)
How Strenuous: Easy
Features: Urban trail

NUTSHELL: This urban trail in south Flagstaff is a pleasant 1.2 mile *1.92 km* walk.

DIRECTIONS:
From Flagstaff City Hall Go:
   East on Route 66 for one block. Turn right on Beaver Street and go south four blocks to Butler Avenue, where there is a stoplight. Turn left on Butler Avenue and follow it east for five blocks to Lone Tree Street (stoplight). Turn right on Lone Tree Street and follow it four blocks south to Brannen Circle. Turn left onto Brannen Circle and then immediately turn to your left on a graveled apron. Park on the apron.

TRAILHEAD: This is a marked and maintained trail. You will see it dipping down into the canyon from the parking area.

DESCRIPTION: Flagstaff is developing an ambitious system of urban trails. This trail shares a common trailhead with the **Sinclair Wash Trail**, which goes west from the parking lot, toward the Northern Arizona University campus, while the Rio de Flag Trail goes east toward a shallow canyon. The Rio de Flag trail was opened in the fall of 1989. The Sinclair Wash Trail was added to the trail system in the fall of 1990 and extended in 1991.
   The trail follows an old road. A row of boulders across the entrance now keeps vehicles from the road, as this path is for pedestrian use (and bicycles) only. The trail follows along the course of the whimsically named Rio de Flag as it curves and recurves along a canyon. The rio's streambed is usually dry, containing water only after the spring snowmelt in April or May or after a summer cloudburst of rain.
   The trail is built mostly above the bottom and the riverbed (riobed?) has been banked and channeled so that the trail should stay dry except in the time of a truly major flood.

The trail is the width of a single lane road and has been graded and surfaced so that the footing is very good.

After the first two hundred yards, you pass out of sight of habitation. Although you are surrounded by industry on the north and residences on the south, the canyon is deep enough so that you don't see any of this and it feels as if you are out in the country.

The walls of the canyon are mostly a buff colored limestone, some of which was crushed to make the surface for the trail. This sedimentary rock is a fairly soft stone that formed in layers. As these layers have eroded they have made ledges. Here and there you will find some interesting formations.

At the end of the hike you are jarred when you come out of the canyon to find that you are under the roaring traffic of Interstate 40 on bridges high overhead at the 1.2 mile *1.92 km* point. Just beyond the second bridge is a sewage treatment plant This is an unwelcome return to "civilization" after a rustic respite.

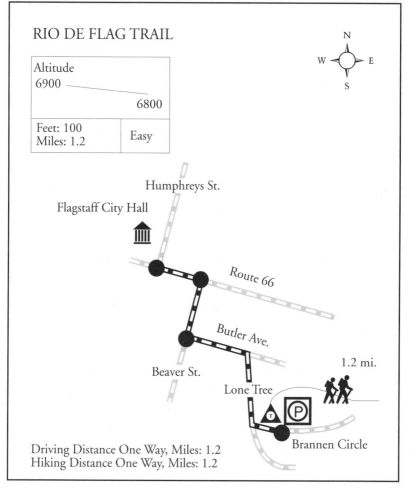

RIO DE FLAG TRAIL

Altitude
6900
                6800

Feet: 100
Miles: 1.2   Easy

Humphreys St.

Flagstaff City Hall

Route 66

Butler Ave.

Beaver St.

Lone Tree

1.2 mi.

Brannen Circle

Driving Distance One Way, Miles: 1.2
Hiking Distance One Way, Miles: 1.2

Mangum

ROCKY RIDGE TRAIL #153

General Information
Location Map E3
Humphreys Peak & Flagstaff West USGS Maps
Coconino Forest Service Map

Driving Distance One Way: 3.9 miles *6.24 km* (Time 20 minutes)
Access Road: All cars, Last .25 miles *0.4 km* medium gravel road
Hiking Distance One Way: 3.0 miles *4.8 km* (Time 1.5 hours)
How Strenuous: Moderate
Features: Shady forest in the hills

NUTSHELL: This is a marked and maintained trail that hugs the base of the south face of the Dry Lake Hills about 4 miles *6.4 km* north of Flagstaff and goes from the Schultz Pass Road to the Elden Lookout Road.

DIRECTIONS:
From Flagstaff City Hall Go:
    North on Humphreys Street for 0.60 miles *1.0 km*. See Access Map, page 10. Turn left at the stoplight onto Columbus Avenue and follow it around a big curve to the north. You will see the street signs call this road Columbus Avenue at first, then Ft. Valley Road and then Highway 180. Stay on Highway 180 to the 3.1 miles *5.0 km* point (MP 218.6), where the Schultz Pass Road, FR 420, goes to the right. Follow the Schultz Pass Road. As it starts around a curve to the left, at the 3.6 miles *5.76 km* point, you will see the unpaved Elden Lookout Road going straight. Ignore this and stay on the paved road. The paving will end soon and the road will become gravel. At the 3.9 miles *6.24 km* point, you will see a gate, which closes the road in winter. Just beyond the gate is FR 9128Y which goes downhill to your right. Take this. At the bottom turn left and follow the road a few yards to a fence, where you park.

TRAILHEAD: You will see a wooden sign for the Rocky Ridge Trail in the fence opening to your right.

DESCRIPTION: This trail starts at the same place that the **Schultz Creek Trail** ends. There are two distinct openings in the fence for the respective trails. They are both signed.
    The trail climbs gradually until it reaches a point about three hundred feet higher than the beginning and then pretty well holds that contour. You will walk through a pine forest which is so thick that you are able to get only a few views through the trees. You will see Buffalo Park and the NAU campus clearly, but most of Flagstaff is below a mesa that cuts off your view of

the town.

The trail takes you around the west toe of the Dry Lake Hills and then follows along their south face. From the one mile point onward you will be aware that the Elden Lookout Road is nearby on your right. Sometimes you can only hear sounds coming from it, while in other places you can see the road and will be a stone's throw from it. Mountain bikers love the road and many of them use the Rocky Ridge Trail as well.

The trail ends where it intersects the Elden Lookout Road at a point that is 3.0 miles *4.8 km* from its beginning.

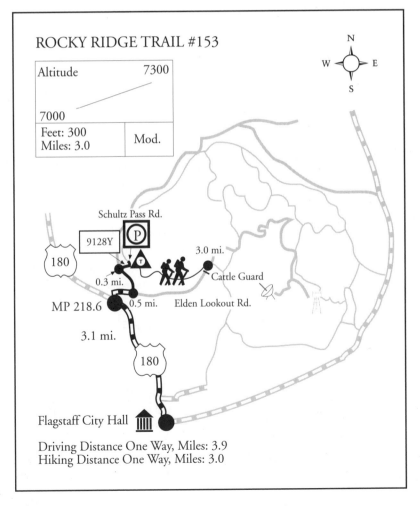

ROCKY RIDGE TRAIL #153

Altitude 7300
7000
Feet: 300
Miles: 3.0
Mod.

9128Y
180
0.3 mi.
Schultz Pass Rd.
3.0 mi.
Cattle Guard
Elden Lookout Rd.
0.5 mi.
MP 218.6
3.1 mi.
180
Flagstaff City Hall

Driving Distance One Way, Miles: 3.9
Hiking Distance One Way, Miles: 3.0

Mangum

ROUTE 66

ROUTE 66

General Information
Location Map E2
Parks USGS Map
Kaibab Forest Service Map

Driving Distance One Way: 18.6 miles *29.76 km* (Time 30 minutes)
Access Road: All cars, Last 0.5 miles *0.8 km* good gravel road
Hiking Distance One Way: 0.75 miles *1.2 km* (Time 30 minutes)
How Strenuous: Easy
Features: Walk along a 1931 portion (now closed) of fabled Route 66.

NUTSHELL: A closed strip of Route 66 near Parks has been turned into a hiking trail. You make an easy walk through a pleasant forest to enjoy a bit of history, then drive the old road.

DIRECTIONS:
From Flagstaff City Hall Go:
    West, then south on Route 66, beneath the railroad overpass. See Access Map, page 10. At 0.50 miles *0.8 km* go right Route 66. You will soon leave town. At the 4.8 mile *7.68 km* point you will merge onto Interstate-40 West. Drive I-40 West to the Parks Exit 178 at the 18.0 mile *28.8 km* point, and take it. Turn right and go up to the next stop sign, which intersects old Route 66. Turn right and drive to the 18.6 mile *29.76 km* point, where you will see a signed parking area to your left. The road will change from paved to gravel-surfaced.

DESCRIPTION: Route 66 came through this area from its first days, but over the years engineers changed its right-of-way in the Williams area, constantly looking for a better, more manageable path. The bit of paved road that still goes by the Parks Store is the 1941 alignment and was used until 1-40 was built in 1964. You will walk the 1931 alignment when you make this hike.
    This little walk starts near the top of 49 Hill. Just east of here was the point where Highway 66 crested at the top of 49 Hill, the absolute high point of Route 66 in its many thousands of miles, and the old cars really strained to pull this grade. Because of the steepness, engineers changed the alignment in the area to go around a flank of 49 Hill instead of over its top.
    You will walk along a disused stretch of old 66 that runs straight downhill. The old pavement survives most of the way, but it is crumbling. At about the 0.5 mile *0.8 km* point you will see a funky stone building to your left. It was a spring house that provided water to a Forest Service campground. The hike ends near the present paved road, at a point where the 1941

route meets the 1931 route. There are a couple of concrete culverts showing how the roads merged here.

When you finish the hike, we suggest that you drive back to Flagstaff on the old highway rather than Interstate 40. You will pass through scenic Brannigan Park, once an active farming area. To do this, keep driving east beyond the trailhead parking spot. At 5.0 miles *8.0 km* from the parking area you will find an interpretive sign to your left at a pullout marked by a pole fence. At about 7.4 miles *12.0 km* you will come to Bellemont, where you re-enter Interstate 40.

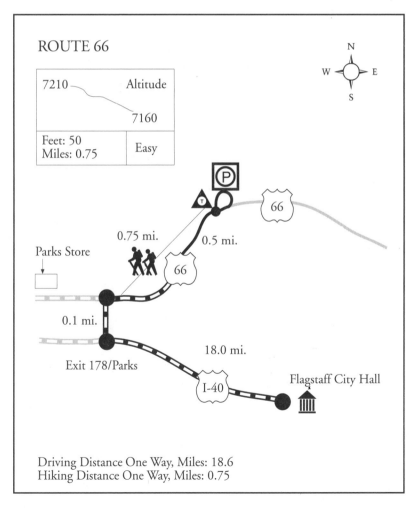

SP CRATER

General Information
Location Map D3
East of SP Mtn., SP Mtn. USGS Maps
Coconino Forest Service Map

Driving Distance One Way: 38.7 miles *61.9 km* (Time 1 hour)
Access Road: All cars, Last 6.5 miles *10.4 km* medium unpaved road
Hiking Distance One Way: 0.5 miles *0.8 km* (Time 1 hour)
How Strenuous: Moderate
Features: Volcano and lava field in midst of volcano belt

NUTSHELL: Located north of Flagstaff in flat country studded with volcanoes, this interesting crater is the most symmetrical of the group. It is relatively easy to climb, with great views from the top.

DIRECTIONS:
From Flagstaff City Hall Go:
    East and then north on Highway 89. See Access Map, pages 10-11. Stay on Highway 89 to the 32.2 mile *51.5 km* point (MP 445.9), where you will see an unpaved road to your left (west) just before you reach MP 446. Hank's Trading Post is in sight to the north. This area is in the middle of a huge ranch run by the Babbitt interests and there are many roads going to tanks and waterholes. The roads are not numbered on maps nor on the ground. Follow the main-traveled road. Be sure to turn left at the first Y. SP Crater will seem dead ahead of you. It stands out because of its shape: a flat top with sloping symmetrical sides. At a point that is 4.8 miles *7.7 km* from the highway, the road forks at the top of a little valley. Go right here, skirting around the valley. At the 38.2 mile *61.1 km* point, you will see a sideroad fork to the right and head straight for a saddle between the crater and SP Mountain, which is joined to the crater by the saddle. This jeep road goes all the way to the top of the saddle but washouts have made it dangerous. We recommend driving 0.50 miles *0.8 km* on it, to the point where it leaves the level land at the base and begins to climb. Park here.

TRAILHEAD: There is no foot trail. You hike the jeep road to the saddle. From the saddle to the top of SP Crater there is no path, but you will see what you have to do: climb straight up about 300 feet.

DESCRIPTION: The saddle offers good views. You will be surprised at the extensive lava field that runs from SP Crater to the north. The crater doesn't seem big enough to have poured out so much lava, but it did. We find that the easiest way to climb one of these cinder volcanic cones is to zigzag, as if you were doing switchbacks with a car. The cinders are loose and the footing is poor.

You will find that your climb is worth the effort. SP Crater itself (we are told that the initials stand for Shit Pot) is quite interesting, the model of what a volcano should be. It is a perfect cone with a depressed center. Many of the volcanoes blasted their sides away or took irregular shapes, but not this one.

Views to the north are splendid. The country is quite flat but dotted with small volcanic eruptions. You see the Painted Desert nicely. The large mesa farthest north is the Coconino Rim, behind which the Grand Canyon is located. To the south you see myriad volcanoes of all shapes and sizes. This place is like a living geology lesson. If you are not interested in the views from a scientific standpoint, then the aesthetics will suffice.

After you come back down to the saddle, you might want to climb to the top of the ridge on the other side of the saddle. This is SP Mountain.

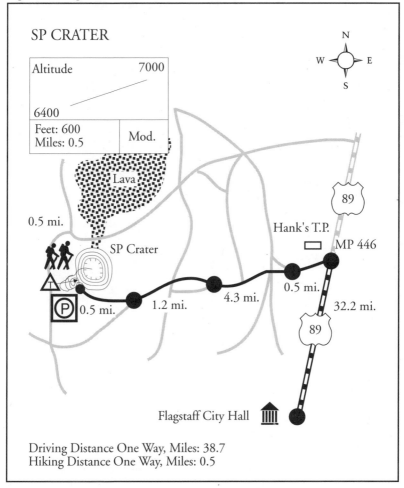

SP CRATER

Altitude   7000

6400

Feet: 600
Miles: 0.5   Mod.

Lava

0.5 mi.

SP Crater

Hank's T.P.
MP 446

0.5 mi.

0.5 mi.   1.2 mi.   4.3 mi.   32.2 mi.

89

89

Flagstaff City Hall

Driving Distance One Way, Miles: 38.7
Hiking Distance One Way, Miles: 0.5

Mangum

SADDLE MOUNTAIN

General Information
Location Map E3
Kendrick Peak & White Horse Hills USGS Maps
Coconino Forest Service Map

Driving Distance One Way: 25.3 miles *40.5 km* (Time 50 minutes)
Access Road: All cars, Last 4.5 miles *7.2 km* good dirt road
Hiking Distance One Way: 2.9 miles *4.64 km* (Time 90 minutes)
How Strenuous: Moderate
Features: Views, Volcanic field

NUTSHELL: Located 25.3 miles *40.5 km* north of Flagstaff, this hike takes you up an abandoned fire lookout road that corkscrews around a bare mountain, giving 360 degree views.

DIRECTIONS:
From Flagstaff City Hall Go:
   North on Humphreys Street for 0.60 miles *1.0 km*. See Access Map, page 10. Turn left at the stoplight onto Columbus Avenue and follow it around a big curve to the north. You will see the street signs call this road Columbus at first, then Ft. Valley Road and then Highway 180. Stay on Highway 180 to the 20.8 miles *33.3 km* point (MP 236.5), where the unpaved road FR 514 takes off to the right. Turn right onto FR 514 and drive it to the 23.4 mile *37.44 km* point where you will see FR 550 to the left. Turn left on FR 550 and take it to the 25.3 mile *40.5 km* point and park there.

TRAILHEAD: Hike the road up the mountain, FR 550A.

DESCRIPTION: Saddle Mountain is located in an ancient volcanic field. The excellent views from the top will show you the scope of the field. The mountains that you see in the region are all extinct volcanoes. Some of them, such as the San Francisco Peaks and Kendrick Mountain are high enough to catch clouds and get a lot of rain and snow. Because of this moisture they support abundant vegetation. In time soil forms on these favored mountains, covering the cinders and lava that formed the mountains with topsoil. On the lesser mountains, hills and cinder cones such as Saddle Mountain, there are only a few areas where soil has formed and most of the mountainsides are still bare cinders.
   A fire swept Saddle Mountain years ago and burned away most of its scant timber growth. The fire was a tragedy but it had its good side. As a result of it, you are able to get unobstructed views. The road circles around the mountain as it climbs, so you are able to see in every direction.

From the 1920s to the 1960s there was a fire lookout tower on the top of Saddle Mountain and the Forest Service built a decent road to the top of the mountain for access to the tower. The tower was replaced with a transmitter after the fire tower was removed. The road is still maintained so that the transmitter can be serviced. You could drive the road if you are a lazy bones, but this is a book of hikes.

At the top you can see all the way to the Grand Canyon when you look north. To the east you can see Sunset Crater and the Painted Desert. To the south you see the north face of the San Francisco Peaks. To the west you can see Kendrick Peak. This is an superb viewpoint.

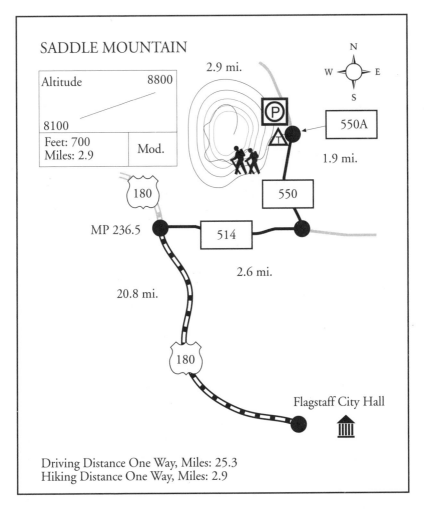

SANDYS CANYON TRAIL #137

General Information
Location Map F3
Flagstaff East USGS Map
Coconino Forest Service Map

Driving Distance One Way: 8.1 miles *13.0 km* (Time 20 minutes)
Access Road: All cars, Last 0.20 miles *0.32 km* good gravel road
Hiking Distance One Way: 3.6 miles *5.76 km* (Time 90 minutes)
How Strenuous: Moderate
Features: Beautiful canyon, Caves, Connection to The Arizona Trail

NUTSHELL: Located south of Flagstaff, only 8.1 miles *13.0 km* out on the Lake Mary Road, this hike requires a brief climb into Walnut Canyon, then an easy walk along the canyon bottom. It features impressive cliffs and a cave that is fun to explore. We formerly called this hike *Fisher Point* but in 1992 the Forest Service created Sandys Canyon Trail, so we have changed the description to match.

DIRECTIONS:
From Flagstaff City Hall Go:
West and then south (left) on Route 66 under the railroad overpass. See Access Map, page 10. At the 0.5 mile point *0.8 km*, go straight on Milton Road. At 1.7 miles *2.72 km* you reach the stoplight at Forest Meadows, where you turn right. At the next corner turn left on Beulah and follow it out of town. Beulah will connect onto Highway 89A. At the 2.4 miles *3.84 km* point (MP 401.6) you will see the turnoff to the Lake Mary Road to your left, where the last stoplight in town is located. Take the turn and follow the Lake Mary Road to the 7.9 mile *12.6 km* point where you will see a gravel road to your left. This is just a few feet past a Flagstaff City Limits sign and the second cattle guard on the Lake Mary Road. Turn left onto the gravel road and take it about 0.20 miles *0.32 km*, where you will see a camp site with parking area. Park there.

TRAILHEAD: Signed. Located near canyon rim.

DESCRIPTION: You will first walk along the rim of the canyon for 0.60 miles *1.0 km*. Then the trail descends a side canyon to the floor of Walnut Creek. Walnut Canyon National Monument is several miles downstream. There is 200 foot drop into the canyon bottom. You reach the streambed at 0.25 miles *0.4 km*. Across it you will find an old road on the other side. Go left on the road.

The trail intersects The Arizona Trail at 0.50 miles *0.8 km* from the creekbed. You keep walking straight north to a bend, where you turn right (east), at 0.90 miles *1.44 km* from The Arizona Trail. At 0.20 miles *0.32 km* from the corner, to your left, is Fisher Point, where there is a half cave under an enormous rounded cliff. Walk on past the cliff to a place where the trail seems to end at a screen of willows.

This screen is at a bend in Walnut Canyon. The trail continues but changes character, going from a jeep road to a foot trail. The canyon becomes very narrow and you wind your way back and forth across the streambed. In 0.25 miles *0.4 km* the trail goes past a large cave to your right. This is fun to explore, and even has an "escape hatch" out the back. In another 0.20 miles *0.32 km* there is a smaller cave that is partly hidden. It is uphill to your right. Look for a short trail to it taking off from the streambed where the bed is wide and full of coarse sand.

We recommend stopping at the 3.6 miles *5.76 km* point, where you will find a large Ponderosa with a silver stripe painted around it.

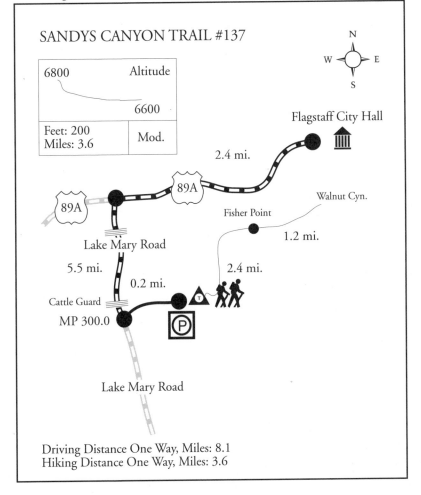

SANDYS CANYON TRAIL #137

6800	Altitude
	6600

Feet: 200 Miles: 3.6	Mod.

N
W ← → E
S

Flagstaff City Hall

2.4 mi.

89A

89A

Walnut Cyn.

Fisher Point

1.2 mi.

Lake Mary Road

5.5 mi.

2.4 mi.

0.2 mi.

Cattle Guard

MP 300.0

Lake Mary Road

Driving Distance One Way, Miles: 8.1
Hiking Distance One Way, Miles: 3.6

Mangum

SCHULTZ CREEK TRAIL

General Information
Location Map E3
Humphreys Peak USGS Map
Coconino Forest Service Map

Driving Distance One Way: 8.5 miles *13.6 km* (Time 30 minutes)
Access Road: All cars, Last 4.5 miles *7.2 km* medium gravel road
Hiking Distance One Way: 4.25 miles *6.8 km* (Time 2.25 hours)
How Strenuous: Moderate
Features: Scenic creekside trail is easy to reach

NUTSHELL: This is a marked and maintained trail that starts high on the Schultz Pass Road north of Flagstaff and follows a creekside downward.

DIRECTIONS:
From Flagstaff City Hall Go:
North on Humphreys Street for 0.60 miles *1.0 km*. See Access Map, page 10. Turn left at the stoplight onto Columbus Avenue and follow it around a big curve to the north. You will see the street signs call this road Columbus Avenue at first, then Ft. Valley Road and then Highway 180. Stay on Highway 180 to the 3.1 miles *5.0 km* point (MP 218.6), where the Schultz Pass Road, FR 420, goes to the right. Follow this road. At 3.6 miles *5.76 km* it curves to the left and you will see the unpaved Elden Lookout Road going straight. Ignore this and stay on the paved road. The paving will end soon and the road will become gravel. As you drive, look down into the canyon to your right and you will see a trail running along the canyon parallel to the road. This is the Schultz Creek Trail. Follow the road to the 8.3 mile *13.3 km* point, where you will see a sign for the Sunset Trail. Turn right on this access and park in the parking area, by the sign board, at 8.5 miles *13.6 km*.

TRAILHEAD: You will see a wooden sign for the Sunset Trail. The Schultz Creek Trail runs in the opposite direction and is marked with a lath showing it to be a trail closed to motor travel but giving no name.

DESCRIPTION: The Schultz Creek Trail follows the course of the old Schultz Pass Road. That road was so near the bottom of the creek that it often flooded, so in the 1930s the present road was built higher up the shoulder, requiring much blasting and earth removal.

Down at creekside you will have a delightful ramble. The path is easy to walk, made of soft soil with few rocks. You will see many wildflowers growing in the upper reaches of the trail where the forest is an interesting mixture of pine, aspen, fir and spruce, with willows in the creek.

This is not really a hiking trail, but a motorcycle trail maintained by a motorcycle club. The members wanted to have at least one trail in this region so an agreement was worked out for them to have this one if they would maintain it. Bicyclists also love the trail.

The trail is always just a stone's throw from the road, which is to your right, and you will see and hear cars pass. This and the presence of bikes mar the natural feeling of this otherwise fine trail.

Near the end of the trail, you will encounter several concrete slabs on the site of a 1930s CCC camp. The workers who lived there built the present road.

Forest Service maps measure this hike at 3.5 miles *5.6 km*, which seems too short. The best way to do this hike is as a two car shuttle, parking one at the Sunset trailhead and the other at the low end on FR 9128Y as shown on the map.

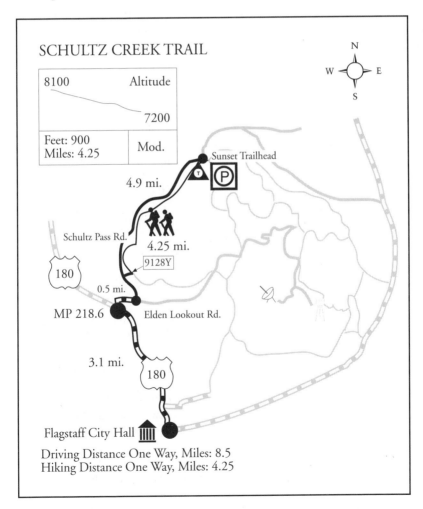

SCHULTZ CREEK TRAIL

| 8100 | Altitude |
| | 7200 |

| Feet: 900 Miles: 4.25 | Mod. |

4.9 mi.

Sunset Trailhead

Schultz Pass Rd.

4.25 mi.

9128Y

180

0.5 mi.

MP 218.6

Elden Lookout Rd.

3.1 mi.

180

Flagstaff City Hall

Driving Distance One Way, Miles: 8.5
Hiking Distance One Way, Miles: 4.25

SECRET MOUNTAIN TRAIL #109

General Information
Location Map F2
Loy Butte, Sycamore Point USGS Maps
Coconino Forest Service Map

Driving Distance One Way: 28.9 miles *46.24 km* (Time 60 minutes)
Access Road: All cars, Last 25.3 miles *40.5 km* dirt road, rough spots
Hiking Distance One Way: 1.6 miles *2.56 km* (Time 1 hour)
How Strenuous: Moderate
Features: Historic cabin, Pristine first growth forest, Views

NUTSHELL: Located 28.9 miles *46.24 km* southwest of Flagstaff, this hike takes you from a scenic lookout on the Mogollon Rim across a ridge to Secret Mountain where you will find a historic cabin and another lookout. **A personal favorite.**

DIRECTIONS:
From Flagstaff City Hall Go:
    West, then south on Route 66, beneath the railroad overpass. See Access Map, page 10. At 0.50 mile *0.8 km* go right on Route 66. You will soon leave town. At 2.6 mile *4.2 km* you will reach a road going to the left. This is the Woody Mountain Road, FR 231. Take it. It is paved about a mile *1.6 km* and then turns into a cinder road. At 16.6 miles *26.6 km* you will intersect FR 538. Turn right onto FR 538 and follow it to the 22.3 mile *35.7 km* point, where FR 538E branches off to the right. Take FR 538 to the left. At 27.7 miles *44.3 km* you will come to the intersection of 538K. Go left here, staying on 538. At 28.9 mile *46.24 km* you will come out onto a ridge. Park by the wilderness boundary sign at the end of the road.

TRAILHEAD: The trail is unmarked. Go east to the toe of the ridge.

DESCRIPTION: The trail is maintained and is easy to follow even though it is not posted. You will find trail-marking blazes on trees along the route as you go. See page 103 for a drawing of a blaze.
    At 0.4 miles *0.64 km*, you drop off a knob onto a saddle where there is a gate. Here the trail splits. The fork to the right is the Loy Canyon Trail (see *Sedona Hikes*) and the fit hiker can follow it about five miles, descending 2,000 feet. Instead, turn left and go uphill. You will reach the top of a knob at 0.6 miles *1.0 km*, then go downhill. In this area you will see damage from an August 1994 forest fire.
    At 1.0 miles *1.6 km* you will enter a fold between three hills. On a small bench of land here you will find an old log corral and a dam. Beyond the cor-

ral you will at all times have a ravine to your right as you hike. Enjoy this forest. It has never been logged. Imagine what northern Arizona would look like if it were all like this. It is breathtaking.

At 1.5 miles *2.4 km* you will come to another shelf of land, with Secret Cabin and another corral. There is also a pond. The cabin is about 20 by 12 feet and only 5 feet high. This remote place was homesteaded unsuccessfully by a family in the 1870s. It was then used by Mormons hiding from polygamy prosecution. After that it was used by horse thieves, who stole horses around Sedona, led them to this hideout via the Loy Canyon Trail and eventually took them to Flagstaff and points north.

From the cabin go west into the ravine and across it. Walk up 0.1 mile *0.16 km* to a lookout on the rim of Secret Mountain for sensational views. There is a satellite trail there going south and east about 0.75 miles *1.2 km* to another viewpoint.

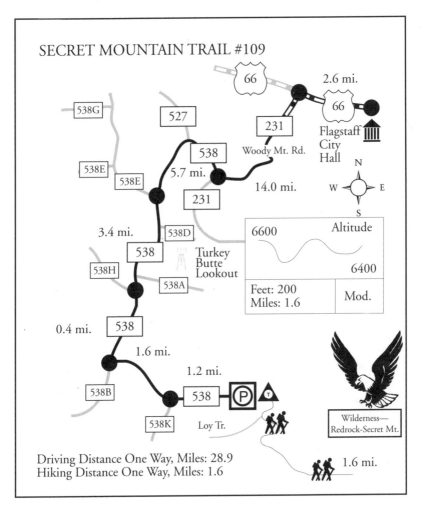

SECRET MOUNTAIN TRAIL #109

66

2.6 mi.

66

538G

527

231

Flagstaff City Hall

Woody Mt. Rd.

538E

538E

538

5.7 mi.

231

14.0 mi.

N

W — E

S

3.4 mi.

538D

538

538H

Turkey Butte Lookout

538A

Altitude

6600

6400

Feet: 200
Miles: 1.6

Mod.

0.4 mi.

538

1.6 mi.

538B

1.2 mi.

538K

538

P

Loy Tr.

Wilderness—
Redrock-Secret Mt.

1.6 mi.

Driving Distance One Way, Miles: 28.9
Hiking Distance One Way, Miles: 1.6

Mangum

SECRET POCKET TRAIL #58

General Information
Location Map F1
May Tank Pocket USGS Map
Kaibab (Williams District) Forest Service Map

Driving Distance One Way: 53.4 miles *85.5 km* (Time 1.25 hours)
Access Road: High clearance needed for last 3.0 miles *4.8 km*
Hiking Distance One Way: 1.0 miles *1.6 km* (Time 30 minutes)
How Strenuous: Moderate
Features: Remote country, Hidden oasis

NUTSHELL: You will drive through miles of beautiful forest, then hike an old cattle trail from the top of the Mogollon Rim to a hidden pond in a "secret" pocket.

DIRECTIONS:
From Flagstaff City Hall Go:
    West, then south on Route 66 under the railroad overpass. See Access Map, page 10. At 0.5 miles *0.8 km*, turn right on Route 66. In about 5.0 miles *8.0 km* you will merge onto I-40 West and stay on it to the 30.3 miles *48.5 km* point, the Williams Exit, #165. Take that exit and at the stop sign go left to Williams. Go into town on Railroad Avenue to the 32.9 mile point *52.6 km* where you will find Fourth Street. Turn left on Fourth Street. As it leaves town its name changes to the Perkinsville Road (FR 173). Stay on this road to the 42.2 mile *67.5 km* point, where you will turn left on FR 354. Stay on FR 354 to the 49.4 mile *79.0 km* point, where FR 354 makes a 90 degree turn to the right. Stay on FR 354. In another mile the road will become quite rough, with lots of exposed rocks. At the 53.4 mile *85.5 km* point, you will see a lath-type marker for Trail 58 on your left, at an old road junction.

TRAILHEAD: Marked by a fiberglass lath.

DESCRIPTION: Once you leave the paved Perkinsville Road, you will drive on FR 354 to reach the trailhead. FR 354 used to be the Perkinsville Road and carried lots of traffic until the present paved road was built in the 1960s. You will see many culverts and other structures indicating the importance of the old road. The road now receives no maintenance and there are many rough spots on the last three miles. If you have a good high clearance vehicle, you might want to follow the road down to its junction with the present paved road after the hike. It's about 10.0 miles *16 km* to the bottom, from where you can turn left and go to Jerome (a great scenic drive) or turn right and go back up the present Perkinsville Road.

The trail is an old ranch road that is now closed to motor vehicles. You will hike over rocky but level ground through a cedar (juniper) forest. As you proceed, the country will open up and you will see that you are on a point near the edge of the Mogollon Rim. Government Canyon, which meets Sycamore Canyon, is prominent before you.

Near its end, the trail dips down and takes you into a fold where you will see green deciduous trees peeking up above the cedars. The hike ends at the pond, the waters of which support the growth of these water-loving trees. It is a delightful place, an open green oasis with a small pond.

We looked hard but could not find any trail going from here to the bottom of the Rim, even though some Forest Service maps indicate that there is such a trail.

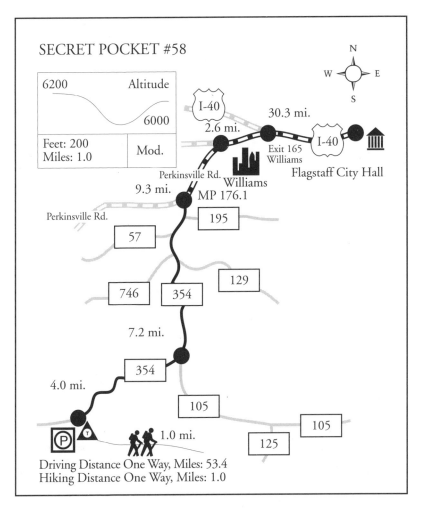

Mangum

SINCLAIR WASH TRAIL

General Information
Location Map F3
Flagstaff West USGS Map
Coconino Forest Service Map

Driving Distance One Way: 2.2 miles *3.52 km* (Time 5 minutes)
Access Road: All cars, All paved
Hiking Distance One Way: 3.0 or 1.0 miles *4.8* or *1.6 km* (Time 1.5 or 0.5 hours)
How Strenuous: Easy
Features: Urban trail

NUTSHELL: This is an urban trail in the south part of town. Starting from the point we have selected, you can go east for an easy one mile hike through NAU's South Campus to Lone Tree Road, or southwest to Ft. Tuthill.

DIRECTIONS:
From Flagstaff City Hall Go:
West, then south on Route 66. See Access Map, page 10. Follow Route 66 beneath the underpass. At 0.5 miles 0.8 km, go straight on Milton Road. Continue on Milton Road to the 1.7 mile *2.72 km* point, where you meet Forest Meadows Street. Turn right. In a block, turn left on Beulah. In another couple of blocks, you will see the Wal-Mart shopping center on your right. Turn right on Woodlands Village Boulevard, and immediately turn right into the Wal-Mart parking lot, parking near the street.

TRAILHEAD: This is a marked and maintained trail. You will see trail signs. Pole fences mark the Flagstaff urban trails.

DESCRIPTION: Flagstaff is developing an ambitious system of urban trails, with several excellent trails already on line, and more to come.
Using Wal-Mart as a starting point, you can go east toward NAU or southwest toward Ft. Tuthill. The scenery is quite different depending on your choice.
The east (NAU) leg is just under one mile. It skirts along the South Campus. Most of the time it stays in a band of trees, but you are always aware that you are in an inhabited area. The trail is kept in good condition and there are no major grades. It is a nice easy walk if you just want a little exercise.
The other leg, going to Ft. Tuthill, is a three-miler. It goes south through more wooded areas. The first portion of this trail passes by the University Heights subdivision, and then through part of the Mt. Dell subdivision, so it

is definitely not what you would call a wilderness experience. There are a few stretches where you cannot see any homes or other man-made artifacts, and these are enjoyable. The trail is much more interesting than the NAU leg.

Just beyond the Mt. Dell subdivision, the trail joins the roadbed of an old logging railroad and goes through a forest. Eventually you will enter the Ft. Tuthill area. At first you will see nothing but an equestrian trail, but soon afterwards, you will come to the main portion of the property.

Ft. Tuthill is an old National Guard camp that is now owned by Coconino County. It is the home of the Coconino County Fair, and other events are sometimes held there.

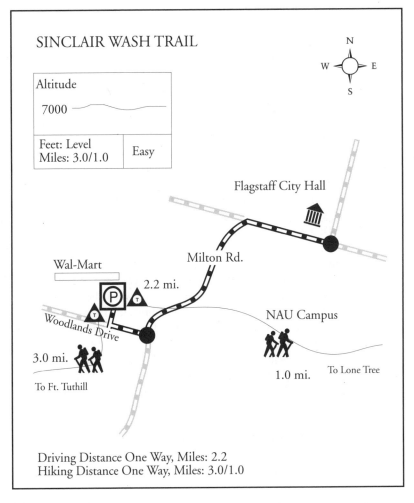

SLATE LAKE LAVA CAVE

General Information
Location Map E2
Kendrick Peak USGS Map
Coconino Forest Service Map

Driving Distance One Way: 28.5 miles *45.6 km* (Time 45 minutes)
Access Road: All cars, Last 2.1 miles *3.36 km* rough dirt road
Hiking Distance One Way: 0.50 miles *0.8 km* (Time 1 hour)
How Strenuous: Moderate
Features: Unusual underground lava tube

NUTSHELL: This underground lava tube located 28.5 miles *45.6 km* north-west of Flagstaff is a unique experience.

DIRECTIONS:
From Flagstaff City Hall Go:
   North on Humphreys Street for 0.60 miles *1.0 km*. See Access Map, page 10. Turn left at the stoplight onto Columbus Avenue and follow it around a big curve to the north. You will see the street signs call this road Columbus at first, then Ft. Valley Road and then Highway 180. Stay on Highway 180 to the 26.4 miles *42.24 km* point (MP 241.9), where an unpaved road takes off to the left. Turn left onto this road, FR 9002H, and follow it to the 28.3 mile *45.28 km* point where you will see an unmarked dirt road taking off to the left. Turn left onto this road and follow it 0.20 miles *0.32 km*, to the 28.5 mile *45.6 km* point, where it ends at a crudely defined loop. Park there.

TRAILHEAD: A big hole in the ground to the left of the parking place.

DESCRIPTION: There is nothing about the topography to alert you to the fact that you are in the presence of the Slate Lake Lava Cave. When you turn off of Highway 180, you enter some flat land between the north side of **Kendrick Peak** and the south side of **Slate Mountain**. The road goes in a generally southwesterly direction toward Kendrick Peak but never comes very close to Kendrick.
   The country is rangeland at first and then you enter into a forest consisting of young pines. You will see three rusted out junked pickup trucks off the road along the way. The road is a primitive one with patches where exposed rocks make you nervous about your undercarriage, but we got through in our trusty Toyota Tercel all right. The majority of the road surface is dirt. Don't try this road when it is wet. At 1.5 miles *2.4 km*, you will hit a logging road created in 1993. Turn right here.
   When you think of a cave, you usually picture an opening in a cliff face,

but that is not the case here. Even after you turn off onto the driveway to the cave, the last 0.20 miles *0.32 km*, there are no cliffs in sight. Instead what you will see is literally a hole in the ground. The exposed rim of lava rock around its opening will attract your attention first. There is no line of stones around it as there is for its nearby cousin, the **Lava River Cave**.

The entrance has not been improved. Rock has fallen from the ceiling of the cave and you have to thread your way around it. A short distance from the entrance you will find a Register in an ammo can.

Typical of such caves, it is very cool. Once you walk beyond the point reached by the light from the opening, the cave is pitch black. You must have reliable lights. Each member of your party should have a good flashlight with fresh batteries and a backup light as well. The floor is very rough, so good shoes are needed. You also need warm clothes. A hard hat is recommended.

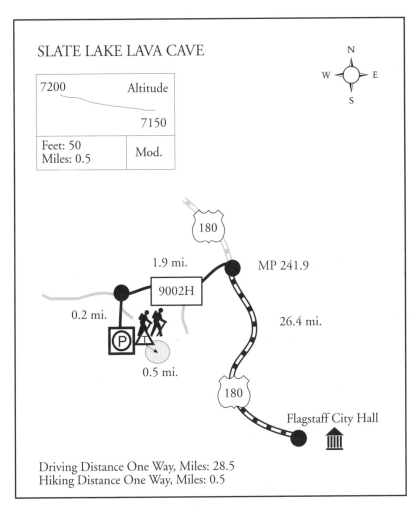

SLATE LAKE LAVA CAVE

| 7200 | Altitude |
| | 7150 |

| Feet: 50
Miles: 0.5 | Mod. |

N
W — E
S

180

1.9 mi.

9002H

MP 241.9

0.2 mi.

26.4 mi.

0.5 mi.

180

Flagstaff City Hall

Driving Distance One Way, Miles: 28.5
Hiking Distance One Way, Miles: 0.5

Mangum

SLATE MOUNTAIN #128

General Information
Location Map E2
Kendrick Peak USGS Map
Coconino Forest Service Map

Driving Distance One Way: 29.1 miles *46.56 km* (Time 40 minutes)
Access Road: All cars, Last 2.2 miles *3.5 km* good gravel road
Hiking Distance One Way: 2.1 miles *3.36 km* (Time 80 minutes)
How Strenuous: Moderate
Features: Excellent views, Nature trail with explanatory signs

NUTSHELL: Located 29.1 miles *46.56 km* north of Flagstaff, this moderate hike follows an old road to the top of a mountain, with signs identifying local flora posted along the way.

DIRECTIONS:
From Flagstaff City Hall Go:
North on Humphreys Street for 0.60 miles *1.0 km*. See Access Map, page 10. Turn left at the stoplight onto Columbus Avenue and follow it around a big curve to the north. You will see the street signs call this road Columbus at first, then Ft. Valley Road and then Highway 180. Stay on Highway 180 to the 26.9 miles *43.0 km* point (MP 242.4), where an unpaved road, FR 191, takes off to the left. Turn left onto FR 191 and follow it to the 28.8 mile *46.1 km* point. There you will see a road to your right that is marked as the trail access. Turn right onto this road and drive it to the 29.1 mile *46.56 km* point, where you will park.

TRAILHEAD: Hike the road going up the mountain.

DESCRIPTION: Like some other hikes in the book, this road was built to provide access to a fire lookout tower that was later dismantled. The road is now closed for vehicular traffic and makes a fine hiking trail.
Slate Mountain is an extinct volcano, like so many other mountains and hills north of Flagstaff. Enough soil has formed on its slopes to support a decent amount of vegetation, but there are also many areas where the black cinders of which the mountain is composed are on the surface.
As you climb the mountain you wind around the two knobs that form a saddle, so that you are able to see in all directions. You will have some great views as you go and will have even better views at the top.
One thing you can count on when you take one of these hikes to a spot where there was (or presently is) a fire lookout tower is that you will have great views, because the Forest Service located the towers in places where

you can see forever. At the top of Slate Mountain there are just a few low-growing pines, so you can see freely to the north, south and west.

Immediately to the north you will see **Red Mountain**. Just a few years ago there was a bit of a stir in Flagstaff when a mining company indicated that it thought that there was gold in the red cinders of Red Mountain and it was going to set up a gold mining operation. Red cinders do contain minuscule quantities of gold, but you have literally to move mountains of it to recover any of the precious metal.

Kendrick Peak is nearby, and an active fire lookout is maintained on its summit during the fire season.

The identified plants we saw (starting from the top of the mountain and working down) were: Oregon Grape, Fremont Holly-berry, Rabbit Brush, Currant, Douglas Fir, Mountain Mahogany, Limber Pine, Ponderosa Pine, Juniper, Alligator Juniper, Prickly Pear, Yucca, Pinyon Pine, Cliff Rose and Dwarf Mistletoe.

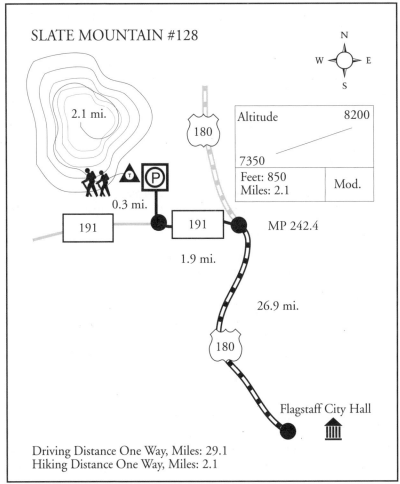

SLATE MOUNTAIN #128

2.1 mi.

180

Altitude   8200

7350

Feet: 850
Miles: 2.1   Mod.

0.3 mi.

191   191   MP 242.4

1.9 mi.

26.9 mi.

180

Flagstaff City Hall

Driving Distance One Way, Miles: 29.1
Hiking Distance One Way, Miles: 2.1

Mangum

General Information
Location Map E3
Humphreys Peak USGS Map
Coconino Forest Service Map

Driving Distance One Way: 14.4 miles *23.0 km* (Time 40 minutes)
Access Road: All cars, All paved
Hiking Distances: Boo Boo Trail—2.0 miles *3.2 km* (1.5 hours); Lodge Run
   Trail—0.63 miles *1.0 km* (45 minutes); Lookout Trail— 0.38 miles
   0.6 km (30 minutes plus ride time)
How Strenuous: All Three Hikes Are Moderate
Features: High mountains, Alpine forests, Excellent views

NUTSHELL: These three hikes start at the Sky Ride at the Arizona Snow
Bowl. The **Boo Boo Loop** and **Lodge Loop** trails move across to Hart
Prairie, then follow the prairie uphill. Lodge Loop crosses back to the
Skyride area about half way up. Boo Boo goes to the top of the prairie, then
turns through an aspen forest and follows a ski run down, to emerge by the
Skyride. **Lookout Trail** requires that you take the Sky Ride, and provides
wonderful sweeping views at the top.

DIRECTIONS:
From Flagstaff City Hall Go:
   North on Humphreys Street for 0.60 miles *1.0 km*. See Access Map, page
10. Turn left at the stoplight onto Columbus Avenue and follow it around a
big curve to the north. You will see that the street signs call this road
Columbus at first, then Ft. Valley Road and then Highway 180. Stay on
Highway 180 to the 7.3 miles point *11.7 km* (MP 223), where the road to the
Snow Bowl branches off to the right. It is well posted. Follow the Snow
Bowl road to the Sky Ride parking area at 14.4 miles *23.0 km.* Park there.

TRAILHEAD: You start **Boo Boo** and **Lodge Run** by using the trailhead
for the **Humphreys Peak Trail.** Starting at the Lodge, walk uphill parallel
to the Sky Ride about 100 paces. The trailhead (marked for the Humphreys
Peak Trail) goes to your left, through the trees. For the **Lookout Trail**, take
the Sky Ride to the top.

DESCRIPTION: The **Boo Boo** and **Lodge Run** trails move northwest,
along a corridor cut through an aspen forest. You will come out of the trees
onto Hart Prairie, where there is a chairlift in the middle. We did not find
any signs for the trails, but they are easy to find. Look for tire tracks to your
right going uphill just as you come out onto the prairie. The trails move

straight uphill. Pause every now and then to look behind you, as you will have sweeping views from the open prairie.

At 0.35 miles *0.56 km* you will find a "catwalk" (a lateral ski trail) cut through the trees to your right. Take this catwalk for the **Lodge Run** Trail. It goes through an aspen forest and comes out into the open above the lodge; then you walk downhill to the starting point..

For **Boo Boo,** continue uphill. At 0.6 miles *1.0 km,* the top of the meadow, the trail curves right (south) through the aspens, making a big S curve. At 0.75 miles *1.2 km* is another catwalk. Turn right and follow it, still climbing. At 1.25 miles *2.0 km* you will reach the high point, at a V-shaped junction of ski runs. Turn right (south) and go downhill. Soon, you will come to a fork in the ski run. Go right, down into a gully. Soon you will walk out into the open just above the base of the Skyride.

For the **Lookout Trail**, take the Sky Ride to the top and follow the signs there. The trail loops around from observation point to observation point.

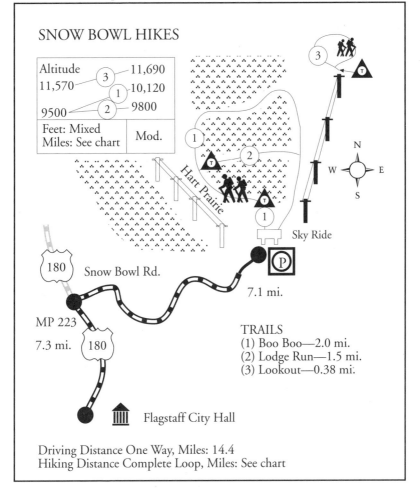

Mangum

SOUTH KAIBAB TRAIL

Driving Distance One Way: 81.4 miles *130.2 km* (Time 2 hours)
Access Road: All cars, All paved
Hiking Distance One Way: 1.5 miles *2.4 km* (Time 3 hours total)
How Strenuous: Hard
Features: Magnificent views of the Grand Canyon

NUTSHELL: This trail is maintained and heavily used. The first leg of the trail, down to Cedar Ridge, makes a perfect day hike.

DIRECTIONS:
From Flagstaff City Hall Go:
   North on Humphreys Street 0.60 miles *1.0 km* to a stoplight. See Access Map, page 10. Go left on Columbus Avenue and follow the curve north. Street signs will show the street first as Ft. Valley Road, then Highway 180, a major road to the Grand Canyon. At 50.4 miles *80.7 km* (MP 265.8), you will intersect Highway 64, coming out of Williams, at Valle. Go right at this junction and follow the highway to the south entrance to the Grand Canyon National Park, where you pay an entrance fee. Then drive on to the East Rim Drive, which you reach at 79.8 miles *128 km*. Turn right (east) on East Rim Drive, away from Grand Canyon Village. At the 80.9 mile *129.4 km* point, you will see the entrance to Yaki Point. Turn left here, then left again at the first fork and follow the sign to the Kaibab Trail parking area, at 81.4 miles *130.2 km.*

TRAILHEAD: At the east side of the parking area. It is posted.

DESCRIPTION: This is the next most famous trail at the Grand Canyon, after the Bright Angel Trail. It is in constant use by hordes of people. Freight-bearing mules coming up from Phantom Ranch use this trail, so it is a busy place, with corrals for the mules at the top. The trail was built by the Park Service 1925-1928, to avoid the tolls charged on the privately-owned Bright Angel Trail. It goes to the river, a trip of 6.5 miles, *10.4 km* with a drop of 4,780 feet, then crosses the river on a bridge, and goes to the top of the North Rim on the other side of the river.
   Overnight backpacking trips in the Grand Canyon require permits (which are scarce and hard to get) and much preparation. Day hikes, such as the one we describe here, do not require permits. You do not need to notify

the Park Service that you are going to be on the trail. Just help yourself. Please take plenty of water. This is a *hot* trail in summer. We avoid it then.

The first part of this trail is an impressive set of switchbacks blasted out of a cliff face, with lots of rock work. Tremendous views open up to the hiker immediately, looking directly into the wide, colorful part of the main canyon.

The footing on the trail is generally good—sandy, with only a few loose rocks, and with many aprons at viewpoints.

The natural stopping point for a day hiker on this trail is at Cedar Ridge, a trip of 1.5 miles *2.4 km*. Here you are in red rock formations, with even better views into the canyon. There is a trail toilet here and a fossil exhibit, as well as hitching posts for the mules. Going out to the toe of the ridge, where you have superb views and a place to sit and soak them in, makes an unforgettable day hike.

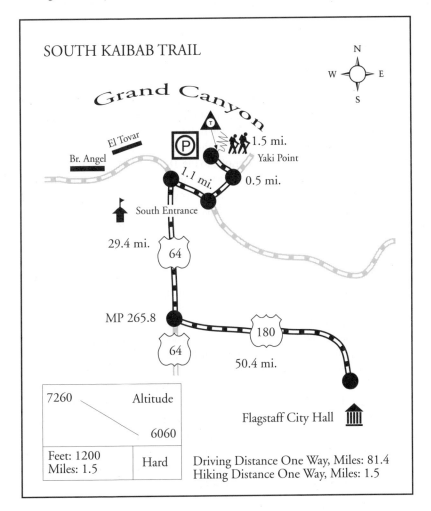

Mangum

SPRING VALLEY TRAILS (3)

General Information
Location Map E2
Parks USGS Map
Coconino Forest Service Map

Driving Distance One Way: 24.7 miles *39.5 km* (Time 40 minutes)
Access Road: All cars, Last 1.5 miles *2.4 km* good gravel
Hiking Distances: See map
How Strenuous: Moderate
Features: Three trails loop through a fine forest, Beautiful meadows, Views

NUTSHELL: These hikes take you on loop routes in the Spring Valley area west of Flagstaff.

DIRECTIONS:
From Flagstaff City Hall Go:
    West a block on Route 66 (Santa Fe), then south, beneath the railroad overpass. The street name will change to Milton Road. At 0.50 miles *0.8 km* you will reach a Y intersection. The right fork is Route 66. Take it. You will soon leave town. At the 4.8 mile *7.7 km* point you will merge onto Interstate-40 West. Look for Exit 178 "Parks" at the 18.0 mile *28.8 km* point, and take it. Turn right at the stop sign and travel to the 18.4 mile *29.5 km* point, where there is a second stop sign. Turn left here and go to the 19.0 mile *30.4 km* point, where you will see the Parks Store to your right. Turn right here, on the Spring Valley Road (FR 141). It is paved to the 23.2 mile *37.12 km* point, and is a good gravel road beyond. At 24.7 miles *39.5 km* you will see a sign for the Cross Country Ski Trail. Turn left here into the parking lot and park.

TRAILHEAD: You will see a large wooden signboard with a trail map.

DESCRIPTION: Three cross-country ski trails in this area make good hiking trails. The **RS Hill Trail** is the easiest. The **Eagle Rock Trail** is harder and a bit longer. The **Spring Valley Trail** is longest.
    For all three trails, you start on a road, then at 0.40 miles *0.64 km* veer off into the woods. You will at times be on roads and at other times off road on this hike. Be sure to follow the triangle trail makers in the trees.
    At 0.75 miles *1.2 km* you will reach a beautiful meadow beyond an aspen grove in the middle of which is Shoot-Em-Up-Dick Tank. At the other side you will come onto FR 76 and walk it to the 1.25 mile *2.0 km* point, where there is a trail fork. At this point, you have options. The best way to understand your choices is to look at the map. Depending on which route you

choose, you can add up the mileage to get the total for the hike you select.

Eagle Rock: Turn left. The trail soon emerges from the woods to join FR 104, which you hike to Eagle Rock Pass. Eagle Rock is to your left just before the pass. You do not go to Eagle Rock. From the gate at the pass you descend steeply on a footpath to join another road, where you turn to the right. We like Eagle Rock best, and recommend it.

RS Hill: This 1.0 mile *1.6 km* trail goes through a typical pine forest. It has a nice rise and fall, then joins the Eagle Rock trail on the old road.

Spring Valley: This starts where the Eagle Rock and RS Hill trails meet near RS Tank. The trail soon leaves the road and goes uphill on a shoulder of RS Hill, through an area rich in obsidian. You find hunks of this coal-like stone everywhere.

As you round the hill you see Spring Valley to your left. From here you walk a road back to the junction of FR 76 and FR 104, then retrace your steps to the parking lot. You never climb RS Hill.

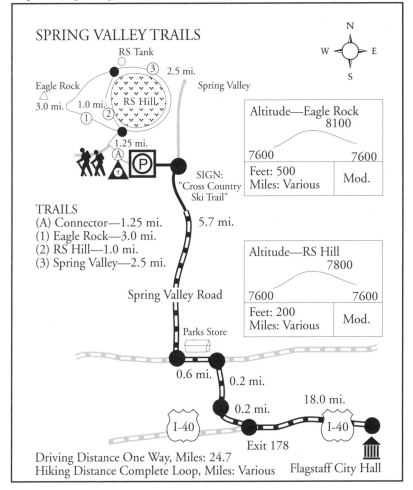

Mangum

STRAWBERRY CRATER

General Information
Location Map D3
Strawberry Crater USGS Map
Coconino Forest Service Map

Driving Distance, One Way: 26.0 miles *41.6 km* (Time 40 minutes)
Access Road: All cars, Last 5.6 miles *9.0 km* gravel, medium condition
Hiking Distance, One Way: 1.0 miles *1.6 km* (Time 45 minutes)
How Strenuous: Moderate
Features: Volcano, Indian Ruins, Painted Desert Views

NUTSHELL: This hike takes you to an extinct volcano located 26.0 miles *41.6 km* north of Flagstaff. You hike up the face of the crater to enjoy great views and Indian ruins.

DIRECTIONS:
From Flagstaff City Hall Go:
East, then North on Highway 89. See Access Map, pages 10-11. Follow Highway 89 north out of town. At 20.4 miles *32.64 km* (MP 434.4), nearly at the bottom of a long downgrade, take FR 546 (unpaved) to the right. Follow FR 546 easterly to the 24.0 mile *38.4 km* point, where it meets FR 779. Here FR 546 veers to the right. Go straight on FR 779, which will take you to Strawberry Crater. You will soon see the crater ahead. At 26.0 miles *41.6 km*, you will reach a huge power line. Just beyond it, roads go left, right and straight ahead. Park at this intersection.

TRAILHEAD: You will see a road heading toward the crater. It is blocked to vehicles by branches, rocks and brush that have been scattered along its route. Walk it. Just short of 0.1 mile *0.16 km* you will come to a fence made of cable. On the other side of the fence is a sign for the Strawberry Crater Wilderness. This is the trailhead.

DESCRIPTION: Step over the fence and keep following the jeep trail. At about 0.15 miles *0.24 km* the road swings to the east (your right). You will see an even fainter jeep trail going northeast (to your left) marked by a line of branches. Follow it. At about 0.25 miles *0.4 km* the track is blocked by a row of stones. Turn right and follow the stones about twenty yards, part way up the slope of the crater. Here you will find a wilderness marker with a distinct footpath going to your left. Follow it.
The trail moves you along northeasterly, making a gentle climb. This gradual climb is appreciated, as the footing is composed of loose cinders, which are hard to walk in. You will come around a wing of the volcano to a

point where you can see into the bowl, a fascinating place. Here the trail ended at about 0.4 miles *0.64 km* from the fence when we were here in July 1992. From this point you can get to the top by bushwhacking. There is no danger of getting lost because you can see everything plainly. The climb to the top from this place is steep. At the top there are some small Indian ruins.

The views from the top are great, with extensive volcano fields on all sides. To the north you can see the Painted Desert. When the light is right, it can be gorgeous.

Strawberry Crater was recently incorporated into a federally protected Wilderness Area. We salute this classification and hope that it will help to preserve this treasure.

You can see that the crater has an open end through which lava flowed and created a large lava field. If you have the energy for it, you might want to go down to the lava field and do some exploring there.

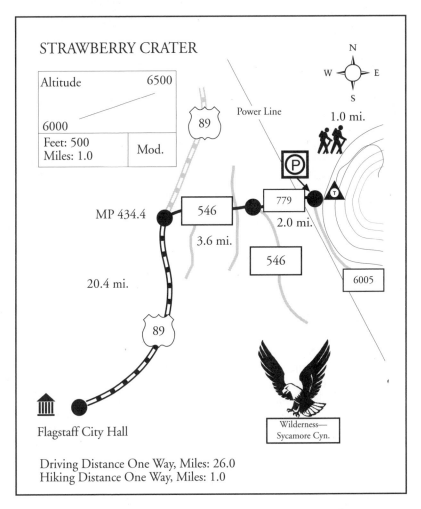

SUNSET TRAIL #23

General Information
Location Map E3
Flagstaff East and Flagstaff West USGS Maps
Coconino Forest Service Map

Driving Distance One Way: 8.5 miles *13.6 km* (Time 30 minutes)
Access Road: All cars, Last 4.5 miles *7.2 km* medium gravel road
Hiking Distance One Way: 3.5 miles *5.6 km* (Time 2 hours)
How Strenuous: Hard
Features: Views, Variety of scenery, Excellent forests

NUTSHELL: This is a marked and maintained trail that starts high on the Schultz Pass Road north of Flagstaff and winds to the top of Mt. Elden. **A personal favorite.**

DIRECTIONS:
From Flagstaff City Hall Go:
    North on Humphreys Street for 0.60 miles *1.0 km*. See Access Map, page 10. Turn left at the stoplight onto Columbus Avenue and follow it around a big curve to the north. You will see the street signs call this road Columbus Avenue at first, then Ft. Valley Road and then Highway 180. Stay on Highway 180 to the 3.1 miles *5.0 km* point (MP 218.6), where the Schultz Pass Road, FR 420, goes to the right. Follow this road. At 3.6 miles *5.8 km* where it curves to the left you will see the unpaved Elden Lookout Road going straight. Ignore this and stay on the paved road. The paving will end soon and the road will become gravel. Follow the road to the 8.5 mile *13.6 km* point, where you will see a sign for the Sunset Trail. Turn right on this road and park in the parking area, by the sign board.

TRAILHEAD: Signed at the parking area.

DESCRIPTION: The Sunset Trail goes to Sunset Park, near the top of Mt. Elden. It is a part of the Dry Lake Hills\Mt. Elden Trail system.
    You will skirt Schultz Tank which is a sizable body of water and then go up a side canyon. Since the canyon faces north and gets lots of water, it is lush and supports a nice forest.
    At the 1.0 mile *1.6 km* point you will cross a road and break into a clearing from where you have good views of the San Francisco Peaks. At the 1.33 mile *2.13 km* point you go over the crest of a hill and from that point onward will be unable to see the Peaks. You follow a shoulder of the Dry Lake Hills to the 1.6 mile *2.56 km* point, where there is a trail junction. Take the fork to the left, downhill. The trail signs here omit the Sunset Trail.

The trail will take you down a fold between the Dry Lake Hills and Mt. Elden and then you will climb steeply up to the top of a ridge on Mt. Elden. On the way up you will pass through a very attractive alpine forest. Once you reach the ridge line you will drop over the other side slightly and walk along the shoulder to a trail junction at 3.5 miles *5.6 km*—just above the Elden Lookout Road. We have the trail stop here, though officially it goes on for another mile to the lookout tower.

At the top of the ridge you enter an area that was badly burned in the catastrophic Radio Fire in 1978. The area is starting to heal and you will see stands of young aspen thriving in favored spots. The only good thing about the fire was that with the tree cover burned away you can now get superior views to the east.

This is a hard hike if you go back the way you came. We love it as a two-car shuttle, parking one at the Sunset Trailhead and the other at a point 5.75 miles *9.2 km* up the Elden Lookout Road; then hike down from the top.

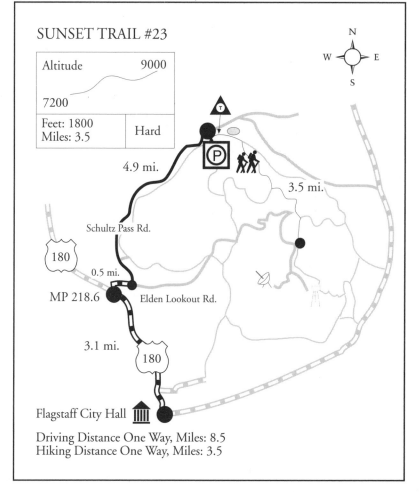

SUNSET TRAIL #23

Altitude	9000
7200	
Feet: 1800 Miles: 3.5	Hard

4.9 mi.

3.5 mi.

Schultz Pass Rd.

180

0.5 mi.

MP 218.6   Elden Lookout Rd.

3.1 mi.

180

Flagstaff City Hall

Driving Distance One Way, Miles: 8.5
Hiking Distance One Way, Miles: 3.5

Mangum

SYCAMORE BASIN TRAIL #63

Driving Distance One Way: 76.4 miles *122.3 km* (Time 2 hours)
Access Road: High clearance needed for last 13.4 miles *21.5 km*
Hiking Distance One Way: 3.0 miles *4.8 km* (Time 1.5 hours)
How Strenuous: Moderate
Features: Gorgeous remote scenic basin framed with redrocks

NUTSHELL: A long drive takes you to the basin of Sycamore Canyon.

DIRECTIONS:
From Flagstaff City Hall Go:
    West, then south on Route 66 under the railroad overpass. See Access Map, page 10. Follow Route 66 when it turns right at the second stoplight. In about five miles *8.0 km* you will merge onto I-40 West and stay on it to the 30.3 miles *48.5 km* point, the Williams Exit, #165. Take that exit and at the stop sign go left to Williams. Go into town on Railroad Avenue to the 32.9 mile point *52.6 km* where you will find Fourth Street. Turn left on Fourth Street. As it leaves town its name changes to the Perkinsville Road (FR 173). Stay on this road to the bottom of the hill, where the paving ends, at 57.4 miles *92 km* and keep going east on FR 492. At 60.6 miles *97.0 km* you will reach an intersection where FR 354 comes down off the rim from your left. Turn right here and stay on the main road to the 63.0 mile *101 km* point, where you turn left at the sign for Henderson Flat on FR 181. Up to this point the roads have been fine for all cars. FR 181 has some rough spots and requires a high clearance vehicle. The road winds around until it reaches an old ranch house at Henderson Flat. This is at the 70.8 mile *113.3 km* point. Keep going on FR 181 to its end at 76.4 miles *122.3 km*, where you will park at the Sycamore Canyon Wilderness boundary.

TRAILHEAD: At the parking spot. There are signs, one reading "Cow Flat 2, Taylor Cabin 8." Go through the fence.

DESCRIPTION: To reach the trailhead, you have driven several miles along the base of the Mogollon Rim, enjoying the sight of beautiful rock formations, which will remind you of the country around Sedona.
    As you begin the hike, you will be see how the Sedona area looked in its pristine condition. You drop down into a vast basin rimmed with colorful cliffs, shaded red in the lower levels, tan and white on the higher levels. The

trail is in good condition and is very easy to walk, with a gradual grade.

You may feel that you are in Sycamore Canyon, but you are not. The basin is so vast that huge Sycamore Canyon occupies only a small part of it. The canyon is to your right (east), and your trail angles toward it, not reaching it until the 4.5 miles *7.2 km* point. At 1.6 miles *2.6 km*, you will come to Cross D Tank, where there is a sign. A few feet beyond is a corral made of juniper poles. This is Cow Flat.

At the 2.2 mile *3.5 km* point, we found a trail marker, "Yew Thicket Trail No. 52," with an arrow pointing NW. (According to maps, this trail climbs the rim and meets the **Lonesome Pocket Trail** at its trailhead in 5.3 miles *8.5 km*).

We end this hike at 3.0 miles *4.8 km* because that makes a good day hike, but you can go farther if you have the time and energy.

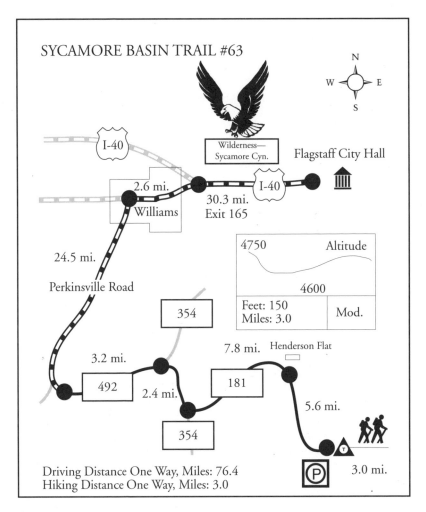

SYCAMORE RIM TRAIL

General Information
Location Map F2
Bill Williams Mountain and Garland Prairie USGS Maps
Kaibab (Williams District) Forest Service Map

Driving Distance One Way: 28.75 miles *46.0 km* (Time 50 minutes)
Access Road: All cars, Last 10.75 miles *17.2 km* good gravel roads
Hiking Distance, Complete Loop: 12.0 miles *19.2 km* (Time 7.0 hours)
How Strenuous: Hard, due to length and rocky places
Features: Cabin and mill ruins, Canyon springs, Views, Waterfall

NUTSHELL: This hike displays the features of the Sycamore Canyon area southwest of Flagstaff, including spring-fed canyon pools, a waterfall, a huge canyon, a prairie and a hill climb.

DIRECTIONS:
From Flagstaff City Hall Go:
    West, then south on Route 66, beneath the railroad overpass. See Access Map, page 10. At 0.50 miles *0.8 km* turn right on Route 66. At the 4.8 mile *7.7 km* point you will merge onto Interstate-40 West. Drive I-40 West to Exit 178, "Parks" and take the exit. It is at the 18.0 mile *28.8 km* point. From the exit turn left and go south to Garland Prairie. When you cross the railroad tracks you will be on FR 141, the main road through Garland Prairie. Stay on it to the 27.6 miles *44 km* point, where it meets FR 131 and FR 13. At this point the road going straight ahead is FR 13. Take FR 13 to the 28.5 mile *45.6 km* point, where it meets FR 56. Turn left on FR 56 and go to the 28.75 mile *46 km* point, where you will see a pole fence marking the parking area to your left. Park there.

TRAILHEAD: Marked at the parking area.

DESCRIPTION: The Sycamore Rim Trail is a loop and you can start it at various places, but the preferred starting point is the one described. The first leg is to go south, where you will first encounter Dow Spring, a perennial water source. It has been captured in a pipe and flows out into a small canyon that is the beginning of gigantic Sycamore Canyon, one of the prominent land features of northern Arizona. The trail crosses the canyon and takes you along the canyon rim. Soon you will see LO Spring, which forms pools in a chain of rock basins, in which water lilies grow.
    Beyond, the canyon deepens drastically. Sycamore Vista, coming up, provides a view into the immensity of Sycamore Canyon and some of its tributaries. From here, you will leave the big canyon and climb a rocky hill-

side and go down into a smaller canyon.

The next point of interest is Sycamore Falls, a sharp chasm. The falls seldom run, but when they do, they are spectacular. The most likely time to see water going over the falls in during the spring snow melt, though the trail may be too muddy to hike then. From the falls, you walk north along the canyon until you come to Pomeroy Tanks, another series of rock basins in which water lilies grow in scenic ponds.

Beyond Pomeroy Tanks, the land is more level. You will cross the Overland Trail, marked by burro symbols burnt into posts. Soon after this, you will cross FR 13 and make the 687 foot climb up KA Hill, from the top of which you will have great views over the countryside. Then it's down KA Hill and back to the parking place.

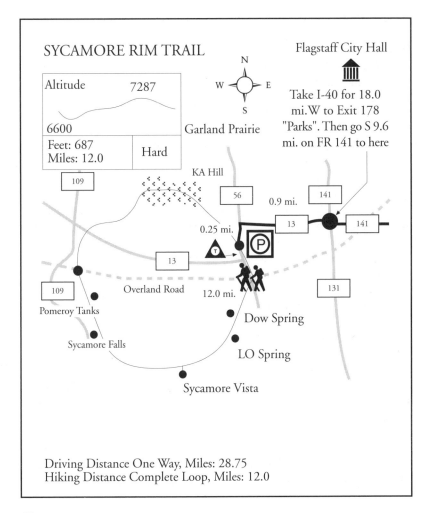

SYCAMORE RIM TRAIL

Flagstaff City Hall

Altitude 7287

6600

Feet: 687
Miles: 12.0

Hard

Garland Prairie

Take I-40 for 18.0 mi.W to Exit 178 "Parks". Then go S 9.6 mi. on FR 141 to here

KA Hill

109

56

0.9 mi.

141

0.25 mi.

13

141

Overland Road

109

13

131

12.0 mi.

Pomeroy Tanks

Dow Spring

Sycamore Falls

LO Spring

Sycamore Vista

Driving Distance One Way, Miles: 28.75
Hiking Distance Complete Loop, Miles: 12.0

Mangum

TAYLOR CABIN TRAIL #35

General Information
Location Map F2
Loy Butte, Sycamore Point USGS Maps
Coconino Forest Service Map

Driving Distance One Way: 29 miles *46.4 km* (Time 1.5 hours)
Access Road: High clearance, Last 25.4 miles *40.6 km* dirt rough spots
Hiking Distance One Way: 2.6 miles *4.2 km* (Time 2.5 hours)
How Strenuous: Hard, Very steep rocky trail
Features: Views, Tremendous wild canyons

NUTSHELL: Located 29.0 miles *46.4 km* southwest of Flagstaff, this hike plunges from the top of Buck Ridge to the bottom of Sycamore Canyon.

DIRECTIONS:
From Flagstaff City Hall Go:
    West, then south on Route 66, beneath the railroad overpass. See Access Map, page 10. At 0.50 miles *0.8 km* turn right on Route 66. At 2.6 miles *4.16 km* you will reach the Woody Mountain Road, FR 231, where you turn left. It is paved about a mile and then turns into a cinder road. At 16.6 miles *26.56 km* you will intersect FR 538. Turn right onto FR 538 and follow it to an intersection at 22.3 miles *35.7 km*. Turn left here, staying on FR 538. At 25.7 miles *41.1 km* you will pass the turn to Winter Cabin. Go straight ahead to the 26.1 mile *42 km* point, where FR 538B branches to the right. Take FR 538B. It follows the path of a huge power line. FR 538B is decent down to the 28.5 mile *45.6 km* point but from there it is one of the worst roads we have seen, virtually impassable, with lots of exposed chassis-ripping rock. Many hikers will want to walk this last half mile. The road ends at 29 miles *46.4 km* at a bare spot on the ridge, where you must park. **Caution**: do not drive down into the canyon, as the road is blocked by a big gate, trapping you in a place where you cannot turn around.

TRAILHEAD: Walk down the road 0.25 miles *0.4 km.*

DESCRIPTION: The trailhead is at a strategic point, located on a thin ridge where three trails come together: the Mooney Trail (see *Sedona Hikes*), the Taylor Cabin Trail and the **Casner Mountain North** trail. The views here are very fine. The ridge divides Sycamore Canyon from the Sedona back country, so you can see into both Sycamore and Sedona.
    There are some false trails at the beginning of the Taylor Cabin trail. From the rusty metal trailhead sign, walk behind it 15 paces to a tree to which a barbed wire fence and Wilderness sign are nailed. Turn right behind

the tree and then turn left at the next trail fork. You will go downhill on a zigzag course. Once established at the beginning, you can follow the trail.

The trail works its way down through a beautiful forest. It contains pockets of maple, beautiful in late October when their leaves are red. The trail is steep and littered with loose rocks, making for tricky footing.

When you have gone down about a mile *1.6 km*, it will seem that you have reached bottom. Not so. From here the trail follows the channel of a side canyon. In many places you walk right in the streambed. Look for cairns and blazes on this leg. Hiking here is slow, hard on the feet, and almost dangerous. As compensation, you pass through a beautiful red-walled canyon that is very colorful. This side canyon eventually merges into the awesome main canyon of Sycamore.

At the bottom of the trail, if you have enough strength left, you can visit Taylor Cabin. It is built of native stone and set against the canyon wall. It is a hard 1.5 miles *2.4 km* to your left (south).

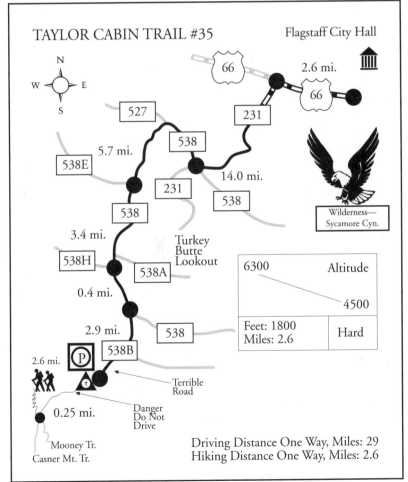

222

THREE SISTERS

General Information
Location Map E1
Williams North USGS Map
Kaibab Forest Service Map

Driving Distance One Way: 38.85 miles *62.2 km* (Time 1.0 hour)
Access Road: All cars, Last 1.75 miles *2.8 km* good unpaved roads
Hiking Distance One Way: 0.50 miles *0.8 km* (Time 1.0 hour)
How Strenuous: Moderate
Features: Interesting volcanic formations, views

NUTSHELL: This group of three hills is a landmark near the City of Williams. You park at a saddle between two of the "sisters" and hike to the top of the tallest. On the way you will see huge boulders and volcanic outcroppings and at the top will enjoy tremendous views.

DIRECTIONS:
From Flagstaff City Hall Go:
South on Route 66 under the railroad overpass. Be sure to turn right on Route 66 at the second stoplight. See Access Map on page 10. In about five miles *8.0 km* you will merge onto I-40 West and stay on it to the 34.5 miles *55.2 km* point, the Golf Course Exit, #163. You will come to a stop sign at 34.9 miles *55.9 km*. Turn right here and go to the 35.4 mile point *56.6 km*, where there is another stop sign. Turn right here and go under the railroad overpass. Stay on the main paved road. Go past the golf course. Soon the paving ends and the road becomes a good gravel road, FR 124. This road winds around the last "sister" and begins to climb. At the 38.1 mile *61.0 km* point take an unsurfaced unmarked road to your right. This road is 1.0 miles *1.6 km* from the end of the paving. The road is not maintained well but isn't bad when dry. Don't try it when it is wet. The road climbs to a saddle where at the 38.85 mile *62.2 km* point you will see a loop pullout to your right. Pull off here and park.

TRAILHEAD: There is no trail. You simply climb to the top of the "sister" to the north.

DESCRIPTION: Generally we like to hike on trails, but if we come across a good non-trail hike we think our readers can handle, we include it. This is such a hike.

As you walk up the hill, you will find that the soil is composed of coarse red cinders. You will think that you see trails through the brush, but actually they are simply natural lanes between bushes. You will pick up game

Flagstaff Hikes

trails only to have them disappear. Don't worry. It is always easy to tell where you are headed. Just keep moving uphill.

At the 0.25 mile *0.4 km* point you will reach the top of a cinder knob. Here you will have your first views, a taste of what is to come. You will see the higher crest before you, made of much different material. Instead of being a rounded cinder hill, it shows exposed volcanic rock, with huge tumbled boulders and a ridge of cliffs along the uplifted east face. It is easy to walk over to the base of this higher face of the hill and begin to climb it.

When you reach the base of the boulders you will have to pick your way more carefully, though we had no trouble finding a route. Once you are on top, you can navigate with ease. Because of bare boulders at places on the top you will have clear views in many spots. The views are splendid. You can see the City of Williams with Bill Williams Mountain behind it. The San Francisco Peaks, Sitgreaves Mountain and Kendrick Peak are all clearly in view. The top is about 0.50 miles *0.8 km* from where you parked.

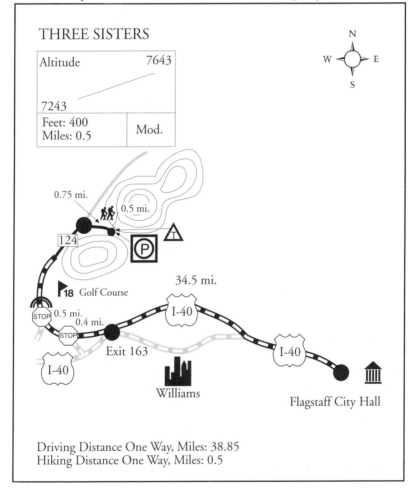

TRAMWAY TRAIL #32

General Information
Location Map G4
Calloway Butte USGS Map
Coconino Forest Service Map

Driving Distance One Way: 57.5 miles *92 km* (Time 1.5 hours)
Access Road: High clearance vehicle, Last 1.7 miles *2.72 km* very rough
Hiking Distance One Way: 0.70 miles *1.12 km* (Time 45 minutes)
How Strenuous: Hard
Features: Views, Beautiful pristine stream, Remote canyon

NUTSHELL: This is one of the few trails into West Clear Creek, a remote canyon 57.5 miles *92 km* southeast of Flagstaff. The hike is short but steep and very beautiful.

DIRECTIONS:
From Flagstaff City Hall Go:
    West, then south on Route 66 beneath the railroad overpass. See Access Map, page 10. At the 0.5 mile *0.8 km* point, go straight on Milton Road. At 1.7 miles *2.72 km* you will reach a stoplight at Forest Meadows Street. Turn right here onto Forest Meadows and go one block to Beulah. Turn left on Beulah and follow it south. Beulah merges onto Highway 89A. At 2.4 miles *3.84 km* (MP 401.6), turn left onto the Lake Mary Road at the stoplight. Follow the Lake Mary Road, going past Lower and Upper Lake Mary and Mormon Lake to the 48.9 mile *78.24 km* point (MP 297.7), where you turn right onto a dirt road, FR 81. The highway sign shows "V Bar V Ranch, Poor Farm and West Clear Creek." Follow FR 81 to the 52.0 mile *83.2 km* point, its junction with FR 81E, turning left on 81E and staying on it to the 55.8 mile *89.3 km* point, where you reach a fork. Take the right fork, on FR 693. You will see a sign for the Tramway Trail soon. FR 693 is a very rough road, requiring high clearance and tough tires. Keep driving FR 693 to the 57.5 mile *92 km* point, a parking area at the very rim of the canyon.

TRAILHEAD: There is a sign at the parking area.

DESCRIPTION: West Clear Creek is a tributary of the Verde River. Its headwaters are on the uplands of the Mogollon Rim, where this hike takes place. Located in a remote area, West Clear Creek canyon cuts a course running from east to west. At its low end it joins the Verde River near Camp Verde.
    At the beginning of the hike, you will see a cable to your left. It goes down to the canyon bottom, and was part of the tram that gives this trail its

name. You will see the cable again farther down the trail.

The canyon is open to view from the beginning. It is not very wide but is deep and colorful—buff sandstone with splashes of a light orangey rust.

The trail is very steep, with a bit of scrambling where you have to climb down ledges.

We were here in late May and there were all sorts of flowers, everything from cactus to penstemon were blooming.

At the bottom, the vegetation is rich. You come out at a big pool at the base of an immense cliff. This is a favorite fishing hole for the speckled and rainbow trout that inhabit the water of Clear Creek. If you want to do any walking along the bottom, we recommend tennies or Tevas, as there are places where you will want to wade. The bottom is a peaceful, beautiful paradise.

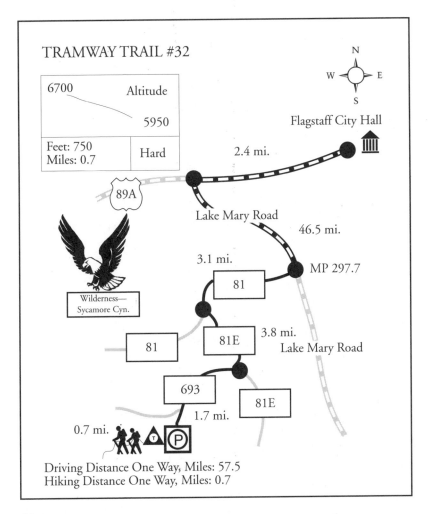

Mangum

TUNNEL (WATERSHED) ROAD

General Information
Location Map E3
Humphreys Peak USGS Map
Coconino Forest Service Map

Driving Distance One Way: 9.4 miles *15.1 km* (Time 30 minutes)
Access Road: All cars, Last 5.8 miles *9.28 km* good gravel road
Hiking Distance One Way: 8.5 miles *13.6 km* (Time 4.5 hours)
How Strenuous: Hard if you go full distance
Features: High mountains, Interesting tunnel, Excellent views

NUTSHELL: Located about 10 miles *16 km* north of Flagstaff, this moderate but long hike takes you through beautiful forests and meadows on the San Francisco Peaks.

DIRECTIONS:
From Flagstaff City Hall Go:
   North on Humphreys Street for 0.60 miles *1.0 km*. See Access Map, page 10. Turn left at the stoplight onto Columbus Avenue and follow it around a big curve to the north. You will see the street signs call this road Columbus at first, then Ft. Valley Road and then Highway 180. Stay on Highway 180 to the 3.1 miles *5.0 km* point (MP 218.6), where you turn right on the Schultz Pass Road. Turn right and follow this road. At 3.6 miles *5.76 km* it curves to the left and you will see an unpaved road going straight. Stay on the paved road. The paving will end soon and the road will become gravel surfaced. Follow it to the 8.8 mile *14.1 km* point, just beyond the **Weatherford Trail** sign, where FR 146 intersects the road from the left. Turn left onto FR 146 and take it to the 9.4 mile *15.1 km* point where you will reach a locked gate. Park off the road by the gate.

TRAILHEAD: Not a marked trail. You walk FR 146 beyond the gate.

DESCRIPTION: The City of Flagstaff maintains FR 146 for access to the city's watershed, particularly the works at Jack Smith Spring, so it is kept in good condition. The only vehicle travel allowed is for city maintenance trucks. Mountain bikers love this road and you are very likely to find them there on weekends.
   The grade of this road is gentle, running along the 8000 foot contour of the mountain for the first couple of miles, then beginning a climb that terminates at about 9400 feet at Jack Smith Spring. When you take the **Inner Basin Trail** hike, you will visit Jack Smith Spring.
   You will reach the tunnel for which the hike is named at 2.0 miles *3.2*

km. At that point the road builders hit a lava dike and decided to bore through it rather than blast it away. The tunnel is about 25 feet long, 10 feet wide and 12 feet high, and adds a pleasing note of interest. Hikers who want a mild but rewarding hike might want to turn back at the tunnel.

There are many fine views from the road, especially off to the hiker's right, into the Sunset Crater area. The volcanic nature of the terrain is plainly displayed and you will see a myriad of cinder cones, which are the remains of small volcanoes.

You can hike all the way to Jack Smith Spring, 8.5 miles *13.6 km*, if you are hardy and quick, but this requires a 17.0 mile *27.2 km* round-trip hike at high altitudes, which may be too arduous for many readers. So, pick your spot anywhere and turn back at your own comfort point.

The road doesn't end at the spring. It continues climbing 5.5 miles *8.8 km* farther to the north face of the Peaks. The **Bear Jaw** and **Abineau Canyon** trails terminate on the far reaches of FR 146.

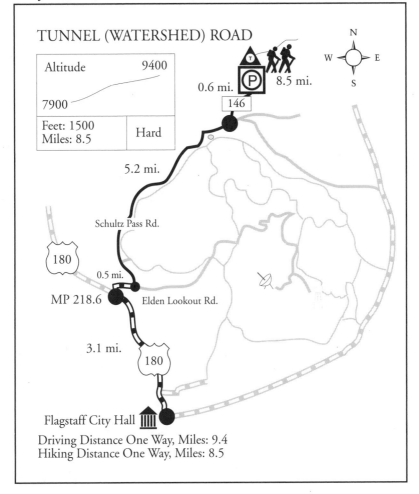

TUNNEL (WATERSHED) ROAD

Altitude 9400
7900
Feet: 1500
Miles: 8.5

Hard

0.6 mi.
146
8.5 mi.

5.2 mi.

Schultz Pass Rd.

180

0.5 mi.

MP 218.6
Elden Lookout Rd.

3.1 mi.

180

Flagstaff City Hall

Driving Distance One Way, Miles: 9.4
Hiking Distance One Way, Miles: 8.5

TUNNEL TRAIL

General Information
Location Map G4
Dane Canyon, Kehl Ridge USGS Maps
Coconino Forest Service Map

Driving Distance One Way: 78 miles *125 km* (Time 2 hours)
Access Road: All cars, Last 12.2 miles *19.5 km* good dirt road
Hiking Distance One Way: 0.6 miles *1.0 km* (40 minutes)
How Strenuous: Moderate
Features: Beautiful Mogollon Rim, Historic railroad tunnel

NUTSHELL: After enjoying a portion of the Rim Drive, you will take a refreshing hike to see a historic relic, an unfinished railroad tunnel boring into the side of the Mogollon Rim.

DIRECTIONS:
From Flagstaff City Hall Go:
    West, then south on Route 66, under the railroad overpass. At 0.5 miles *0.8 km*, go straight on Milton Road. See Access Map, page 10. At 1.7 miles *2.72 km* you will reach a stoplight at Forest Meadows Street. Turn right here onto Forest Meadows and go one block to Beulah. Turn left on Beulah and follow it south. Beulah merges onto Highway 89A. At 2.4 miles *3.84 km* (MP 401.6), turn left onto the Lake Mary Road. Follow the Lake Mary Road (also known as FH 3) to its end at the junction with State Route 87, 56.6 miles *90.6 km*. Turn right here on Highway 87, a paved road, and follow it to the 65.8 mile *105.3 km* point MP 280, where you turn left on FR 300, which is posted. FR 300 is surfaced with gravel and is a good road. Follow it to the 78 mile *125 km* point, where you will see a monument to the Battle of Big Dry Wash. Park near the monument.

TRAILHEAD: Across the road from the battle monument.

DESCRIPTION: You will see the trail running beneath the power line that goes down a canyon. On the way down the trail, be sure to leave the power line at the second pole and move to your left, where you will find an old service road that was built for the purpose of tunnel construction.
    The hike is steep, but the footing is not bad. It is short. The trail goes down about 0.33 miles *0.53 km*, and then makes a sharp turn to your left, going uphill. There were markers for the trail when we took the hike.
    After you make the turn, the trail doubles back uphill, going up 0.25 miles *0.4 km* to the tunnel, which sits on a scenic shelf of land. In front of the mouth are the remains of a hut built of sandstone slabs, and evidence of

the tunnel construction all around. The sight of the tunnel is quite a shock, as it sits in isolation, far from the world. The first reaction of any visitor is to ask, "How in the world did this get here?"

The tunnel was part of an 1885 plan to build a railroad from Flagstaff to Globe. Rim area residents were recruited to dig this tunnel in advance of the rails, taking their wages in stock rather than cash. After reaching Mormon Lake, the bankrupt railroad was abandoned, leaving this tunnel high and dry, miles away from anything, and the crews with nothing but worthless paper.

The Rim Drive is a scenic must for northern Arizona. If you have not taken it, we highly recommend finishing it, by continuing east on FR 300 after the hike. The entire drive is 34.5 miles *55.2 km.* The drive ends at Highway 260, a good paved highway, where you turn right and go down into Payson. From Payson you can return to Flagstaff via Camp Verde or on Highway 87. A detour to the Tonto Natural Bridge is well worthwhile. Take a long full day to do all of this.

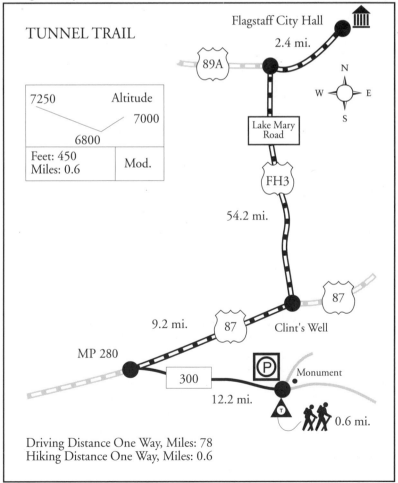

Mangum

230

TURKEY HILL

General Information
Location Map F3
Flagstaff East USGS Map
Coconino Forest Map

Driving Distance One Way: 8.65 miles *13.8 km* (Time 20 minutes)
Access Road: All cars, Last 1.1 miles *1.8 km* rough cinder road
Hiking Distance One Way: 1.0 miles *1.6 km* (Time 30 minutes)
How Strenuous: Moderate
Features: Easy access, Views

NUTSHELL: This cinder hill is located so as to give good views around the Flagstaff area. You hike an abandoned road that goes around the hill to the top.

DIRECTIONS:
From Flagstaff City Hall Go:
    East on Route 66. See Access Map, pages 10-11. At 3.8 miles *6.1 km* (MP 418.2/MP 200) you will come to a fork, where Route 66 goes to the right. Turn right onto Route 66 and follow it to the 7.5 mile *12.0 km* point, where there is a cinder road to the left. Turn left onto this road, FR 791, and follow it to the 8.3 mile *13.3 km* point, where the road splits. Both the left and right forks are marked FR 510B. Take the left fork. Up to this point the road has been good, but it now turns pretty bad, as there are ruts and exposed rocks. If you are not in a high clearance vehicle, you should park at the 510B fork. If you can make it, go up to the 8.65 miles *13.8 km* point, where there is an unmarked road going to the left. Park on the right shoulder here.

TRAILHEAD: There are no trail signs. You hike the road.

DESCRIPTION: At one time there was a cinder pit operation on this hill. The road you will hike was built to service the pit. You will see a number of side roads as you walk along. At every junction take the right fork, always staying on the outside of the hill and moving upward.
    You will soon come to the pit. There you will see that a road keeps going up the hill to the right of the pit. Stay on it and continue the ascent. From this point onwards it is easy to tell what the roads are doing and to follow the correct one.
    The road literally winds completely around the hill as it climbs. The vegetation is mostly low so that you can see clearly. The views are good. You are looking at some interesting landscapes: volcano fields, and beyond them, the Painted Desert. You can get a good look at Anderson Mesa. To the west

Flagstaff Hikes

you can see parts of Flagstaff.

The top of Turkey Hill is a true top. There are no false tops or benches. You suddenly pop up onto a small flat summit from which you can see out on all sides.

On the maps, you will see references to Turkey Hills. The other hill is quite a bit smaller and is to the north of the one you can hike.

You will also see the Turkey Hills Pueblo on maps. This is located north of the hiking hill also. The best way to reach it is by going east on the Townsend-Winona Road for 3.0 miles *4.8 km* from the stoplight, then turning right on an unmarked gravel road and following it for 0.15 miles *0.24 km*. There you will see a burglar-proof chain-link fence surrounding about a half acre of ground to your right. Unfortunately there isn't much to see: just low lines of rubble marking pit houses and you can't get inside for a closer look.

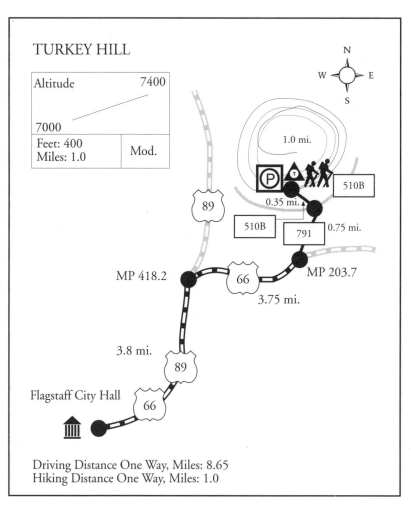

TURKEY TANKS—COSNINO CAVES

General Information
Location Map F4
Sunset Crater East, Winona USGS Maps
Coconino Forest Service Map

Driving Distance One Way: 18.6 miles 29.8 km (Time 30 minutes)
Access Road: All cars, Last 0.2 miles *0.32 km* good gravel road
Hiking Distance One Way: 0.6 miles *1.0 km* (Time 45 minutes)
How Strenuous: Easy
Features: Caves with ruins, Historic site

NUTSHELL: Located 18.6 miles *29.8 km* east of Flagstaff, this easy hike takes you along a portion of San Francisco Wash to visit Turkey Tanks (natural ponds) and Cosnino Caves (Indian ruins). You will also see a fragment of the historic Beale Road.

DIRECTIONS:
From Flagstaff City Hall Go:
East, curving to north on Highway 89. See Access Map, pages 10-11. At 6.5 miles *10.4 km* (MP 420.5) you will reach the last stoplight in town at the junction of the Townsend-Winona Road. Turn right here onto the Townsend-Winona Road and follow it to the 14.7 miles *23.52 km* point (MP 428.7) where it intersects Leupp Road. Turn left on the Leupp Road and go to the 18.4 mile *29.44 km* point (MP 432.4). Turn right on an unmarked black gravel road and follow it to the 18.6 mile *29.8 km* point, where you will be on the rim of the canyon at San Francisco Wash. Park there.

TRAILHEAD: Look for trees marked with white diamonds about two inches square. Park by the diamond-marked tree closest to the canyon, where you will see an old road cut down to the canyon floor. This is the trailhead.

DESCRIPTION: The white diamonds on the trees mark the route of the historic Beale Road. This road was built in 1858 by the U.S. Government to open up the recently acquired Arizona territory. It ran from Ft. Wingate, New Mexico to the Colorado River. The road came through this point to take advantage of the water at Turkey Tanks. You can follow the diamonds east about a mile *1.6 km* to Cochrane Hill if you want a little side trip.

The place where you parked was once a ranch operated by the Sykes brothers who had a post office in the ranch house in 1881. Now you can see nothing of the dwelling except a small pile of stones, the remains of the chimney. Godfrey Sykes's autobiography, *A Westerly Trend*, University of Arizona Press, 1984, describes this place, and is a good read.

Walk down onto the canyon floor (it's easy) and then turn right, following the canyon bottom. At 0.4 miles *0.64 km* you will come to a bend where the highway is just above your head. On the bank under the road you will encounter the Cosnino Caves. These are lava blowouts. The entire bank is honeycombed with them. Early archaeologists made significant finds of museum quality artifacts in these caves, but by the 1950s they were disregarded to the extent that the present road was run right over the top of them, doing extensive damage. Early travelers using the Beale Road were fascinated with these caves and all the diarists commented on them.

From the caves go back to where you started and walk upstream. In 0.2 miles *0.32 km* you will come to a stone dam located at the last tank in the chain of Turkey Tanks. It is easy to skirt the dam on the right and come up on top of it. The dam seems almost comically deep. It was built in the 1930s. Before that, travelers relied on the natural ponds.

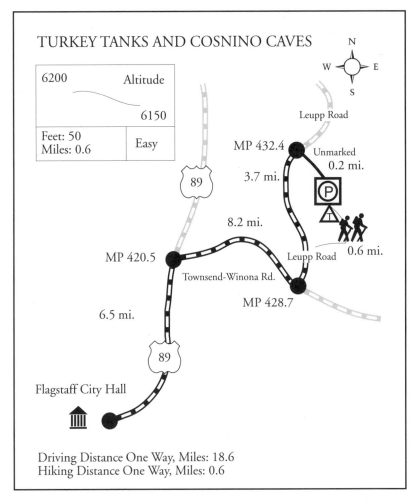

TURKEY TANKS AND COSNINO CAVES

Driving Distance One Way, Miles: 18.6
Hiking Distance One Way, Miles: 0.6

Mangum

VEIT SPRINGS

General Information
Location Map E3
Humphreys Peak USGS Map
Coconino Forest Service Map

Driving Distance One Way: 11.8 miles *18.9 km* (Time 30 minutes)
Access Road: All cars, All paved
Hiking Distance One Way: 0.75 miles *1.2 km* (Time 30 minutes)
How Strenuous: Easy
Features: Alpine forests, Historical cabin, Rock art

NUTSHELL: The hike takes you to an old cabin site on the San Francisco Peaks about 11.8 miles *18.9 km* north of Flagstaff, a lush, peaceful Shangri-La. **A personal favorite**.

DIRECTIONS:
From Flagstaff City Hall Go:
   North on Humphreys Street for 0.60 miles *1.0 km*. See Access Map, page 10. Turn left at the stoplight onto Columbus Avenue and follow it around a big curve to the north. You will see the street signs call this road Columbus at first, then Ft. Valley Road and then Highway 180. Stay on Highway 180 to the 7.3 miles *11.68 km* point (MP 223), where the road to the Snow Bowl branches off to the right. It is well posted. Follow the Snow Bowl road to the 11.8 miles *18.9 km* point. There you will see a driveway to your right to the Lamar Haines Memorial Wildlife Area. Pull in and park there.

TRAILHEAD: Posted at the gate.

DESCRIPTION: At the parking area there is a gate. Go through it. There is a large sign beyond the gate telling about the area. The trail goes uphill to the right behind the sign, not straight ahead along the old jeep road.
   Although a lot of snow falls on the San Francisco Peaks, very little of the water produced by the snow appears there in streams, ponds or springs. Due to their volcanic origin, the Peaks are quite porous and most of the water produced by snow melt sinks in and goes into underground rivers. Here and there you will find a spring. This hike takes you to such a site.
   The early settlers in the area looked carefully for springs and used most of them as sites for sheep or cattle operations. One such settler was Ludwig Veit, who homesteaded the area reached by this hike in 1892. You can see his name chiseled into the face of a lava boulder to the right of the cabin.
   As you walk the trail you will come to a fork at about 0.20 miles *0.32 km*. Take the right fork here. You will follow an old wagon road to the cabin

from this point. At 0.70 miles *1.1 km* the road winds around to a plaque set into a boulder. The plaque honors Lamar Haines, a Flagstaff outdoorsman.

There is a basalt ridge running behind the cabin site, furnishing a sort of wall or backdrop to it. One of the richest stands of aspens on the Peaks is located to the east of the plaque.

Follow the road from the plaque up to the old log cabin. The cabin is very low. It has been cut down so that adults can't stand up in it. Above the cabin is a pond formed by the water from the main spring. Between the pond and the cliff is a small stone shed. In the face of the cliff a frame has been built around the opening to the spring.

If you walk the face of the cliff to your left (as you face the spring), you will go around a bend and find a secondary spring. There are pictographs on the rock walls surrounding it.

This is a terrific place to enjoy changing aspen leaves in October.

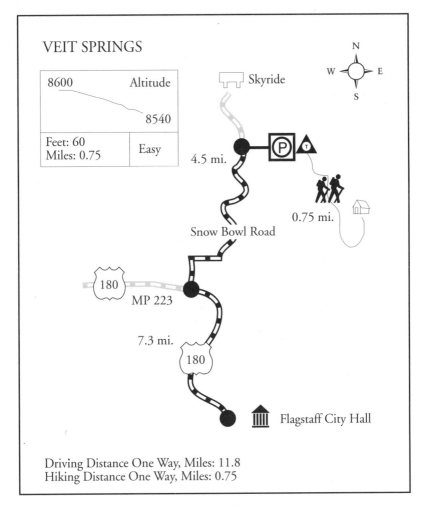

WALKER LAKE

General Information
Location Map E3
Humphreys Peak and Wing Mt. USGS Maps
Coconino Forest Service Map

Driving Distance One Way: 21.8 miles *34.9 km* (Time 40 minutes)
Access Road: All cars, Last 2.2 miles *3.52 km* good dirt road
Hiking Distance One Way: 0.50 miles *0.8 km* (Time 1 hour)
How Strenuous: Easy
Features: Views, Scenic crater

NUTSHELL: This is a gentle hike to the crater of an ancient volcano located about 20 miles *32 km* north of Flagstaff.

DIRECTIONS:
From Flagstaff City Hall Go:
   North on Humphreys Street for 0.60 miles *1.0 km*. See Access Map, page 10. Turn left at the stoplight onto Columbus Avenue and follow it around a big curve to the north. You will see the street signs call this road Columbus at first, then Ft. Valley Road and then Highway 180. Stay on Highway 180 to the 19.6 miles *31.36 km* point (MP 235.2), where the unpaved upper Hart Prairie Road branches off to the right. Turn right onto this road, which is also identified as FR 151, and follow it to the 21.2 miles *33.92 km* point. There FR 418 branches to the left. Take FR 418 and follow it just 0.20 miles *0.32 km*, to the 21.4 mile *34.24 km* point. There you will reach an unmarked dirt road to the left. Turn left onto it and follow it to the 21.8 miles *34.9 km* point, where you will park.

TRAILHEAD: There are no trail signs. You will see a blocked road going up to the top of a cinder cone. You hike this road.

DESCRIPTION: The road is easy walking, being broad with a gradual grade. It is about 0.20 miles *0.32 km* to the top, where you will find yourself on the rim of a volcanic crater. This was a small volcano so the crater is fairly shallow. Walker Lake is in the center of the crater. The lake, never very big, often dries up completely in the summer. The best time of year to find water in it is in the spring, after the snow melts, which is usually in April or May.
   The road forks at the top and you can walk either left or right on it. The left fork goes directly down to the lake, while the right fork sweeps around through a stand of aspen and firs and is more scenic. It is only about 0.10 miles *0.16 km* to the lake by the left fork, slightly longer than that by the

right fork.

The north rim of the crater is rather bare due to a forest fire. It is higher than the south rim. It is worth a climb up the north rim if you are willing to make the effort, for fine views from the top unimpeded by trees. There is no trail to the north rim but it is easy to bushwhack your way there. You can't get lost.

This is a pretty and little known spot. The San Francisco Peaks area is dotted with over one hundred volcanic craters. This is one of the most accessible and scenic of them, with the bonus of a lake. Most craters are pretty bare, but this one has lots of vegetation and a nice friendly feel.

There is a strange pit lined with steel panels near the pond. Our guess is that it is an old well site. Take a look and see what you think.

The cinders in most Northern Arizona volcanic craters are black or red, but at Walker Lake they are brown. This gives the place more of an earthy, less moonlike appearance and is less stark, more inviting.

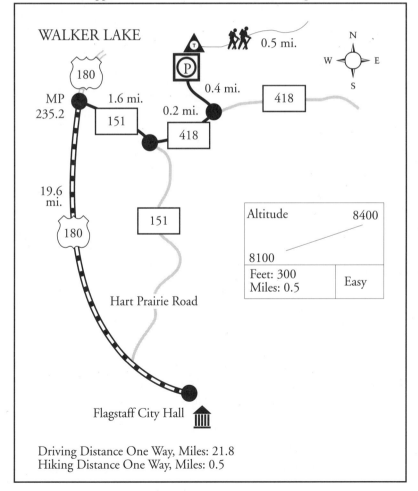

WALNUT CANYON TRAILS (4)

General Information
Location Map F3
Flagstaff East USGS Map
Coconino Forest Service Map

Driving Distance One Way: 17.3 miles *27.7 km* (Time 25 minutes)
Access Road: All cars, All paved
Hiking Distance, See below
How Strenuous: Easy to Moderate
Features: Indian ruins, Scenic canyon

NUTSHELL: There are four hiking trails in the Walnut Canyon National Monument, located just a few miles east of Flagstaff. All allow the hiker to enjoy scenery and ruins.

DIRECTIONS:
From Flagstaff City Hall Go:
East, then north on Highway 89. See Access Map, pages 10-11. At 4.2 miles *6.7 km* you will see a sign to your right marking the entrance to Interstate-40. Take this entrance and at 4.3 miles *6.8 km* turn left on the Interstate-40 East Exit. This will place you on I-40 headed east. At 14.3 miles *22.9 km* (MP 204) you will reach the Walnut Canyon turn, Exit 204. Turn right on this and follow the paved road to Walnut Canyon. You will reach the parking lot at the Visitor Center at 17.3 miles *27.7 km.*

TRAILHEAD: The Visitor Center.

DESCRIPTION:
Island Trail. Length, 0.8 miles *1.28 km* complete loop. Paved. Altitude change 300 feet. This is the main trail, and is really enjoyable. To take it, you must go into the Visitor Center and pay a fee. Then you go out the back door of the center, where you will find an endless flight of steps (there are 240). The steps take you down to a ledge that was undercut by erosion, creating a series of shallow caves. The trail winds around the toe of a ridge and loops back up to the Visitor Center. Along the way you are able to inspect the extensive ruins of ancient cliff dwellings.
Rim Trail. Length, 0.4 miles *0.64 km*, one way. Level. Paved. Interpretive signs along the trail. This trail moves east along the rim of the canyon. It is a very easy short walk. The scenery is beautiful. You will not walk right by ruins as you do on the other trails, but you can see many ruins across the canyon. On the way back, detour to the Pit House.
Ranger Cabin Trail. Reservation required. Summer only. Length 1.6

miles *2.56 km* complete loop. Altitude change of 300 feet. Unpaved except for last portion. This hike is guided by a ranger. Starting from the Visitor Center, you walk west along the rim to the old Ranger Cabin, a historic site that is fun to visit. Then you enter Walnut Canyon the old way, going down through a side canyon. From there you hike along a ruin-studded ledge to join the Island Trail at the foot of the steps and return to the Visitor Center. This is our favorite trail.

Ledge Trail. Reservation required. Summer only. Length 0.5 miles *0.8 km* complete loop. Altitude change of 300 feet. Half of trail is paved. This hike is guided by a ranger. Starting from the Visitor Center, you go down the steps on the Island Trail, then branch off to the west, where you visit a number of cliff dwellings, returning the way you came. This same ledge is included on the Ranger Trail.

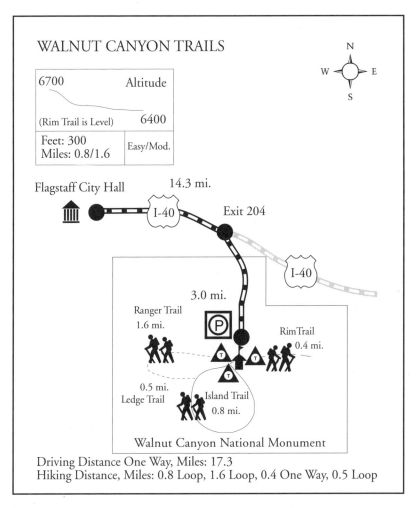

WALNUT CANYON TRAILS

6700   Altitude

(Rim Trail is Level)   6400

Feet: 300
Miles: 0.8/1.6   Easy/Mod.

Flagstaff City Hall   14.3 mi.

I-40   Exit 204

I-40

3.0 mi.

Ranger Trail
1.6 mi.

RimTrail
0.4 mi.

0.5 mi.
Ledge Trail   Island Trail
0.8 mi.

Walnut Canyon National Monument

Driving Distance One Way, Miles: 17.3
Hiking Distance, Miles: 0.8 Loop, 1.6 Loop, 0.4 One Way, 0.5 Loop

Mangum

WEATHERFORD CANYON

Driving Distance One Way: 8.7 miles *13.9 km* (Time 30 minutes)
Access Road: All cars, Last 5.0 miles *8.0 km* medium gravel road
Hiking Distance One Way: 2.0 miles *3.2 km* (Time 1 hour)
How Strenuous: Moderate
Features: High mountains, Aspen groves

NUTSHELL: This trail climbs through a scenic canyon on the southeast face of the San Francisco Peaks 8.7 miles *13.9 km* north of Flagstaff.

DIRECTIONS:
From Flagstaff City Hall Go:
     North on Humphreys Street for 0.60 miles *1.0 km*. See Access Map, page 10. Turn left at the stoplight onto Columbus Avenue and follow it around a big curve to the north. You will see the street signs call this road Columbus Avenue at first, then Ft. Valley Road and then Highway 180. Stay on Highway 180 to the 3.1 miles *5.0 km* point (MP 218.6), where a paved road goes to the right. This is the Schultz Pass Road, FR 420. Turn right and follow this road. At 3.6 miles *5.8 km* you reach a curve to the left where you will see an unpaved road going straight. Stay on the paved road. The paving will end soon and the road will become gravel surfaced. Follow the Schultz Pass Road to the 8.7 mile *13.9 km* point, where you will see a sign for the **Weatherford Trail**. Park anywhere near the Weatherford trailhead.

TRAILHEAD: Begin this hike by taking the Weatherford Trail.

DESCRIPTION: The trailhead for this hike is also the "official" trailhead for the Weatherford Trail, the one indicated by the Forest Service on its maps and guides.
     You will hike the closed road for about 0.75 miles *1.2 km*, just beyond the place where a logging road takes off to the left.
     You will see a blocked road to your right going down into a shallow canyon at this point. Follow it. The canyon is Weatherford Canyon. Soon after you begin this new trail you will see a road forking to the right. Do not take it. Go straight up the canyon, walking along the canyon floor. The trail seems to have been an old wagon road, as it is broader than a footpath. Higher up it does turn into a footpath.
     You will pass through incredible aspen groves on this hike. In the lower

reaches of the canyon there is a stand of aspen saplings thick as hair that all seem to be the same height and age. This would indicate that they are the product of some bumper year, and from their age we would speculate that they are the result of the huge snowfall that hit the Flagstaff area in December, 1967. This dumped over twenty feet of snow on the San Francisco Peaks and caused a correspondingly wet spring in 1968.

Just before the trail ends you come to Aspen Spring, where a pond has been created. In a wet year this pond holds water year around and is a great place to spot animals.

The trail ends where it comes out into an open park and intersects the Weatherford Trail. The Weatherford Canyon Trail can be used as an interesting approach to or return from the Weatherford Trail.

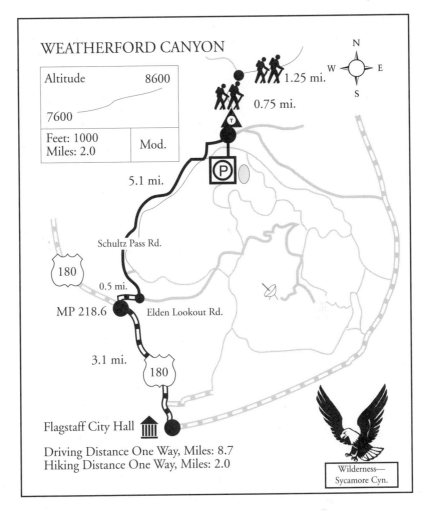

WEATHERFORD CANYON

Altitude	8600
7600	
Feet: 1000 Miles: 2.0	Mod.

1.25 mi.
0.75 mi.

5.1 mi.

Schultz Pass Rd.

180

0.5 mi.

MP 218.6

Elden Lookout Rd.

3.1 mi.

180

Flagstaff City Hall

Driving Distance One Way, Miles: 8.7
Hiking Distance One Way, Miles: 2.0

Wilderness—
Sycamore Cyn.

Mangum

WEATHERFORD TRAIL #102

General Information
Location Map E3
Humphreys Peak USGS Map
Coconino Forest Service Map

Driving Distance One Way: 13.7 miles *21.92 km* (Time 40 minutes)
Access Road: All cars, Last 4.0 miles *6.4 km* rough cinder road
Hiking Distance One Way: 6.0 miles *9.6 km* (Time 3.5 hours)
How Strenuous: Hard
Features: Highest mountains, Alpine forests, Excellent views

NUTSHELL: This is the easiest trail to the top of the San Francisco Peaks, 13.7 miles *21.92 km* north of Flagstaff.

DIRECTIONS:
From Flagstaff City Hall Go:
   North on Humphreys Street for 0.60 miles *1.0 km*. See Access Map, page 10. Turn left at the stoplight onto Columbus Avenue and follow it around a big curve to the north. The street signs call this road Columbus at first, then Ft. Valley Road and then Highway 180. Stay on Highway 180 to the 7.3 miles *11.7 km* point (MP 223), where the road to the Snow Bowl branches to the right. It is well posted. Follow the Snow Bowl road to 9.7 mile *15.52 km* point, where you will see an unpaved road, FR 522, branching to the right. Turn right onto FR 522, which is also known as the Friedlein Prairie Road. At 9.8 miles *15.7 km* this road will fork. Take the left fork and drive FR 522 to the 13.7 mile *21.92 km* point. There you will find a parking lot and road's end. Park in the lot.

TRAILHEAD: You will see a blocked road just beyond the parking lot. Hike the blocked road. There is a trail sign.

DESCRIPTION: These directions are for our easy way to the Weatherford Trail. For the "official" Forest Service way, which is longer and harder, see the entry for **Weatherford Canyon**.
   When you have hiked 0.33 miles *0.5 km* up the Weatherford Trail, take note of a trail coming onto the road from your left. This is the end of the **Kachina Trail**, a favorite hike. Beyond this is a big meadow. There are several roads branching off the main road. Follow the road that takes you across the meadow and moves uphill.
   At the end of the meadow the road will enter a shaded area framed by aspens and marked by a sign. When you see these you will know you are on the Weatherford Trail. Up the trail from here about 0.20 miles *0.32 km* you

will find a trail logbook in an ammunition can chained to a log. Please make an entry for yourself in this book. It is fun to read it and see who has been here.

The Weatherford Trail was built as a private toll road, construction lasting from 1920 to 1928. The Great Depression wiped out any chances of success the road might have had. It fell into disuse and was incorporated into the Kachina Wilderness Area in 1984. The trail tops out at 6.0 miles *9.6 km* at Doyle Saddle (formerly called Fremont Saddle) where you get great views out over the countryside and down into the Inner Basin of the Peaks.

The trail goes another 3.0 miles *4.8 km* to meet the **Humphreys Peak Trail,** from where you can go another half mile *0.8 km* to the highest point in Arizona, at 12,643 feet.

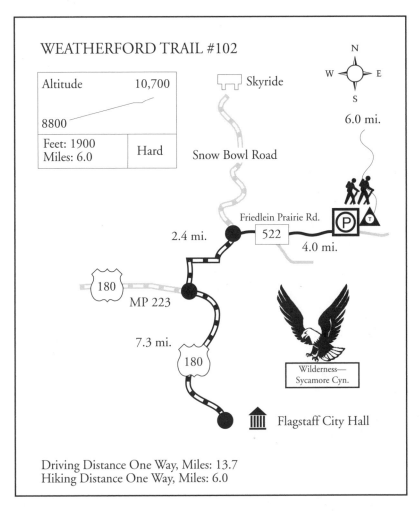

WEST FORK HEAD

Driving Distance One Way: 21.1 miles *33.8 km* (Time 40 minutes)
Access Road: All cars, Last 18.5 miles *29.6 km* good gravel road
Hiking Distance One Way: 1.0 miles *1.6 km* (Time 40 minutes)
How Strenuous: Moderate
Features: Extremely attractive canyon, Lush vegetation

NUTSHELL: The West Fork of Oak Creek is a beautiful canyon. The hike at its end, where it meets Highway 89A is famous. See *Sedona Hikes*. This hike is at the beginning of the canyon, 21.1 miles *33.8 km* south of Flagstaff and has its own considerable attractions.

DIRECTIONS:
From Flagstaff City Hall Go:
    West, then south on Route 66, beneath the railroad overpass. See Access Map, page 10. At 0.50 miles *0.8 km,* go right on Route 66. You will soon leave town. At 2.6 miles *4.16 km* you will reach a road going to the left. This is the Woody Mountain Road, FR 231. Take it. It is paved about a mile and then turns into a cinder road. Stay on FR 231 to the 21.1 mile *33.8 km* point, where the road crosses a bridge. Go just past the bridge and park on the right shoulder.

TRAILHEAD: Not marked. Go down into the canyon.

DESCRIPTION: As you travel FR 231 you will encounter many side roads. The best way to describe the route is to tell you to stay on FR 231 at all times. It winds around in a bewildering way, but generally is the main traveled road everywhere. It is well posted.
    When you get to the bridge over West Fork you will see a canyon to your left which is fairly shallow right at the bridge. This is the head or beginning of West Fork. Those who are familiar with West Fork at its mouth where it meets Oak Creek will be surprised by West Fork's humble beginnings, as it seems to be just another ravine in country full of ravines. Go down into the canyon and start walking along the right hand bank of the streambed. You will pick up the trail there.
    At 0.2 miles *0.32 km* you will come to a large sign that reads, *"WEST FORK OF OAK CREEK. You are entering a very remote canyon. There is no developed hiking trail. Only experienced hiking parties should attempt*

this hike. DO NOT go alone." Don't worry. The first mile of the canyon does have a trail and is plenty safe. We feel that the warning on the sign is appropriate only if you go beyond the first mile. After the first mile the trail disappears and you have to hop the rocks in the streambed as the canyon narrows and the shoulders and shelves disappear.

It is possible for fit hikers to hike the whole length of the canyon in a day, about 12 miles *19.2 km*, meeting a car that they have previously parked at the West Fork trailhead in Oak Creek Canyon, but we do not recommend this for the average hiker.

This canyon is incredibly lush. You will think you are in a Pacific Northwest rain forest. Many of the trees are festooned with Spanish moss. The variety of plant life is mind boggling (including poison ivy). This is a special place and a magic hike.

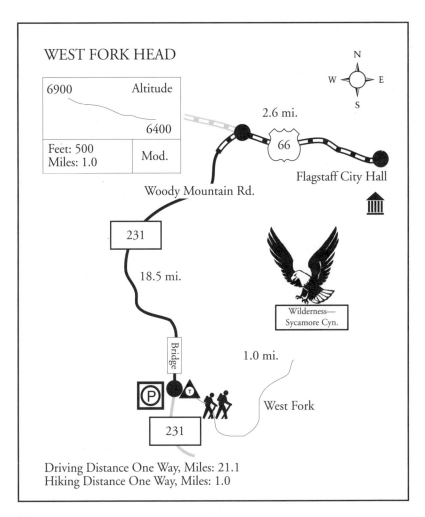

WEST FORK HEAD

6900	Altitude
	6400
Feet: 500 Miles: 1.0	Mod.

2.6 mi.

66

Flagstaff City Hall

Woody Mountain Rd.

231

18.5 mi.

Wilderness— Sycamore Cyn.

Bridge

1.0 mi.

P T

West Fork

231

Driving Distance One Way, Miles: 21.1
Hiking Distance One Way, Miles: 1.0

Mangum

WHITE HORSE HILLS

General Information
Location Map E3
White Horse Hills USGS Map
Coconino Forest Service Map

Driving Distance One Way: 23.35 miles *37.36 km* (Time 45 minutes)
Access Road: All cars, Last 3.75 miles *6.0 km* good gravel road
Hiking Distance One Way: 1.0 miles *1.6 km* (Time 45 minutes)
How Strenuous: Moderate
Features: Views

NUTSHELL: This moderately strenuous hike to the top of a mountain located just north of the San Francisco Peaks gives great views.

DIRECTIONS:
From Flagstaff City Hall Go:
    North on Humphreys Street for 0.60 miles *1.0 km*. See Access Map, page 10. Turn left at the stoplight onto Columbus Avenue and follow it around a big curve to the north. You will see the street signs call this road Columbus at first, then Ft. Valley Road and then Highway 180. Stay on Highway 180 to the 19.6 miles *31.36 km* point (MP 235.2), where you will turn right onto the unpaved upper Hart Prairie Road, FR 151. Follow FR 151 to the 21.2 miles *33.92 km* point, where you turn left onto FR 418. Follow FR 418 to the 23.35 mile *37.36 km* point, where you will see a sign and the entrance to the trailhead on your left. Pull into the driveway and park.

TRAILHEAD: You will see a large sign announcing the trail at the parking place.

DESCRIPTION: The trail climbs gradually except for one steep haul from about 0.50 miles *0.8 km* to 0.70 miles *1.12 km* . It is easy to follow. You are on one mountain that has four knobs. The trail forks to go to the two highest knobs. You will reach the first fork at 0.50 miles *0.8 km*. Take the left hand trail there. It climbs steeply up the mountain. At 1.0 miles *1.6 km* you will reach another fork at a saddle. From that point you can go left for about 0.10 miles *0.16 km* to the top of an 8700 foot high knob or right for 0.20 miles *0.32 km* to the top of a 9000 foot high knob. We recommend that you do both.

    From either of the tops you are treated to magnificent views of the north face of the San Francisco Peaks. Mt. Humphreys, the tallest peak, really shows its stuff from here and is very imposing. The lower top of White Horse is a splendid viewpoint from which to see the changing aspen leaves in October. Visibility is not so good on the higher top because of trees growing there.

From the lower top you can enjoy views into Kendrick Park, the Hochderffer Hills, **Saddle Mountain**, the Grand Canyon Plateau, the Vermillion Cliffs and countless cinder cones. To the east you can see sweeping views of Deadman Flat and **O'Leary Peak**.

While the soil, terrain and vegetation look typical of the area when you start climbing on this trail, you become aware about half way up the trail that the earth beneath your feet has turned red. It looks like the soil in southern Utah or Sedona. In fact, the Flagstaff area would be part of an unbroken belt of red stone had it not been for the volcanic eruptions that covered it with lava and cinders and wrenched things askew with violent uplifts.

Near the top of White Horse you will find a white limestone layer. This limestone seems identical to the stone found around Walnut Canyon and Lake Mary many miles to the south.

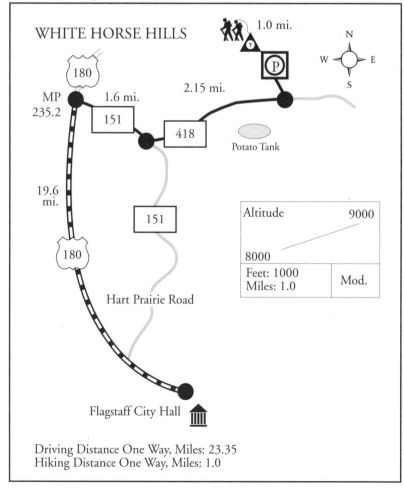

WHITE HORSE HILLS

1.0 mi.

N
W — E
S

180

MP
235.2

1.6 mi.

151

2.15 mi.

418

Potato Tank

19.6
mi.

151

Altitude   9000

8000

Feet: 1000
Miles: 1.0   Mod.

180

Hart Prairie Road

Flagstaff City Hall

Driving Distance One Way, Miles: 23.35
Hiking Distance One Way, Miles: 1.0

WILD BILL HILL

General Information
Location Map E2
Wing Mountain USGS Map
Coconino Forest Service Map

Driving Distance One Way: 21.85 miles *35 km* (Time 40 minutes)
Access Road: High clearance only, Last 2.0 miles *3.2 km* rough dirt road
Hiking Distance One Way: 1.5 miles *2.4 km* (Time 1 hour)
How Strenuous: Moderate
Features: Hoodoos in volcano's center, Views

NUTSHELL: This mountain 21.85 miles 35 km west of Flagstaff is located at the east edge of Government Prairie and is an extinct volcano. It is easily climbed to enjoy a look into the heart of the volcano and views over the prairie. **A personal favorite**.

DIRECTIONS:
From Flagstaff City Hall Go:
   North on Humphreys Street for 0.60 miles *1.0 km*. See Access Map, page 10. Turn left at the stoplight onto Columbus Avenue and follow it around a big curve to the north. You will see the street signs call this road Columbus at first, then Ft. Valley Road and then Highway 180. Stay on Highway 180 to the 14.5 miles *23.2 km* point (MP 230), where an unpaved road takes off to the left. Turn left onto this road, FR 245, and follow it to the 17.6 mile *28.16 km* point where it intersects FR 171. Turn left onto FR 171 and follow it to the 19.7 mile *31.5 km* point, where FR 156 goes off to the right. Turn right on FR 156 and take it to the 21.35 mile *34.16 km* point. Turn left on a primitive unmarked road and follow it to the 21.85 miles point *35 km*, where you park. You will be 0.25 miles *0.4 km* away from the hill.

TRAILHEAD: You will see Wild Bill Hill to your left. There is no trail. Just walk across country to the hill and climb it to the saddle.

DESCRIPTION: Wild Bill Hill is one of many hills that form a ring around Government Prairie.
   This hill is shaped like a three-leaf clover. When you reach the top of the saddle, at an aspen grove, about 0.75 miles *1.2 km* from where you parked, you will see a bare knob to your right, a wooded knob (the highest) to your left, and the smallest knob to the north. We suggest that you climb the bare knob first. The views from there are great. You have good lines of sight in all directions except to the north, where the lowest knob blocks your view. Out over Government Prairie you can see for miles. If you know where to

look, you can see the Beale Road coming across from Government Mountain. In fact, you can see it here better than you can as you walk the old road. See **Beale Road on Government Prairie**.

Then come back to the saddle. You will see a game trail there headed to the west. Follow it about 0.15 miles *0.24 km* and you will come to a place where you look down into the core of the volcano. Here is a wonderful moonlike landscape of hoodoos. You can walk to the north knob on a game trail from there, though the views are not so good because of the timber,

If you want to climb the highest knob, don't do it from the hoodoos even though you see a game trail going west, because it is very steep there. Come back to the first saddle and ascend it from there.

These three knobs are fascinating. The soil of which each is composed is quite different. The highest knob, loose red cinders; the lowest knob, brown cinders; the bare knob, red cinders.

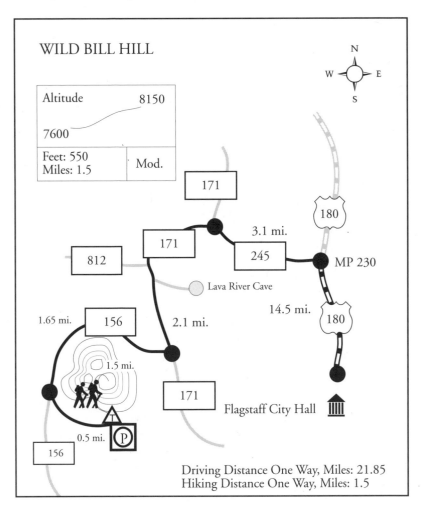

Mangum

WILDCAT HILL

General Information
Location Map F3
Flagstaff East USGS Map
Coconino Forest Map

Driving Distance One Way: 7.0 miles *11.2 km* (Time 20 minutes)
Access Road: All cars, Last 0.20 miles *0.32 km* rough cinder road
Hiking Distance One Way: 0.1 miles *0.16 km* (Time 30 minutes)
How Strenuous: Moderate
Features: Cave, Pit house ruins, Rock Art, Scenic canyon

NUTSHELL: Located on the fringe of town, this canyon suddenly appears as a deep slash. On its steep lava walls are several panels of rock art and a cave. On top are the remains of several pit houses.

DIRECTIONS:
From Flagstaff City Hall Go:
 East, then north on Route 66. See Access Map, pages 10-11. At 3.8 miles *6.1 km* (MP 418.2/200) you will come to a fork, where Route 66 goes to the right. Turn right onto Route 66 and follow it to the 5.8 mile *9.3 km* point (MP 202).where you will see a street sign to your left marked *El Paso Flagstaff* and beyond that a sign for the *Wildcat Hill Waste Water Treatment Plant.* Turn left onto this good gravel road. At 5.95 miles *9.52 km* you will see a road going left. Ignore it. At 6.4 miles *10.24 km* you will see the turnoff to the El Paso Station. Ignore it. The road will curve around the back of the El Paso property and you will reach another fork at 6.8 miles *10.9 km*. You can see the canyon from here. Take the right fork, which runs along the rim of the canyon and follow it to the 7.0 mile *11.2 km* point where you will see an old barbed wire fence. Park here.

TRAILHEAD: There are no trail signs.

DESCRIPTION: You have parked on a high point just off the rim of the canyon. Walk over to the canyon and take a look at it. It is a strange gash in the earth. On each end of the canyon is gentle wide country; then suddenly the earth's crust split and made this steep narrow rock-lined canyon. You will see a stream flowing in the bottom of the canyon. Beware! The water you see there is treated sewage coming out of the wastewater treatment plant.
 You do not actually walk down to the bottom of the canyon on this hike, but stay up on a bench about a third of the way down.
 Begin by walking downhill, looking to your left. You will see the

Flagstaff Hikes

remains of pithouses on the rim of the canyon to the left of where you parked, at a place where the canyon walls are not so steep and sheer. From there come back toward the parking spot, working your way down to a lower ledge at the base of the cliffs and boulders. You will see a fairly deep cave here, its roof blackened by the smoke of countless fires. Beyond, look on every smooth boulder face for rock art. The art seems scattered without a pattern.

There are several panels. We counted at least six. The art is rather basic, not as elaborate as that encountered at other sites.

When you reach the end of the area of the sheer cliffs, walk back up to the top and return to your car. There is a bit of rock art across the canyon, but it is hardly worth the effort. The most interesting sights are on your side.

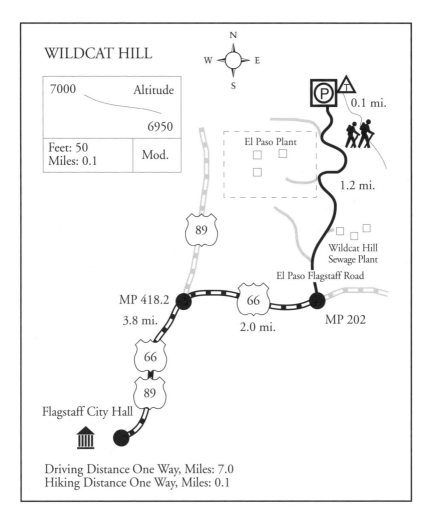

Mangum

WILLOW CROSSING TRAIL #38

General Information
Location Map G4
Calloway Butte USGS Map
Coconino Forest Service Map

Driving Distance One Way: 53.65 miles *85.84 km* (Time 1.5 hours)
Access Road: High clearance best, Last 4.75 miles *7.6 km* unpaved road
Hiking Distance One Way: 1.0 miles *1.6 km* (Time 45 minutes)
How Strenuous: Moderate
Features: Beautiful pristine canyon, Back country

NUTSHELL: This little-used trail takes you into and across Willow Valley Canyon, a tributary to West Clear Creek. The canyon is beautiful, and the trail in and out is on a moderate grade.

DIRECTIONS:
From Flagstaff City.Hall Go:
     West, then south on Route 66, beneath the railroad overpass. See Access Map, page 10. At 0.5 miles *0.8 km*, go straight on Milton Road. At 1.7 miles *2.72 km* you will reach a stoplight at Forest Meadows Street. Turn right here onto Forest Meadows and go one block to Beulah. Turn left on Beulah and follow it south. Beulah merges onto Highway 89A. At 2.4 miles *3.84 km* (MP 401.6), turn left onto the Lake Mary Road at the stoplight. Follow the Lake Mary Road, going past Lower and Upper Lake Mary and Mormon Lake to the 48.9 mile *78.24 km* point (MP 297.7), where you turn right onto a dirt road, FR 81. The highway sign shows "V Bar V Ranch, Poor Farm and West Clear Creek." Follow FR 81 to the 52.0 mile point *83.2 km*, its junction with FR 81E. Turn left on 81E and stay on it to the 53.15 mile *85 km* point, where you reach a fork. Take the left fork. This is FR 9366M, though we saw no markers. Go to the 53.65 mile *85.84 km* point, where you will see a barbed wire fence, with a cattle guard. Just beyond the cattle guard, to your left (east), is the trailhead. Park here.

TRAILHEAD: There is a sign and wire-bound cairn where you park.

DESCRIPTION: The first leg of this trail is the approach to the rim of Willow Valley Canyon. The approach is eastward along level ground. The trail is not very distinct here, but it is easy to find your way: all you have to do is walk along the fence. This part of the trail is rather drab.
     When you reach the 0.4 mile *0.64 km* point, you will enter into an area where a sheep wire fence creates an enclosure. You can see that you are very

near the canyon here. A big blaze on a pine tree marks the trail here, which dips down into the canyon, moving away from the barbed wire fence. From this point, the trail is clear and easy to follow.

You descend along the bank of a side canyon. The hike is not steep, and the area becomes more and more beautiful as you go. Finally, you drop down into the streambed, where you can enjoy some impressive views. The canyon walls here are very sheer, though not terribly deep. We saw a huge variety of plants, including many flowers.

Go straight across the canyon, where you will see the trail going up the other side. From this point, you climb to the opposite rim. Again, the grade is not very steep, and it is a pleasant hike.

The hike terminates in a park in a pretty valley, where you will find a trail marker sign.

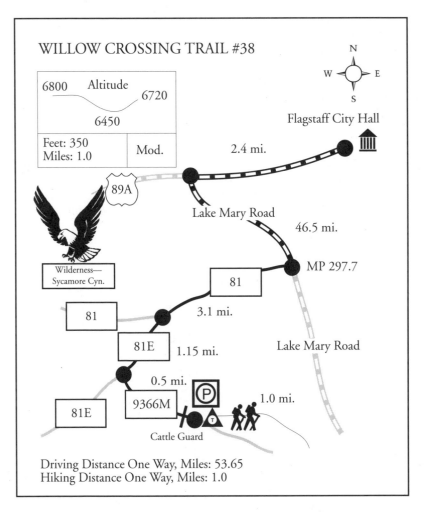

WILLOW CROSSING TRAIL #38

Altitude
6800
6720
6450

Feet: 350
Miles: 1.0   Mod.

2.4 mi.

Flagstaff City Hall

89A

Lake Mary Road

46.5 mi.

MP 297.7

Wilderness—
Sycamore Cyn.

81

81

3.1 mi.

81E   1.15 mi.

Lake Mary Road

0.5 mi.

9366M

1.0 mi.

81E

Cattle Guard

Driving Distance One Way, Miles: 53.65
Hiking Distance One Way, Miles: 1.0

Mangum

WILSON MEADOW

General Information
Location Map E3
Humphreys Peak and Wing Mountain USGS Maps
Coconino Forest Service Map

Driving Distance One Way: 14.9 miles *23.84 km* (Time 35 minutes)
Access Road: All cars, Last 4.7 miles *7.5 km* good gravel
Hiking Distance One Way: 1.0 miles *1.6 km* (Time 30 minutes)
How Strenuous: Easy
Features: Aspen groves, Meadow Views

NUTSHELL: Located on the San Francisco Peaks, 14.9 miles *23.84 km* north of Flagstaff, this easy walk displays the area's alpine beauty.

DIRECTIONS:
From Flagstaff City Hall Go:
   North on Humphreys Street for 0.60 miles *1.0 km*, to the stoplight. See Access Map, page 10. Then take a left onto a street marked Columbus Avenue, which changes to Ft. Valley Road as it makes a curve to the north. Outside the city limits, the road becomes Highway 180, a major route to the Grand Canyon. At 10.2 miles *16.3 km* (MP 225.1), turn right onto FR 151, the lower Hart Prairie Road, and follow it to the 14.7 miles *23.5 km* point, where an unmarked gravel road takes off to the right. This access is rough because of exposed rocks, but it is only 0.2 miles *0.32 km* long. Turn right and drive to the 14.9 miles *23.84 km* point, where you will find a fenced parking place. Park there.

TRAILHEAD: You will see a "Road Closed" sign at a gate in the parking area fence. Walk up this road.

DESCRIPTION: The sign at the parking lot identifies this merely as a "Wildlife Habitat Area" and it is not named on any map that we could find. You will see a reference to the Wilson Foundation on the sign. As we made this beautiful hike, enjoying the flowers, the meadow and the views, it occurred to us that it would be fitting to call it the Wilson Meadow hike in honor of The Wilson Foundation, for it spearheaded a fight two decades ago to prevent the commercial development of Hart Prairie, under the slogan, "Save the Peaks." Had it not been for it bearing the brunt of years of costly litigation, this pristine area would now be covered with condos. Thanks, folks! This is a wonderful place and we are grateful that you saved it for nature lovers.
   The hike consists of following a closed road up the meadow. This is a

wet area with underground water marked by lines of water loving shrubs. After one half mile *0.8 km* the tracks peter out near a large metal water tank lying on its side. No problem. Just keep hiking toward the top of the meadow, to the tree line.

From the half mile point *0.8 km* you begin to get wonderful views. Turn around every so often and enjoy them. Three major mountains and an infinity of hills cover the landscape. Beginning on your right hand, the tallest mountains are Kendrick, Sitgreaves and Bill Williams. The hike ends at a fence at the top of the meadow.

We made the hike in mid-August and the meadow was full of flowers and high grass. Instead of going to the fence, we veered to the right near the top, into a grove of spruce and aspen, so cool on a hot day. The rippling of the wind in the aspen leaves sounded like water running. Almost every aspen in the grove shows signs of having been rubbed by antlers.

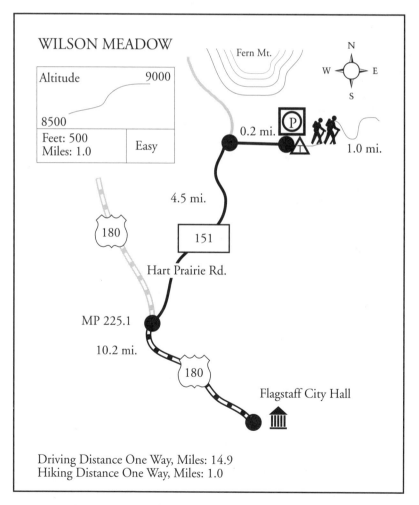

Mangum

WING MOUNTAIN

General Information
Location Map E2
Bellemont and Flagstaff West USGS Maps
Coconino Forest Service Map

Driving Distance One Way: 12.4 miles *20 km* (Time 30 minutes)
Access Road: All cars, Last 3.7 miles *6 km* good gravel road
Hiking Distance One Way: 0.75 miles *1.2 km* (Time 40 minutes)
How Strenuous: Hard
Features: Landmark crater north of Flagstaff provides wonderful views

NUTSHELL: A hard climb straight uphill brings the hiker to the rim of a crater, the bowl of which is a grassy meadow with a lake (sometimes) in the bottom.

DIRECTIONS:
From Flagstaff City Hall Go:
   North on Humphreys Street for 0.60 miles *1.0 km*. See Access Map, page 10. Turn left at the stoplight onto Columbus Avenue and follow it around a big curve to the north. You will see the street signs call this road Columbus at first, then Ft. Valley Road and then Highway 180. Stay on Highway 180 to the 8.7 miles *14 km* point (MP 224.3), where an unpaved road takes off to the left. Turn left onto this road, FR 222, and follow it to the 10.4 mile *16.7 km* point where it intersects FR 519. Turn left on FR 519 and follow it to the 12.2 mile *19.5 km* point, where you turn right, on a primitive unmarked road. This is pretty rough, but you can probably follow it to the 12.4 mile *20 km* point, which is a good place to park.

TRAILHEAD: Unmarked. No official trailhead.

DESCRIPTION: From the point where you parked, the primitive road continues up the side of the mountain. You will see signs of tree cutting. It is hard to tell whether this was a logging operation or just tree thinning. Where the road ends, you will be part way up the mountain. From there, it is just a question of scrambling to the top, up the south face of Wing. The pitch is very steep, and you might want to zigzag rather than go in a straight line.
   Once at the top, turn around and enjoy the views behind you, to the south. You will find a large cairn of stones here, bound together with sticks and wire. This is a good marker. Use it to locate the place to go back down the mountain when you are finished. At this point, you will have hiked 0.75 miles *1.2 km.*
   From here, you can walk around the rim. We suggest going counter-

clockwise, to the northeast. You will find a clear place just in front of a fence, where you have good views of the San Francisco Peaks.

The barbed wire fence you will find here is unexpected. The Forest Service map does not show that it is private property.

Wing Mountain and **A-1 Mountain** are near neighbors. In Flagstaff's early years, the Arizona Cattle Company had a huge ranch in the Ft. Valley area. Its brand was the A-1, which is how A-1 Mountain got its name. Wing was one of the owners of the Arizona Cattle Company.

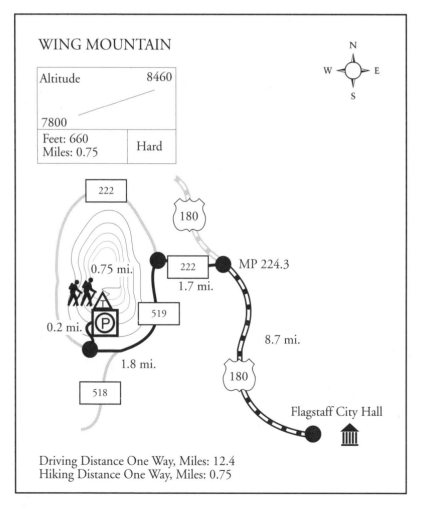

WING MOUNTAIN

Altitude	8460
7800	
Feet: 660 Miles: 0.75	Hard

222

180

0.75 mi.

222
1.7 mi.

MP 224.3

519

0.2 mi.

8.7 mi.

1.8 mi.

180

518

Flagstaff City Hall

Driving Distance One Way, Miles: 12.4
Hiking Distance One Way, Miles: 0.75

WINTER CABIN TRAIL

Driving Distance One Way: 26.3 miles *42.1 km* (Time 1 hour)
Access Road: All cars, Last 22.7 miles *36.3 km* dirt road, rough spots
Hiking Distance One Way: 1.1 miles *1.76 km* (Time 1 hour)
How Strenuous: Moderate
Features: Views, Sycamore Canyon access, Historic cowboy cabin

NUTSHELL: Located 26.3 miles *42.1 km* southwest of Flagstaff, this is a scenic trail in its own right as well as being an access trail into Sycamore Canyon. There is an interesting cabin in an idyllic glade at the end of this hike.

DIRECTIONS:
From Flagstaff City Hall Go:
    West, then south on Route 66 beneath the railroad overpass. See Access Map, page 10. At 0.50 miles *0.8 km* turn right on Route 66. At 2.6 miles *4.16 km* you will reach the Woody Mountain Road, FR 231, going to the left. Take it. It is paved about a mile and then turns into a cinder road. At 16.6 miles *26.56 km* you will intersect FR 538. Turn right onto FR 538 and follow it to the 22.3 mile *35.7 km* point, a T junction. Turn left, still on FR 538, and drive to the 25.7 mile *41.1 km* point, where it intersects FR 538H. Turn right on FR 538H and go to its end at 26.3 miles *42.1 km*. FR 538H is rather rough. Park at the end of the road.

TRAILHEAD: You will see a sign at the parking area.

DESCRIPTION: The trail is maintained and passes through an attractive mixed forest with oaks, maples and other trees adding variety to the prevailing Ponderosa pines. This is a colorful trail in mid-October. The trail is mostly soft, covered with soil, though there are a few rocky patches.
    Forest Service signs give the mileage to Winter Cabin as 1.5 miles *2.4 km*. We measured it as 1.1 miles *1.76 km*. The cabin is located in a peaceful glade on a little shelf of land, a remote peaceful paradise far from the cares of the world. You may not want to come back out.
    The cabin is an old log relic with a corrugated metal roof, and is still in good condition. It is hard to tell how the place got its name, Winter Cabin, because one can't imagine cowboys surviving the winter here. Heavy snows fall in this area and once the snow season begins in the autumn, this place

would be totally cut off from the outside world.

The cabin is a trail intersection. The trail to the southwest goes on down 1.5 miles *2.4 km* to **Ott Lake,** and from there goes another 2.0 miles *3.2 km* into the bottom of Sycamore Canyon. (Don't try hiking into Sycamore Canyon unless you are really prepared for it. Unprepared people die there). The trail to the west goes to Dorsey Spring and then on to Kelsey Spring on the 5.5 mile *8.8 km* long **Kelsey-Winter Trail**.

Stopping at Winter Cabin makes a dandy day hike that can be handled by almost anyone who is reasonably fit.

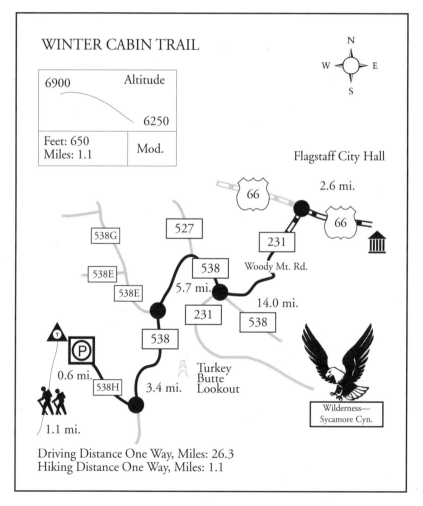

Mangum

WUPATKI RUIN TRAIL

Driving Distance One Way: 37.8 miles *60.48 km* (Time 60 minutes)
Access Road: All cars, All paved
Hiking Distance Complete Loop: 0.40 miles *0.64 km* (Time 45 minutes)
How Strenuous: Easy
Features: Views, Best pueblo Indian ruins in the Flagstaff area

NUTSHELL: This is a fascinating easy trail starting at the Visitor Center in Wupatki National Monument 37.8 miles *60.48 km* north of Flagstaff. It features pueblo ruins, a ball court, an amphitheater and a unique blow hole.

DIRECTIONS:
From Flagstaff City Hall Go:
    East, curving to north on Highway 89. See Access Map, pages 10-11. Follow Highway 89 north out into the country. At 16.4 miles *26.24 km* (MP 430.3) you will reach the entrance to Sunset Crater National Monument. Turn right on the road into Sunset Crater. This road is also known as FR 545. At 18.4 miles *29.44 km* you will reach a ticket booth where you will have to pay admission. Just beyond that is the Visitor Center, which is worth a look. At 26.0 miles *41.6 km* you reach the Painted Desert Vista. This is a lookout point where we recommend stopping to enjoy the view. Under the right lighting conditions it is superb. At 37.8 miles *60.48 km* you enter the Wupatki National Monument, which adjoins Sunset Crater, and you will see the road to the Wupatki Visitor Center to your left. Take the road to the Visitor Center and park in the parking lot.

TRAILHEAD: The trail starts at the right hand side of the Visitor Center.

DESCRIPTION: Even though this is a "tame" hike, being the furthest thing from a wilderness adventure, it is very interesting and well worth taking. This is a favorite excursion for visiting relatives. It will keep even the small fry happy.
    The setting is lovely. The ruins are situated on the side of a small valley, where exposed layers of red sandstone provided plentiful building materials. The Sinagua Indians, who built the pueblo, fitted their construction around some of the existing boulders in fascinating ways so that they could use the boulders as much as possible to serve as walls and buttresses. Across the valley you can see a couple of small pueblos, but you are not permitted to visit

them. Beyond the far end of the valley you can see the Painted Desert, a vast multicolored area.

From the pueblo at the top of the valley you walk downhill to an amphitheater, then to the valley floor to a ball court and a blow hole. The blow hole is wonderful. During the cool hours of the day, in the morning and evening, the blow hole draws in air. When the day is hot, during the afternoon, the blow hole expels air. It is like some giant breathing. The breaths can be quite forceful, causing a loud rushing noise.

Along the trail are posted several markers which are keyed into a trail guide. You pick up the guide at the beginning of the trail. If you want to keep it, you put fifty cents into the box at the end of the trail. If you do not want to keep it, you return it to the box.

We recommend visiting other Wupatki sites: Wukoki, Lomaki and the Citadel.

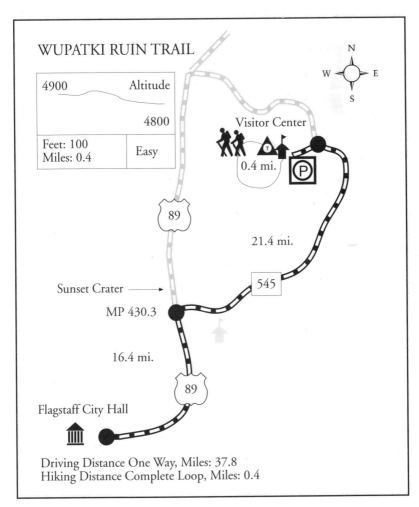

Driving Distance One Way, Miles: 37.8
Hiking Distance Complete Loop, Miles: 0.4

Mangum

Index